IMAGES
of America

World War II Italian Prisoners of War in Chambersburg

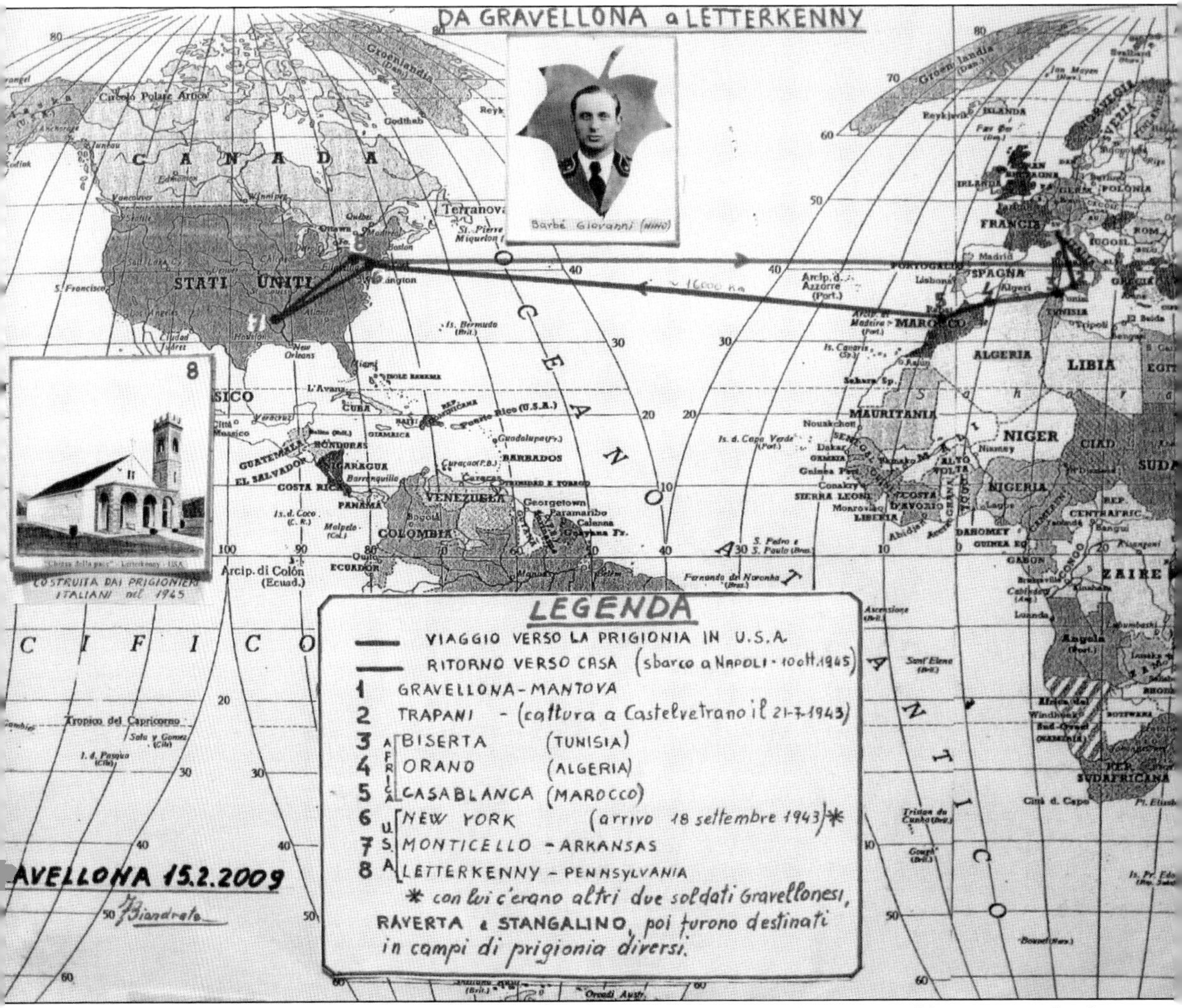

This map belonging to Giovanni Barbè shows his movements during World War II as both a soldier and POW when he departed for Sicily and later returned from the United States. Visible on the left is the Letterkenny chapel, which was built by the prisoners. Barbè was very attached to the small church, and it represented one of his most endearing memories of his POW experience. (Courtesy of Giancarla Barbè Biandrate.)

On the Cover: Letterkenny Army Depot Italian Service Unit prisoners pose at the Caledonia State Park located near Chambersburg, Pennsylvania, on July 14, 1944. The soldiers had arrived at Letterkenny in March and April of that year from other detention camps in the United States. The recreation area at Caledonia had a large swimming pool that many groups of POWs often frequented during good weather in the summer months. (Courtesy of Frances Tonolo MacAvoy and Eva Cittadini.)

IMAGES
of America

WORLD WAR II ITALIAN PRISONERS OF WAR IN CHAMBERSBURG

Flavio G. Conti and Alan R. Perry

ARCADIA
PUBLISHING

ISBN 978-1-4671-2723-3

Published by Arcadia Publishing
Charleston, South Carolina

Printed in the United States of America

Library of Congress Control Number: 2017937003

For all general information, please contact Arcadia Publishing:
Telephone 843-853-2070
Fax 843-853-0044
E-mail sales@arcadiapublishing.com
For customer service and orders:
Toll-Free 1-888-313-2665

Visit us on the Internet at www.arcadiapublishing.com

We dedicate this book to all those Italian POWs who, through their perseverance and sacrifice, collaborated with the United States during World War II to ensure the defeat of Nazi Germany and the rebirth of Italy after the bleak experience of fascism.

Contents

ACKNOWLEDGMENTS

We could not have written this book without the multitude of photographs and documents that the scores of family members of ex–Letterkenny POWs generously provided us over these last two and a half years. The greatest numbers live in Italy, but several, having emigrated with their families as children following the war, have reached out to us from here in the United States and other countries such as Canada, Australia, Brazil, Argentina, and France. We share our sense of earnest gratitude to all of them for their great enthusiasm and willingness to participate in this special project. Because of sheer numbers, we cannot list them all, but readers can find their individual names listed after each caption we have provided to accompany our photographs.

We also gathered material from an important archive in Italy—Il Ministero della Difesa, Direzione Generale di Commissariato e di Servizi Generali, Ufficio Spese Generali Nazionali ed Estere, Archivio Generale di Deposito, Roma, listed henceforth as MDDGCSGA when appropriate in the captions. We wish to thank all the staff members who were always available and highly professional in providing us information. In particular, we would like to mention the archivists Mauro Fagiani, Angelina Puccio, Elisabetta Giudice, Enrico Tuzzi, and Paolo Frezza.

A few key individuals in the Chambersburg community gave us great support. We need to mention Dave Goodman for his initial help in providing us first-source materials that the Letterkenny command had kept over the years; Dave Sciamanna, former president of the Greater Chambersburg Chamber of Commerce, for his organizational and leadership abilities; and the Reverend Dr. William H. Harter and Paul Cullinane, respectively president and secretary of the Historical Letterkenny Chapel and Franklin County Veterans and 9/11 Memorial Park, for their acumen in generating community interest for this book.

Two archivists stateside helped us with scanning important images. Our thanks go out to Catherine Q. Perry at Gettysburg College and Bob Dunkelberger at Bloomsburg University.

Finally, we are most grateful to Erin Vosgien and Caroline Anderson at Arcadia Publishing, who carefully considered the merit of our work and ensured the highest quality of presentation for each of our photographs.

INTRODUCTION

A symposium took place in Milan, Italy, on November 13, 2015, to commemorate the 70th anniversary of the end of World War II and the repatriation of some 1,200 Italian soldiers who had been detained at the Letterkenny Army Depot, located near Chambersburg, Pennsylvania, from May 1944 to October 1945. On this occasion, organizers of the conference, including one of the authors of this book, Flavio G. Conti, inaugurated a photographic exhibit that offered viewers an intimate portrait of POW life at Letterkenny. Beyond family members of ex-POWs and Dr. Conti, several political representatives of the Lombardy region and the City of Milan were present, along with academic experts and Italian diplomatic exponents who joined the festivities from all over the country.

These special events in Milan took place not long after a very special celebration had unfolded in Chambersburg on October 24, 2015, to honor the Letterkenny Italian prisoners. Here, too, a photographic display played a vital role in recounting this fascinating World War II story, when a set of permanent images was placed inside the back atrium of the chapel the Italian POWs had built during the war. This place of worship is still used today and is considered a historic landmark. The event garnered welcomed media attention: representatives from the US Congress, Italian embassy, Chambersburg Chamber of Commerce, Franklin County, and Corpus Christi Church spoke at Mass, exchanged official gifts, and recounted important aspects of prisoner life during the war. Several scores of Italian Americans were also present, including children and grandchildren of former POWs who had returned to live in the United States after the war. Most significantly, an Italian delegation comprised of family members and friends of ex-prisoners had traveled from Italy to revel in the memories and listen to Dr. Conti deliver the keynote address.

The great interest in the subject matter of these Italian POWs, both abroad in Italy and here in the United States, helped to generate a historical study titled *Italian Prisoners of War in Pennsylvania: Allies on the Home Front, 1944–1945*, that Farleigh Dickinson University Press published in October 2016. Simultaneously, there arose a great parallel need to publish a full-length photographic history that could furnish a precise picture of typical POW life for these Italian soldiers.

Photographs have a wonderful power to tell stories, and these presented here aim to reconstruct an aspect of the American home front during World War II that has not received much historical analysis until recently. At Letterkenny, as in general with other POW detention camps, and especially those that hosted cooperating soldiers, the Italian POWs could take pictures and be photographed with great freedom—even when Italian American relatives and friends came to the depot from towns and cities both near and far. We hold, therefore, that this present photographic study can be of great interest to scholars and the wider public in general and not solely to family members of these prisoners. Indeed, to the best of our knowledge, ours is the first full-length photographic study dedicated to cooperating Italian POWs in World War II.

The Italian soldiers detained at Letterkenny were only a small part of the total numbers of Italian POWs taken during the war. After September 8, 1943, the Germans captured around 600,000 Italian military members. The Allies imprisoned another 600,000, and of this number, 51,000 were sent to the United States. They had mainly been captured in North Africa in the spring of 1943, and in particular during the last weeks of the Tunisia Campaign that ended with the surrender of Axis forces on May 13 of that year. The Americans detained the huge numbers at holding camps, from which they were transported to Casablanca and Oran in order then to be shipped to the United States.

Most of the POWs were loaded aboard Liberty ships that had been hastily outfitted to carry human cargo. After a voyage that lasted about three weeks, the POWs arrived at the ports of New York City, Boston, or Norfolk, Virginia. When they disembarked, they underwent personal hygiene and medical checks. Barbers shaved their hair, while other personnel disinfected their clothes and assigned them new uniforms, if necessary, that carried the printed letters "PW." The prisoners also took showers with hot water and soap, an experience that many of them had almost forgotten, having faced combat conditions in the desert for more than two years.

Then the Americans interrogated them, snapped their official identification photographs, registered their fingerprints, and assigned official POW serial numbers to those who did not already have one. The International Red Cross, through US authorities, also provided them with a postcard to send to their family and loved ones in Italy that documented their status and communicated the mere fact that they were still alive. Finally, the POWs, still under guard, then boarded trains where they often received their first, abundant, hot meals in weeks.

As they traveled through the heartland of the United States to their various camps, most of them had their first true encounter with America, and it was simply unforgettable. They spied huge cities with automobiles that traveled everywhere over expansive roads. Skyscrapers, one after the next, wowed them with their height and massiveness. They sat and slept in train cars that were carpeted and covered with plush fabric, and polite African American attendants served them enormous portions of food at breakfast, lunch, and dinner, often generously giving them seconds and maybe even thirds. These wonders truly struck the Italian POWs, and many of them immediately realized two things. First, they gathered that they had been duped by Fascist propaganda that often depicted only the seedier side of American life, and second, they had their first real inkling of the US economic power that undergirded the American armed forces.

The trains headed to camps dispersed throughout the United States. For the POWs who refused to collaborate with the Americans, these camps would serve as their definitive places of detention for the duration of the war, while the cooperators were sent to other camps. Beginning in March 1944, in fact, American military authorities offered Italian prisoners the opportunity to aid in fighting against Nazi Germany through all activities connected to the US war effort with the exception of combat.

This decision to offer Italian POWs the chance to cooperate actually contravened the 1929 Geneva Convention Accords that governed the proper and ethical treatment of prisoners of war. The US advanced the chance to cooperate unilaterally without prior coordination with the Italian government. Indeed, many authorities in Italy officially protested and opposed this program. Nevertheless, many of them reluctantly approved the cooperation system as a means for Italy to contribute to Germany's defeat and thus earn greater leverage during deliberations that would craft a peace treaty after the war.

The Italian government's ambiguous position regarding cooperation caused uncertainty among its prisoners, who tried to decipher what their government's most authentic position regarding the matter might be. Regardless, the majority of the 51,000 POWs present in the United States opted to cooperate, but only 36,000, or about 71 percent of the total, were actually utilized. These soldiers who did take an oath of allegiance were then organized into Italian Service Units (ISUs) and sent to bases, camps, forts, and depots where the greatest need for labor existed. They donned American uniforms with the only distinguishable feature being a large patch with "Italy" stitched upon it that was worn both on the left sleeve and on the left front side of the garrison cap. They earned $24 a month, of which $8, or a third, was paid in cash with the other $16 issued in coupons to be used at base, post, or depot exchanges.

Cooperating ISU soldiers also enjoyed further special liberties. For example, on weekends they could receive guests or travel off base to visit Italian American friends and relatives in nearby towns and cities. They could also fraternize liberally with fellow US soldiers and civilians, including women. In exchange for these greater freedoms, the cooperating soldiers gave the United States a ready labor pool that offset the wartime labor shortages and contributed in a meaningful way to the powerful production efforts on the home front.

About 1,200 cooperators, organized into the 321st Italian Quartermaster Battalion, commanded at first by Lt. Col. Salvatore Campa and then by Maj. Angelo Bassi, were sent to the Letterkenny Army Ordnance Depot, located less than six miles from the quaint Pennsylvania town of Chambersburg. There, they were further divided into six ISUs to provide wartime assistance at what was one of the largest and newest military depots in the country—Letterkenny had only been constructed out of 20,000 acres of gentle farmland two years prior in 1942. Spread out over the entire depot, 30 warehouses and 800 underground storage units held munitions, weapons, and other military equipment of all types that personnel packaged and sent to the European and Pacific theaters of war. American military power, shown simply through the quantity of weapons that flowed through Letterkenny, further confirmed to many Italian POWs the absurdity of Mussolini's choice to go to war with the United States.

The cooperators at Letterkenny performed various duties. Although they operated and maintained the small railroad that served the depot, they mainly loaded, unloaded, and stocked the war materials that freight trains brought to the depot. Several POWs hurt themselves in the course of their work, often on equipment that they used to perform their official duties, but fortunately no accidental deaths occurred, and most injuries were not life threatening. As they went about their jobs, they worked side by side with American civilians, many of whom were African American, and often, as previously stated, they were in the presence of many women. This situation, as could be expected, favored sentimental attachments that even the women often initiated.

During their free time after work and on weekends, the cooperators pursued many leisure activities that interested them. Some gravitated to sport, others to music, and many had hobbies that involved arts and crafts. As for sport, many played soccer, often with fiery passion. Matches were frequent, and company-level teams participated in several tournaments. With regard to music, the ISU members organized an orchestra, a band, and a choral group. On weekends, those soldiers who liked to dance often had dates, and especially escorted Italian American women who came to the depot to visit them with their families.

Italian POWs detained in the United States were, simply put, the best treated anywhere in the world during the war, and a few important factors ensured that this was the case. The United States had the highest standard of living among all countries, and since international regulations held that the detaining power treat its prisoners on par with its own soldiers, Italian soldiers truly benefited from the highest of standards that US soldiers enjoyed. Italian POWs had superior food, billeting, uniforms, and health care that far outdistanced what the Italian military could give them.

The singular experience of Italian American immigration provides a second motive for their outstanding treatment. At the time of World War II, more than five million Italian Americans, mainly comprised of first- and second-generation immigrants, played a decisive role in providing help of all kinds to the Italian soldiers to whom they often felt bonded emotionally if they were not so in fact by blood. From a political perspective, Italian Americans tried to influence US congressional representatives and local authorities to ensure proper treatment was accorded, and they also assisted the POWs personally by visiting the camps and hosting Italian soldiers in their homes when possible.

A final, powerful motive further explains the high quality of life Italian POWs experienced—that pertaining to the Roman Catholic Church and its crucial help. Since the greatest numbers, by far, of the Italian POWs were Catholic, they could count on the church's infrastructure to give them aid of all sorts: local bishops and priests celebrated Mass with them, heard their confessions, wrote letters to loved ones back in Italy on their behalf, and otherwise cared for them in extraordinary ways. In this regard, they could especially count on the Vatican's apostolic delegate, Msgr. Amleto Cicognani. He often visited Italian soldiers in various camps throughout the county and represented their needs time and time again to American authorities.

The ISU soldiers of the 321st Italian Quartermaster Battalion were stationed at Letterkenny for 17 months, and initially, their relative liberty did, from time to time, provoke hostilities between them and the local populace. Indeed, many disgruntled American civilians saw the Italian prisoners as overly pampered, and they brought their grievances to military authorities. In reaction, the POWs had many of their freedoms curtailed, such as only being able to leave the depot on Saturdays after work and on Sundays. For the ISU soldiers, these negative measures greatly disturbed them, and only the frequent visits that civilians, and especially Italian Americans, paid to them on the depot could assuage their bitterness. They had been in combat for several years under dire conditions and were relieved to become cooperating prisoners. But detention was nonetheless growing longer by the week, and "barbwire" disease—a pernicious form of melancholy—also hit the troops at Letterkenny. Numerous POWs suffered bouts of depression and faced other psychological trauma. Such is the tragic case with Pasquino Savini, who committed suicide on June 3, 1944, when he hurled himself beneath a road grader as he and other POWs were helping to construct a new depot road.

The greatest antidote to depression, beyond getting any news from home via the mail, was to keep occupied, and fortunately, the POWs had the chance to help build the depot itself after normal duty hours while using secondhand materials from civilian houses and farms that had been knocked down. The most important building project involved the construction of the chapel and bell tower, to be sure, but the POWs also built the Post Assembly Hall, still extant today, where movies and theatrical plays were shown and where Mass was held prior to the construction of the chapel. In addition, the soldiers constructed an amphitheater where with good weather the battalion orchestra could play. The weekend dances they hosted brought fun entertainment and, importantly, American women who provided them company.

Letterkenny POWs were among the earliest to repatriate to Italy. A first contingent that left in September 1945 arrived in Naples on October 6. The rest departed at the beginning of October and disembarked on the 20th of that month. The last Italian POWs around the country were repatriated in March 1946. As such, even in this way the POWs were extraordinarily fortunate when considering that the last Italian POWs held in the British Commonwealth arrived in Italy in March 1947, almost two full years after the end of the European war.

By and large, Italian prisoners who lived in the United States judged their experience in very positive terms. As soldiers, they recognized how fortunate they had been to escape harm and death and be able at times to put on weight even while being classified as prisoners. Once home, given that they had seen aspects of democratic institutions that functioned very well, they both gravitated themselves toward and helped others to support Italian political orientations in line with such institutions, a critical point if we consider that the largest Communist Party in Europe outside of the Soviet Union was found in Italy. These returning soldiers, in other words, helped socially instill an awareness that the United States provided the best ally for their country's economic recovery. They then further contributed to helping foster good relations between the United States and Italy during the Cold War. Finally, the decision of several ex-POWs to return to the United States to make a life after the war, for many of them with American brides who sailed to Italy to marry them, confirms at another level their positive experience at the hands of their American captors.

One

From War to Imprisonment

Italian soldiers fought with great tenacity and courage during World War II, despite the fact that their equipment and arms were decisively inferior to weapons and machinery that their Allied foes employed. To prove this point, note a few photographs of Italian tanks. The troops called them "sardine cans," and they stand in marked contrast to the size of American M4 Shermans and various models of German Panzers. Much of the equipment Italians used was also outdated. Indeed, many artillery pieces and transportation vehicles were first employed during World War I.

By mere chance, most likely because of circumstances and location of capture, numerous Letterkenny POWs belonged to a special infantry corps. The bersaglieri were elite foot soldiers easily identifiable in garrison by their large plumed hat and highly disciplined running regimen; bersaglieri never marched but jogged everywhere they went, and their esprit de corps was matchless. Fierce fighters, they often were called upon for special assault operations.

Several prisoners, before being sent to America, were first transported to England. Such is the case of Giovanni Serpe, whose submarine *Galileo Ferraris* was sunk in the Atlantic Ocean.

Once the POWs arrived in the United States, each had an identification card issued to him that consisted of his photograph along with annotations concerning his personal data, place of detention, and assigned unit. A soldier had to carry his ID with him wherever he went.

It was not uncommon for relatives and even brothers to be captured together, and these troops naturally did all they could to stay together during their term of imprisonment. At Letterkenny, there were two sets of brothers—Domenico and Luigi Sambrotta, who were originally from San Buono, a town in the province of Chieti; and Cirillo and Ismo Beggi, who came from Casalgrande in the province of Reggio Emilia. Two photographs in this chapter detail the information that Americans registered for the Sambrottas during administrative in-processing along with their assigned prisoner serial numbers. Finally, a few examples are provided of individual POW photographs that accompanied official US prisoner documentation.

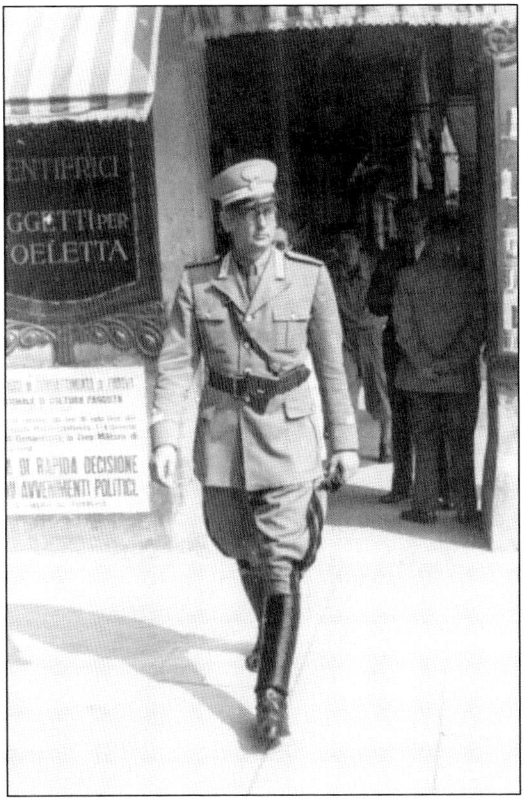

Lt. Roberto Cardinale, a carabiniere (member of the Italian national police force) is seen here in Florence in 1938. Together with the Italian army, navy, and air force, the carabinieri are Italy's fourth armed service. During the war, they primarily undertook military policing. While at Letterkenny, Cardinale served as a captain and commanded the 85th ISU. Since he was a carabiniere, he was one of the first to be repatriated to Italy, where he arrived on March 13, 1945. (Courtesy of Giuseppe Grasso.)

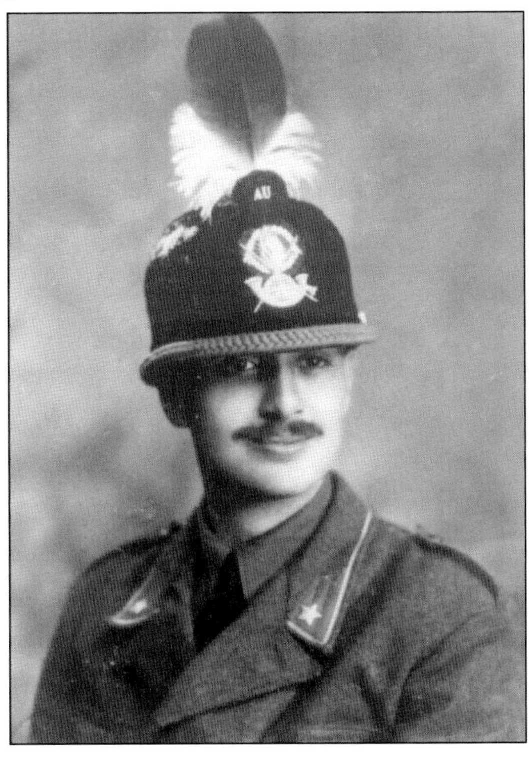

Massimo Jappelli is seen here in his officer candidate school photograph, dressed in his decorative hat with a large feather. At Letterkenny, Jappelli, as second lieutenant, served with the 83rd ISU, a unit later sent in July 1945 to the Sioux Ordnance Depot, Sidney, Nebraska. After the war, Jappelli lived in different countries for work, and in 2000 he emigrated to Brazil, where his daughter Deborah and her family still live today. (Courtesy of Deborah Jappelli.)

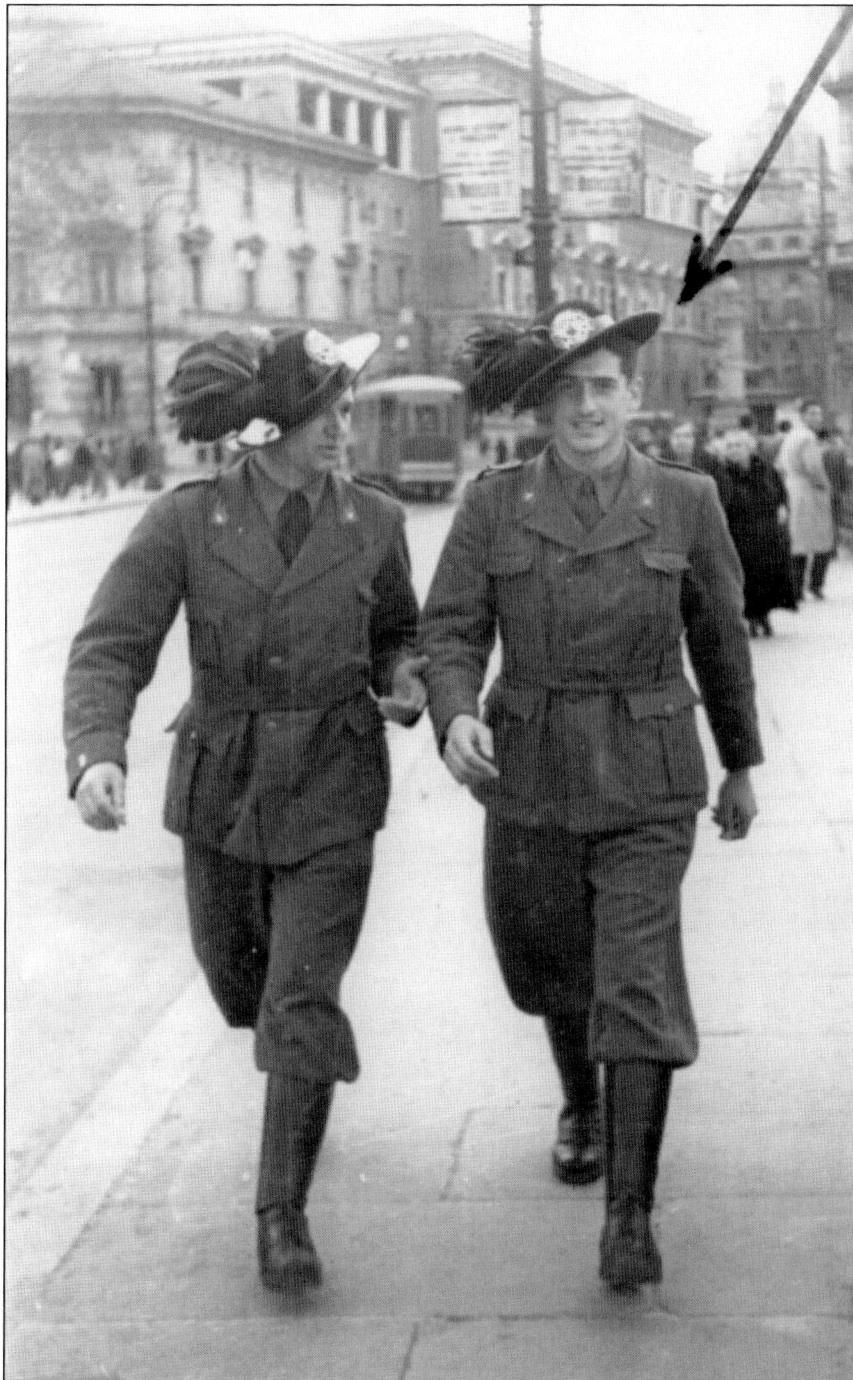

2nd Lt. Alfredo Tonolo, right, walks with a fellow bersagliere on Rome's Via Arenula, most likely in 1941 or early 1942. The Bersaglieri are a special infantry unit of the Italian army and very beloved by the Italian public still today. Indeed, one of the corps' distinguished traits is to parade at double time with unique bugle calls while donning special feathered hats. (Courtesy of Frances Tonolo MacAvoy.)

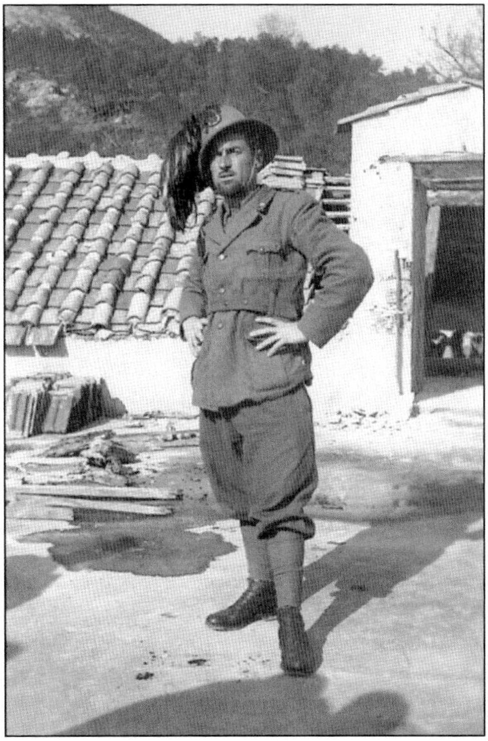

Aldo Lorenzi poses somewhat arrogantly in his bersagliere uniform for this photograph. Lorenzi, born on October 22, 1913, in Mozzecane, a town near Verona located in the Veneto region, served with the Italian army in the 8th Bersaglieri Regiment. He was captured on March 20, 1943, in North Africa when US tanks surrounded his unit. As a Letterkenny POW, he served with the 84th ISU. (Courtesy of Keti Melotto.)

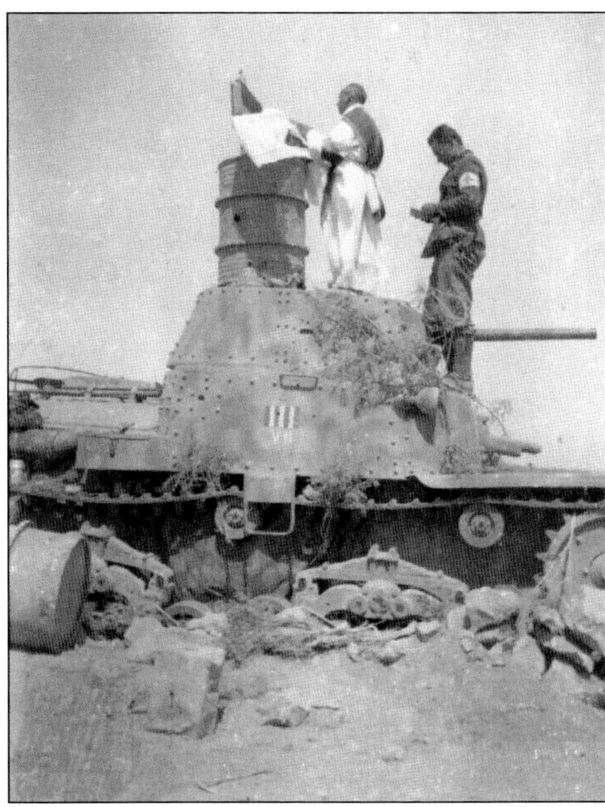

A military chaplain of the 8th Bersaglieri Regiment, assisted by another Italian soldier wearing a Red Cross band on his left arm, celebrates an improvised field Mass on the Tobruk front on May 2, 1941. Note that the priest is using the turret of a tank as an altar. (Courtesy of Vittoria Buffoni.)

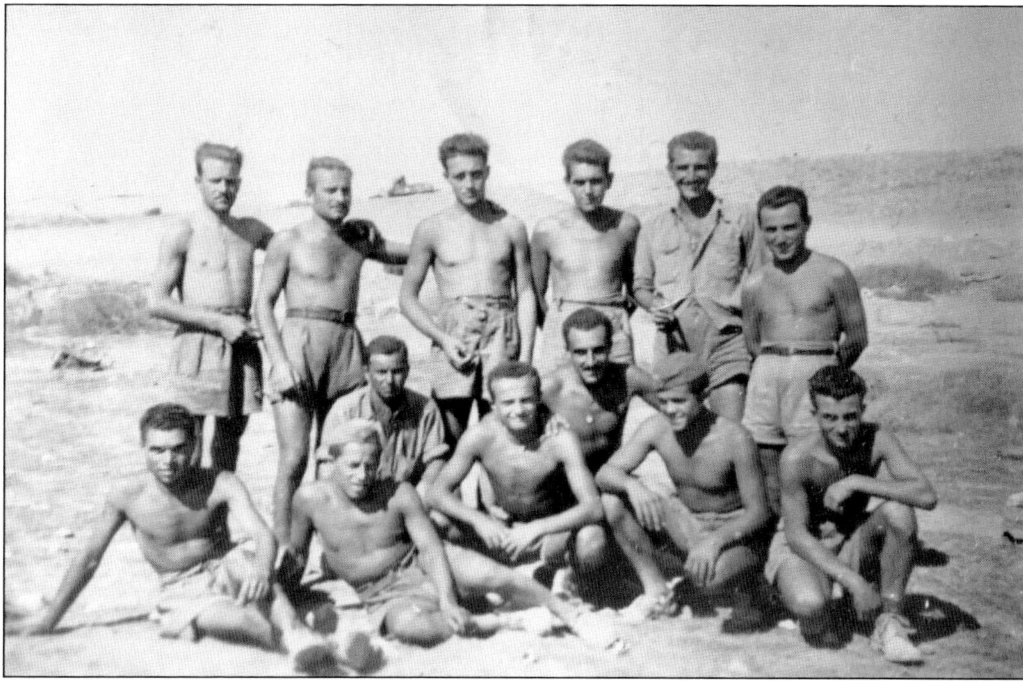

Donato Pietra, seated second from the left, poses with a few military buddies at Tobruk (Libya) on July 17, 1942. English troops took him prisoner on May 11, 1943, in Tunisia. Born on October 22, 1921, Pietra still enjoys excellent health, and, as of April 2017 he lives with family members in Bergamo, a city in the Lombardy region. (Courtesy of Donato and Massimo Pietra.)

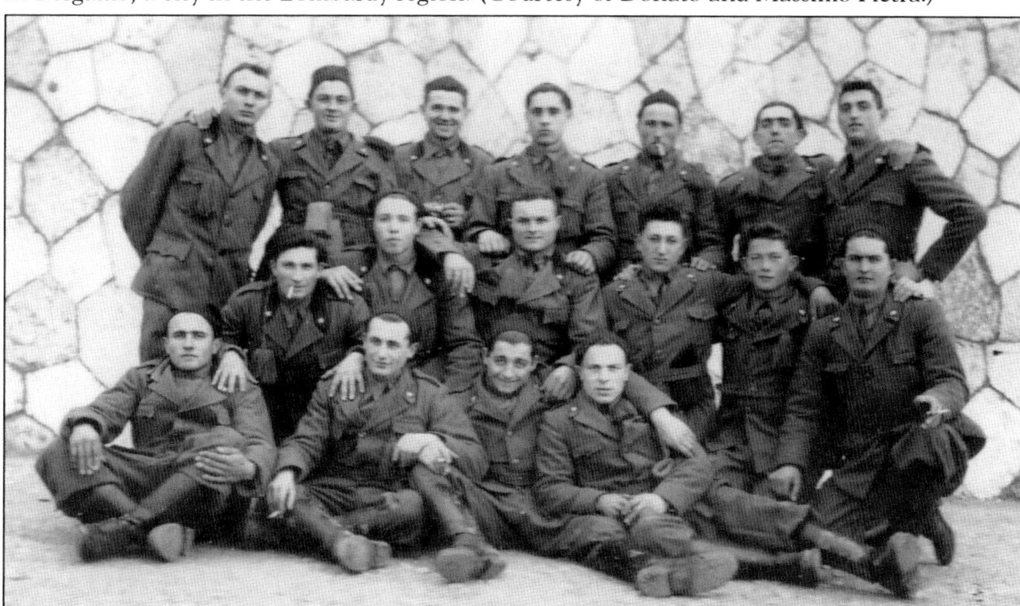

Innocente Salini stands, first on the right, with other bersaglieri troops. Besides the feathered hat, bersaglieri at times wore the fez. In the 19th century, during the first years after this branch formed in 1834, they also wore knickerbockers. Salini was born on August 20, 1922, in the province of Bergamo, in the Lombardy region. (Courtesy of Mariantonia Salini.)

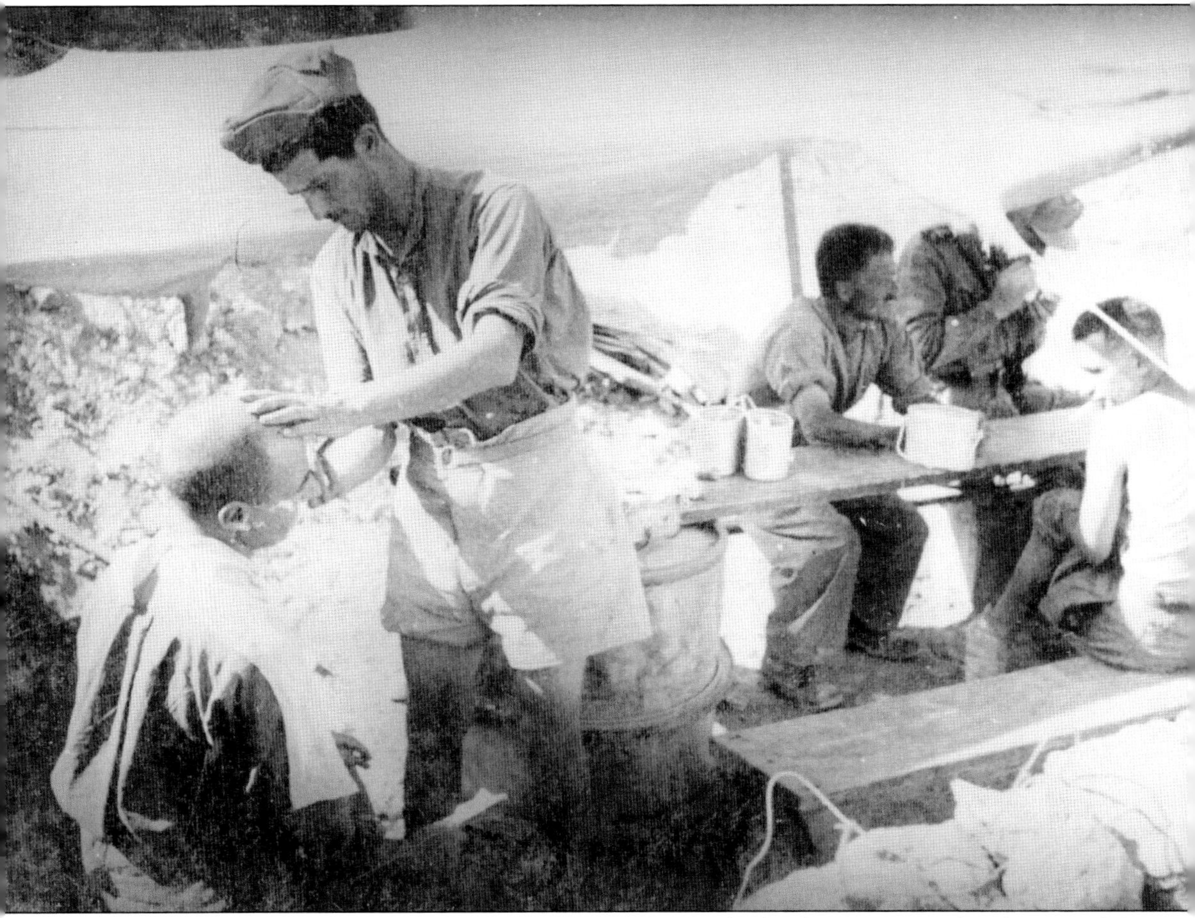

Antonio Arganetto here shaves a fellow soldier under the shade of a tent in North Africa. English forces captured Arganetto shortly after the Battle of El Alamein, on November 3, 1942. Upon capture, his barber tools were confiscated, but in the United States Arganetto received a completely new set and continued to exercise his barber trade. (Courtesy of Michael Arganetto.)

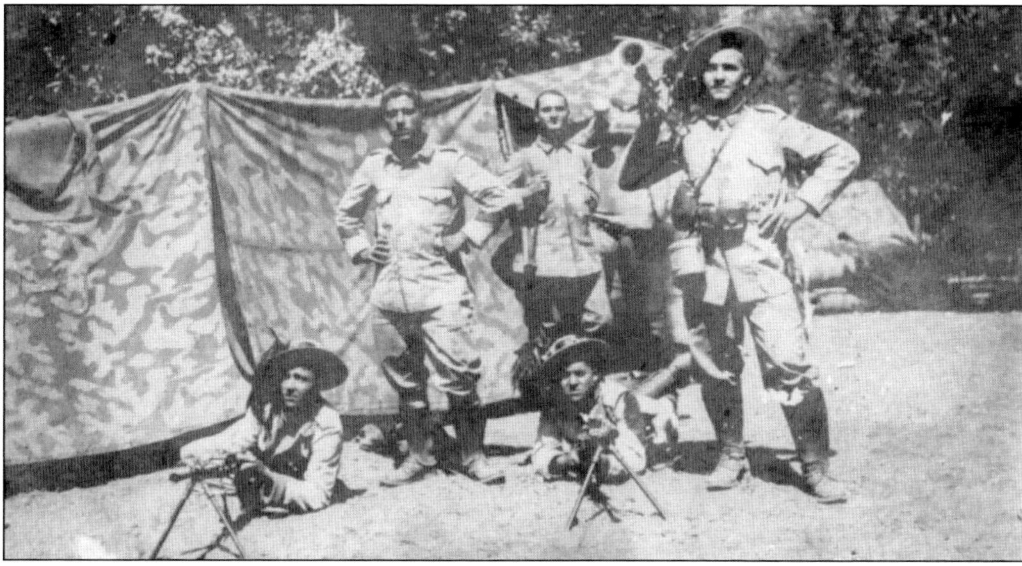

Mario Luigini is first on the left standing with other bersaglieri and seen here during military maneuvers. Luigini was born in Pescara, and at Letterkenny he was the sergeant major of the 321st Italian Quartermaster Battalion. In 1945, for almost six months, he was hospital bound recovering from thromboangiitis (Buerger disease), first at Carlisle Barracks and then subsequently at the Ashorf General Hospital in West Virginia. (Courtesy of Mario Luigini [grandson].)

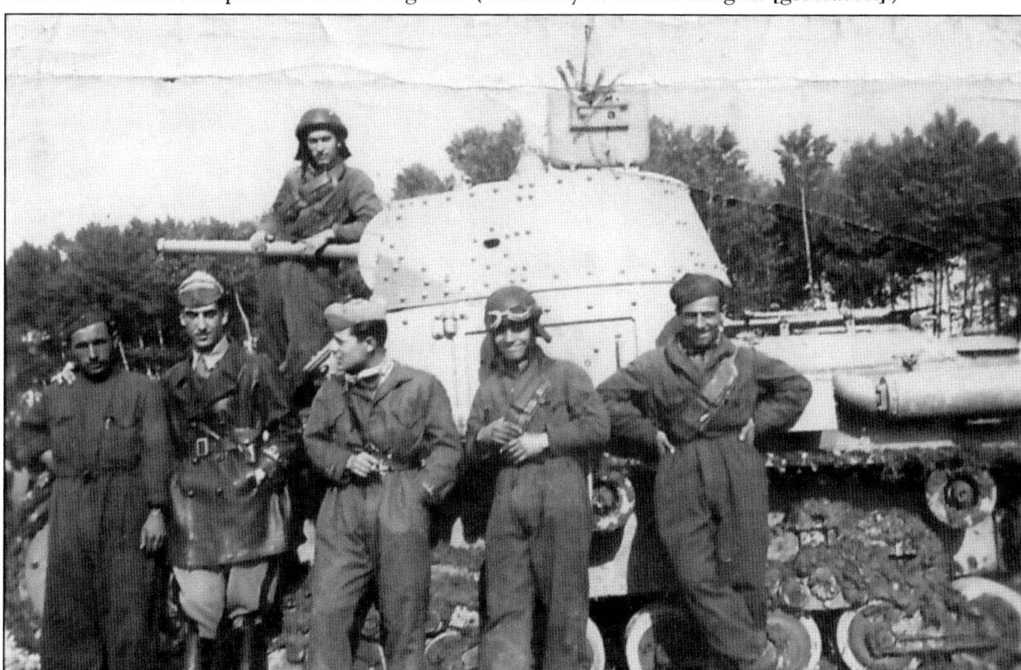

Leo Siligardi, far right, poses with other soldiers in front of a tank in Africa in 1942. Siligardi hailed from the Emilia Romagna region. The English captured him on May 10, 1943, in Tunisia and two weeks later turned him over to US custody. After being sent to Camp Hereford, Texas, and then Camp Monticello, Arkansas, he arrived at Letterkenny and was assigned to the 86th ISU. (Courtesy of Sandra Siligardi.)

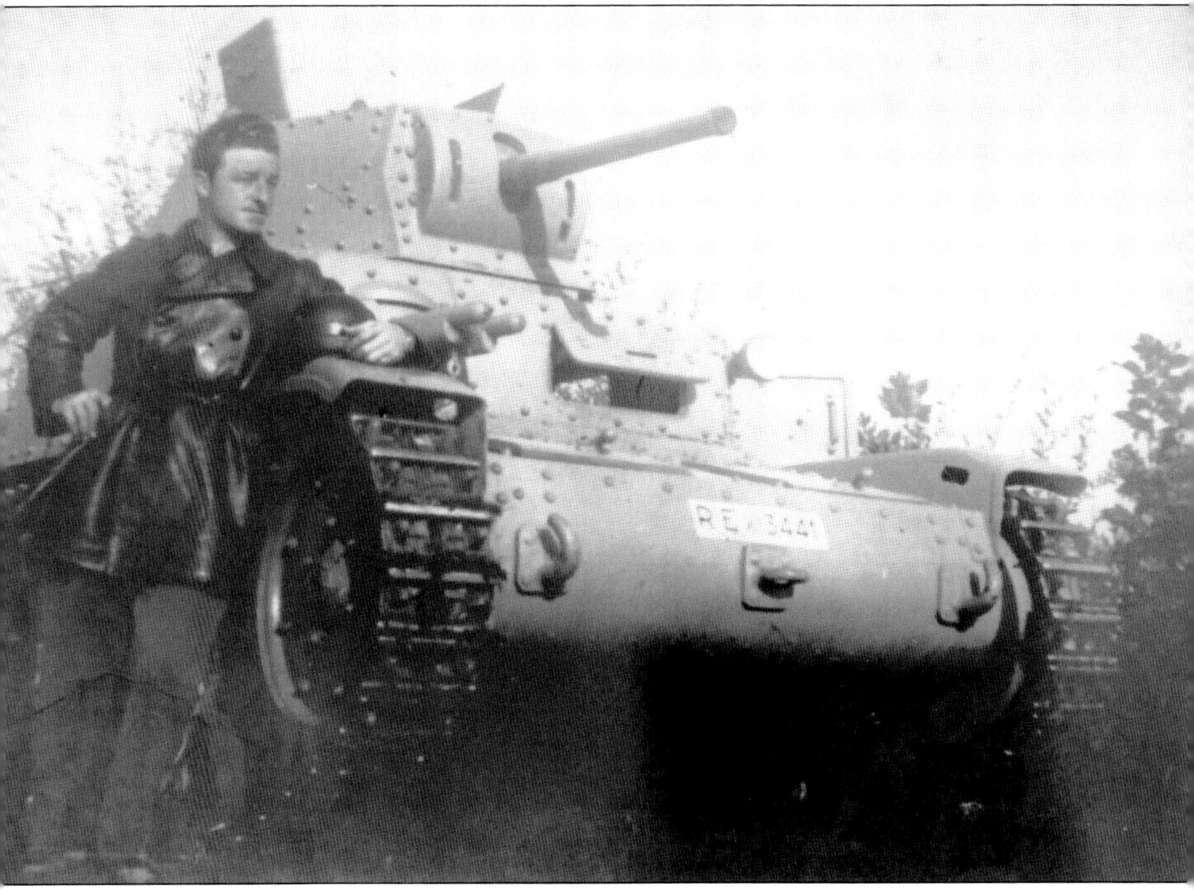

This photograph shows Luciano Boneschi leaning on an Italian M13/40 tank. In comparing this tank to American or English ones of the same period, one can easily tell that the Italian military went into combat with decisively inferior armed vehicles. The state of material unpreparedness upon Italy's entry into the war was one of Mussolini's most serious faults. (Courtesy of Valeria Conconi.)

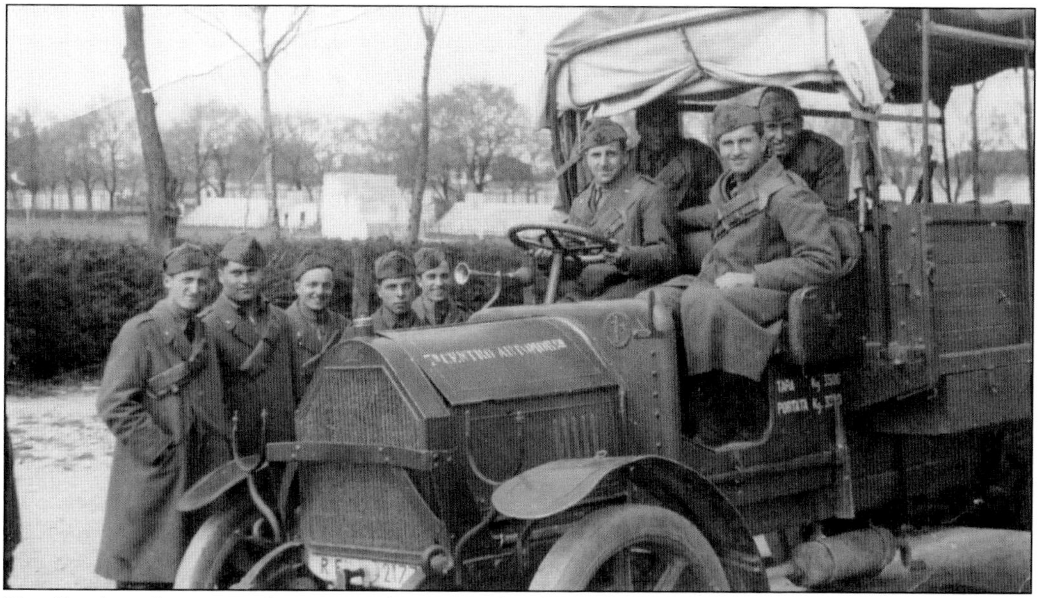

Elio De Angelis is seen here seated next to the driver of an old military utility truck in Italy. Italian military means of transportation, just like with weapons, were in part old and used during World War I. Despite the Fascist regime's propaganda about its military power, Italian soldiers were sent into combat highly unprepared and inferior to Allied troops with respect to material, leadership, and training. (Courtesy of Roberto De Angelis.)

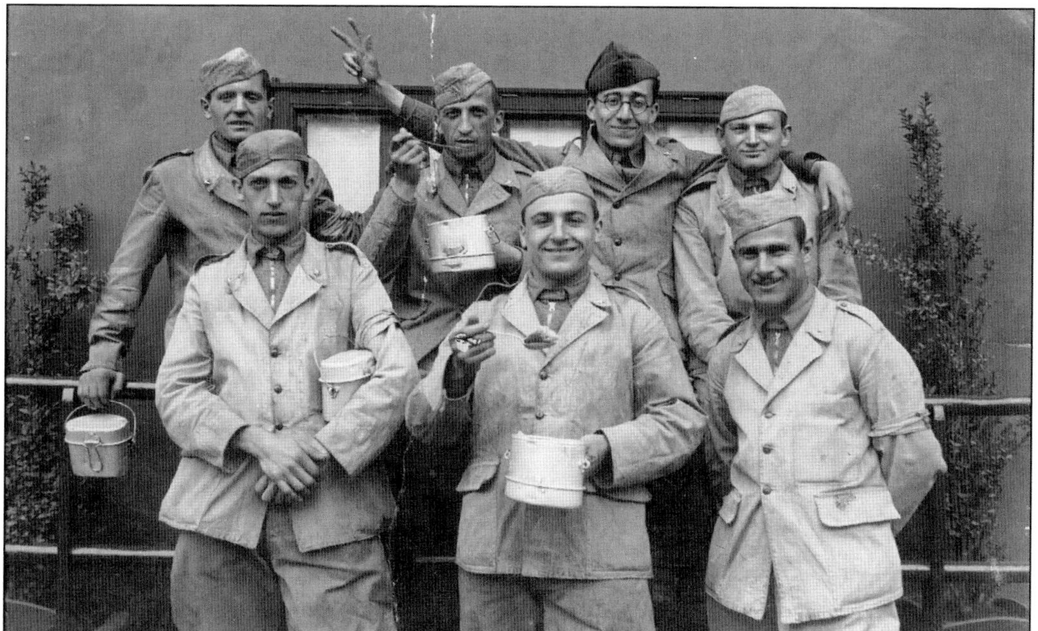

Holding a mess tin and happy to taste his rations in front of his barracks in Turin on May 5, 1938, Pvt. Egidio Dall'Aglio poses in the first row, center, with other soldiers in his unit. Born on May 24, 1917, in Masi (Padua), Dall'Aglio was captured by the Americans on March 23, 1943, in Meknassy, Tunisia, after having survived for a few days by nibbling on rosemary bushes. (Courtesy of Franco Cosentino.)

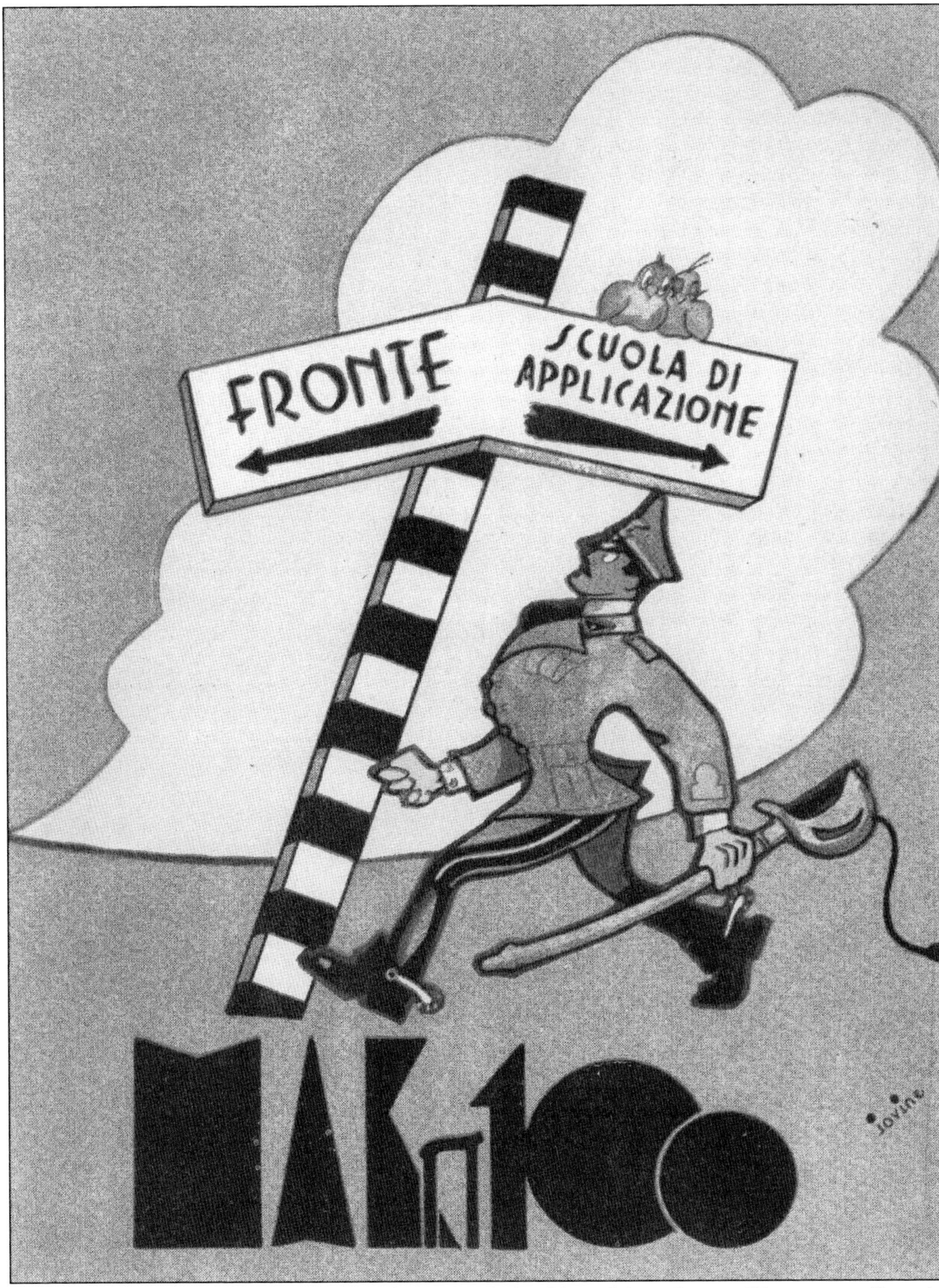

Marcello Iovine designed this propaganda postcard. A self-confident Corps of Engineers officer (as was Iovine himself) preferred to head to the 1942 front lines instead of finishing his specialization training. With this artistic example, one can already note Iovine's refined artistic abilities that destined him to become a well-known artist and medallion crafter in the United States after the war. (Courtesy of Flavio G. Conti.)

Marcello Iovine, in uniform as a second lieutenant of the Italian Corps of Engineers, poses on a horse, most likely in Italy. Iovine was born in Naples on July 26, 1921. He studied engineering in college but worked as a mural painter and cartoonist for newspapers and magazines. The English captured him in Tunisia on May 13, 1943. (Courtesy of Marcia and Andrea Jovine. © 2017.)

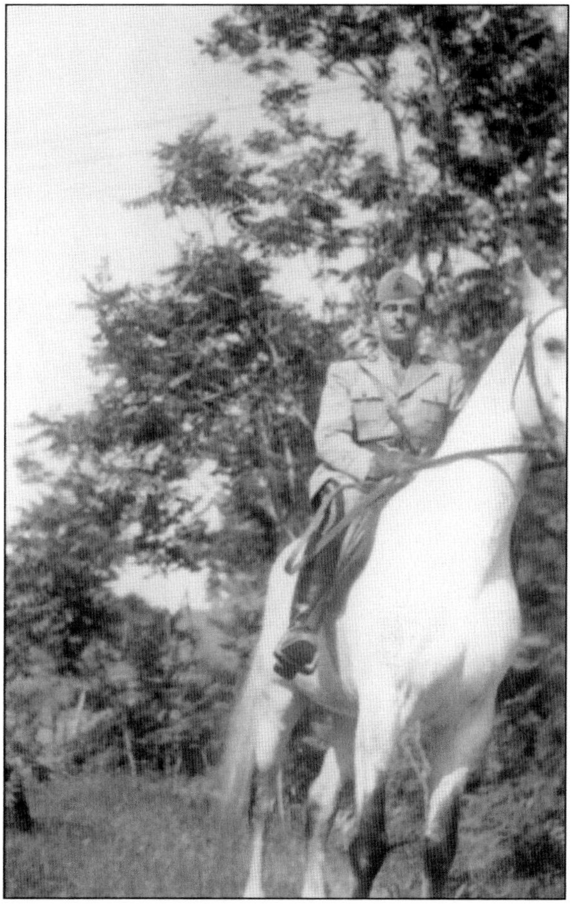

Antonio Arganetto is at far left in Tarhuna, Libya, in December 1942. Cesare Almagioni is at far right, to the right of the second camel. Almagioni, originally from Bergamo, was a sergeant major in the field artillery when he was captured. At Letterkenny, he served with the 82nd ISU. (Courtesy of Maurizio Almagioni.)

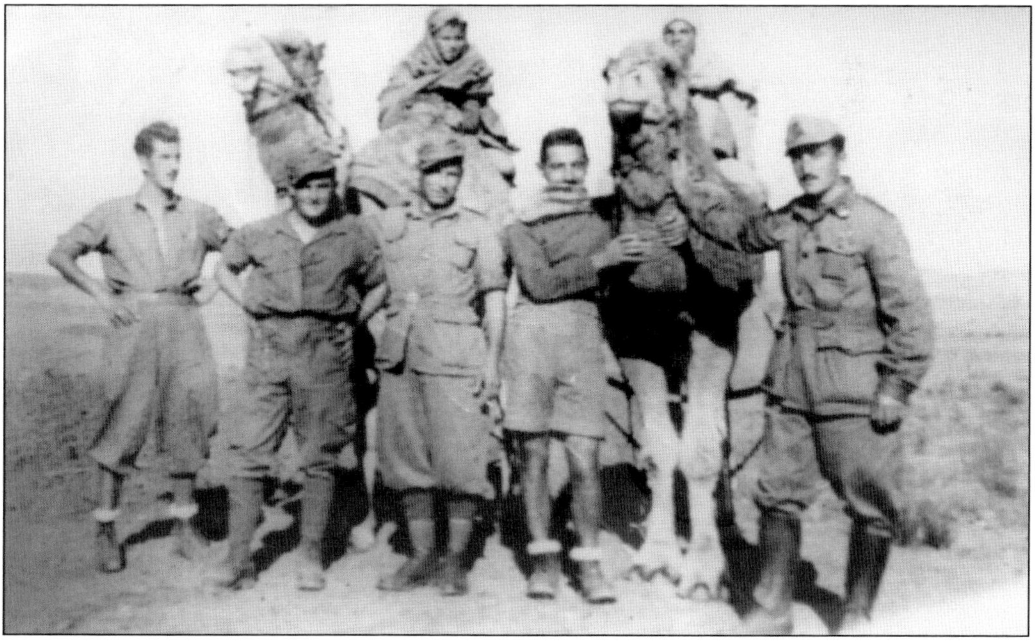

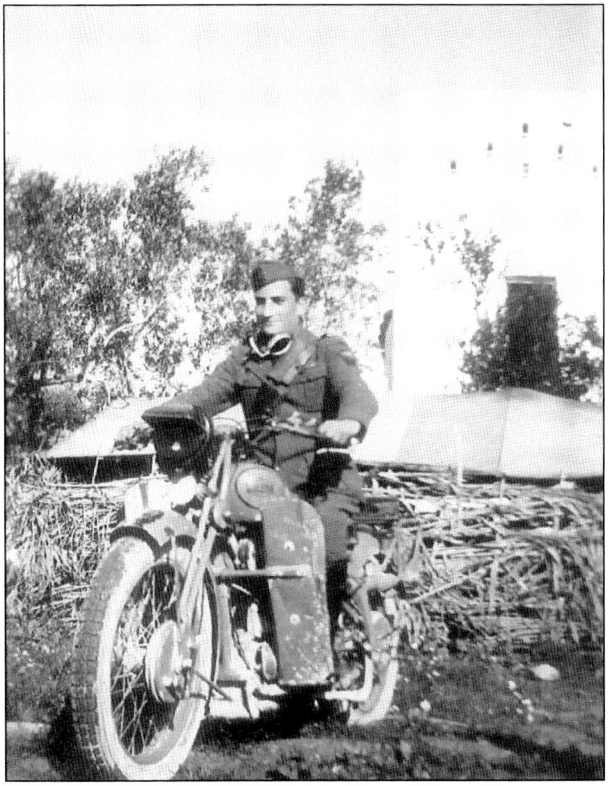

Cpl. Giuseppe D'Argenio sits on a motorcycle in Mazara del Vallo, Sicily, on February 5, 1943. D'Argenio was born in Ospedaletto d'Alpinolo (Avellino) on April 7, 1921. American forces captured him in Sicily on July 21, 1943. He arrived at Letterkenny on March 1, 1944, in transit from Camp Monticello, Arkansas, and was assigned to the 83rd ISU. (Courtesy of Maria Rosaria D'Argenio.)

Antonio Santambrogio, born in Seveso (Milan) on June 13, 1911, is standing fourth from the left with a few soldiers in his unit, most likely in Sicily. Santambrogio was captured by the English in Sicily on July 10, 1943, and turned over to the Americans. By September 7, a few weeks later, he was already on the POW rosters at Camp Butner, North Carolina. (Courtesy of Natale Santamborgio.)

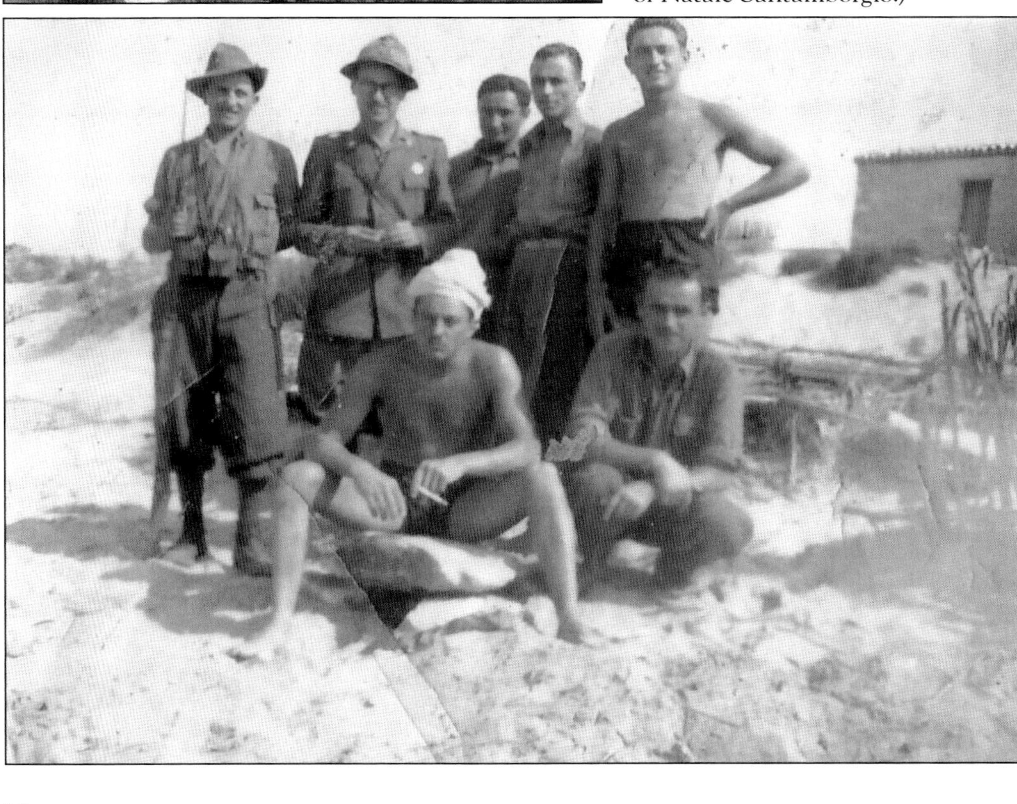

Sergeant major of engineers Federico Cavicchi, born in Bologna on August 12, 1919, was captured by the English Eighth Army on May 11, 1943, at Hammamet, Tunisia, and the following October was sent to the United States. Here, he poses in a colonial helmet that Italian forces in Africa wore. Many soldiers got rid of them upon arrival because they were cumbersome and utterly useless for protection. (Courtesy of Sonia Cavicchi.)

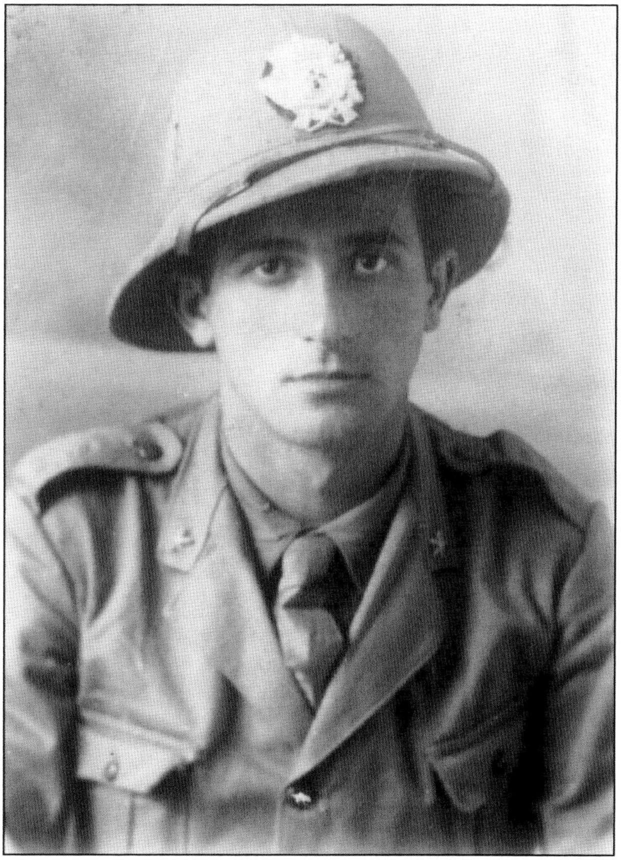

Italian soldiers playfully pose together with three North African youths, most likely in Tunisia or Libya. Andrea Cecchini stands in the center while smoking a cigarette. Born on February 6, 1916, in Trevignano, a small town near Rome, Cecchini was captured by the British Eighth Army at Enfidaville, Tunisia, on May 12, 1943. (Courtesy of Massimo Cecchini.)

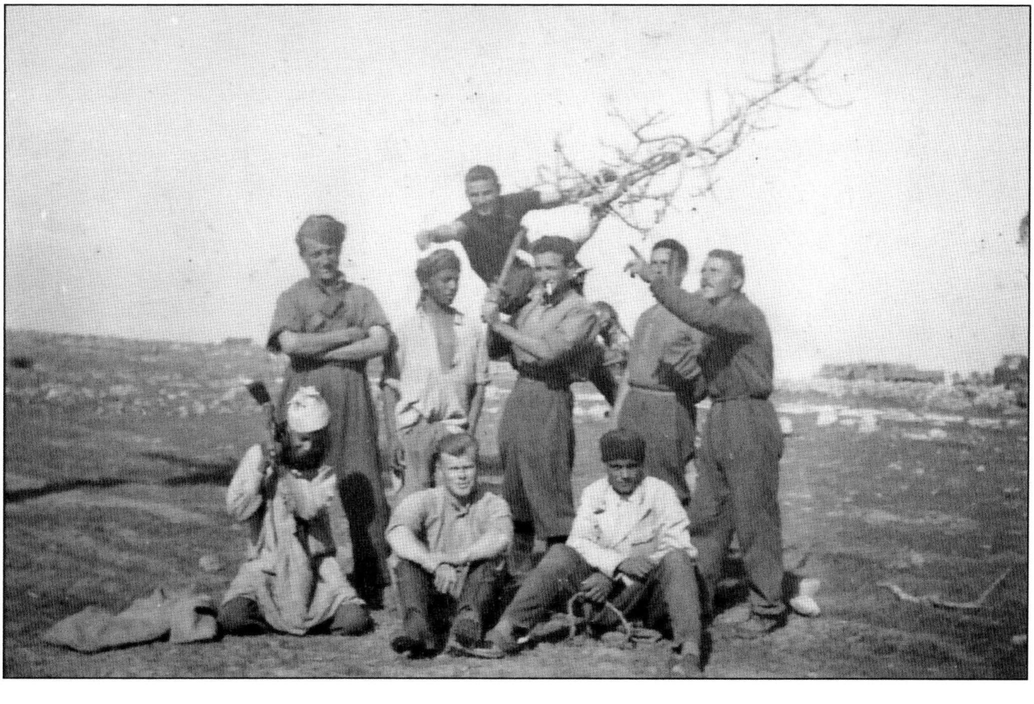

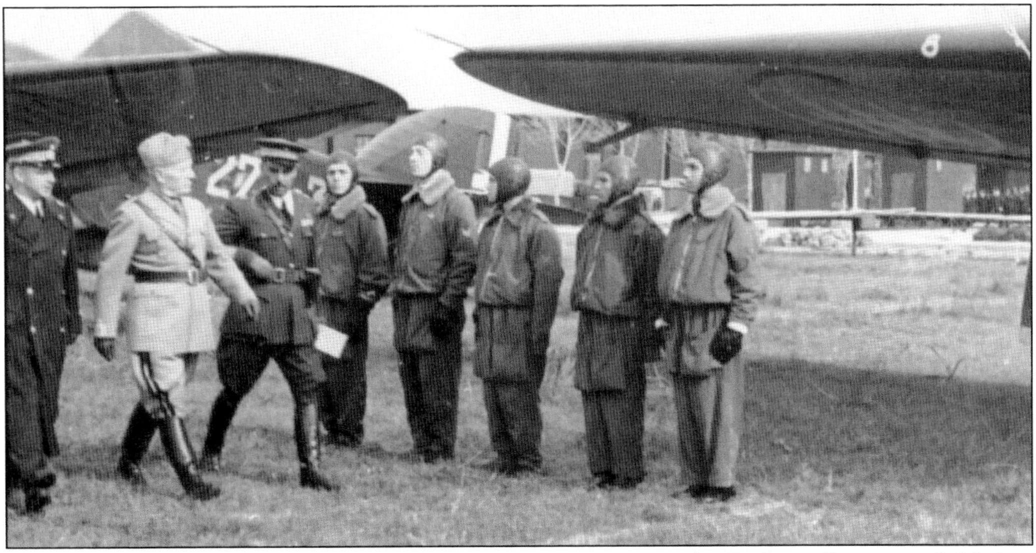

Il Duce, Italian dictator Benito Mussolini, reviews aircrews at the Furbara, Rome, airfield that are leaving for Sicily on March 28, 1943. Lt. Giovanni Fresta, wearing his flight jacket, is the first on the left with his crew. Fresta was shot down on May 20, 1943, and had to ditch his airplane not far from Bona (also known as Annaba), Algeria. One member of his crew died, and several others were severely wounded. (Courtesy of Isidoro Fresta.)

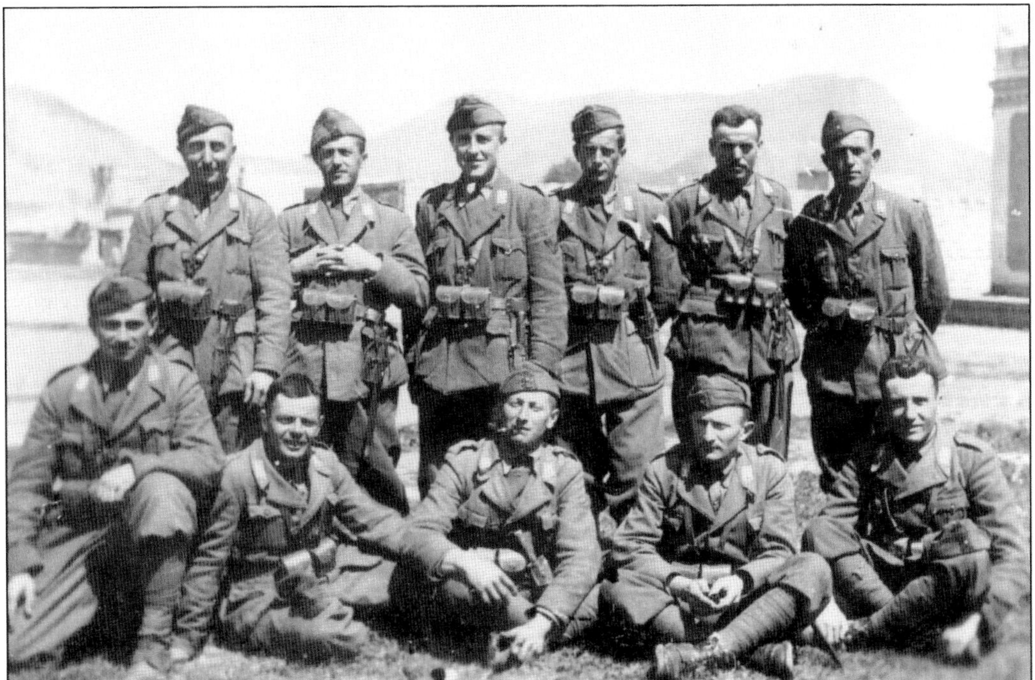

Several Valsesian members of the 465th Costal Battalion pose for a photo souvenir in Bagheria (Palermo) in April 1943. Pietro Bracchi is sitting second from the left. Valsesia is a valley in the province of Vercelli, in the Piedmont region. When possible, soldiers from the same geographical region, including the ones pictured here, tried to stay together while imprisoned. (Courtesy of Carmela Bracchi and Sara De Giorgis.)

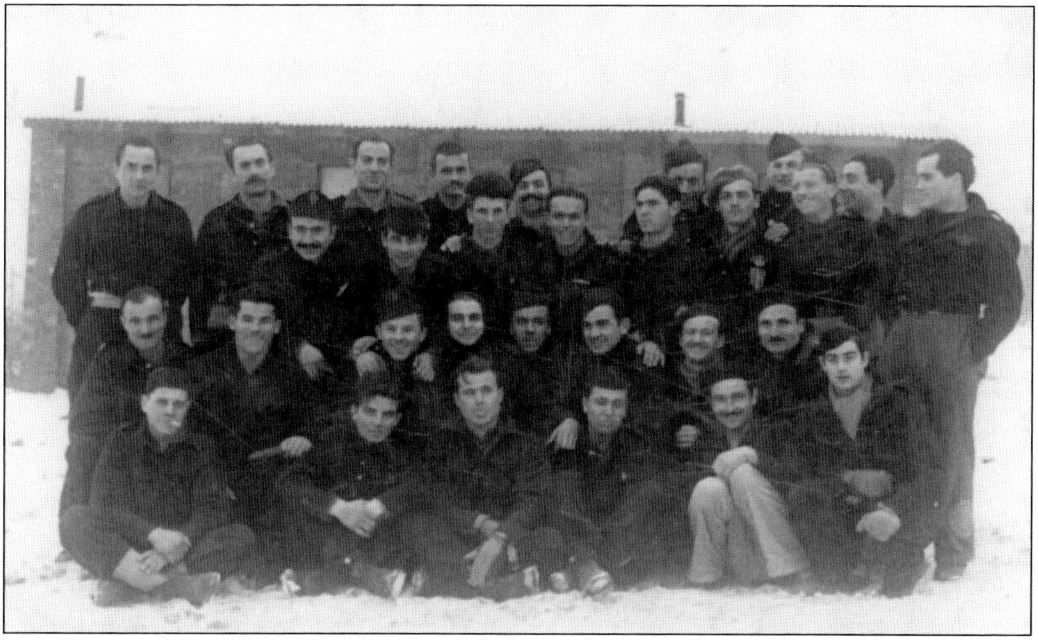

Giovanni Serpe, kneeling in the first row on the far right, is with part of his *Galileo Ferraris* submarine crew as a prisoner at POW Camp 17, Sheffield, England, on January 17, 1942. The *Galileo Ferraris* was sunk by the English destroyer *Lamerton* and RAF aircraft on October 25, 1941, east of the Azores, and six members of the crew died. In December 1942, Serpe was sent to the United States. (Courtesy of Giovanni Serpe.)

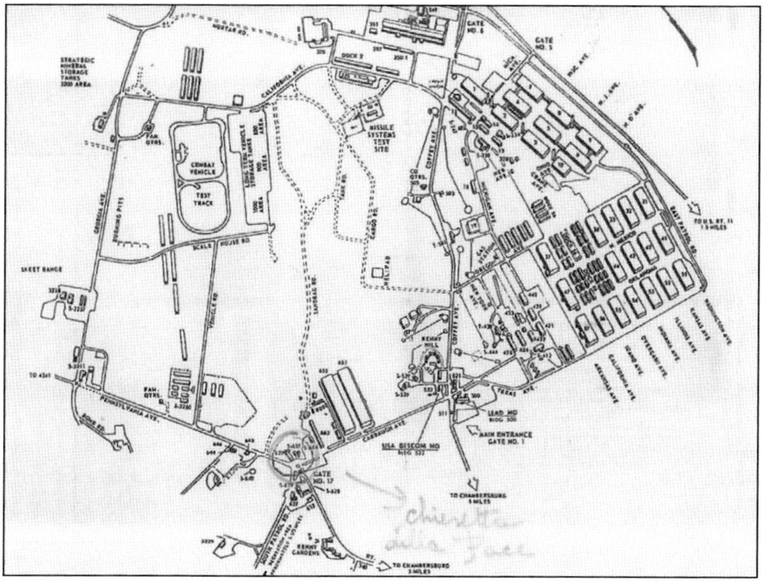

Renato Volpi indicated with a green circle on his small map of Letterkenny the general area of POW billeting, the chapel, and Post Assembly Hall—all of which were located near Gate 17. Volpi wrote "la chiesetta della pace" (the little church of peace). The streets of the depot were named after the 48 states that at the time comprised the Union. (Courtesy of Luisella Volpi.)

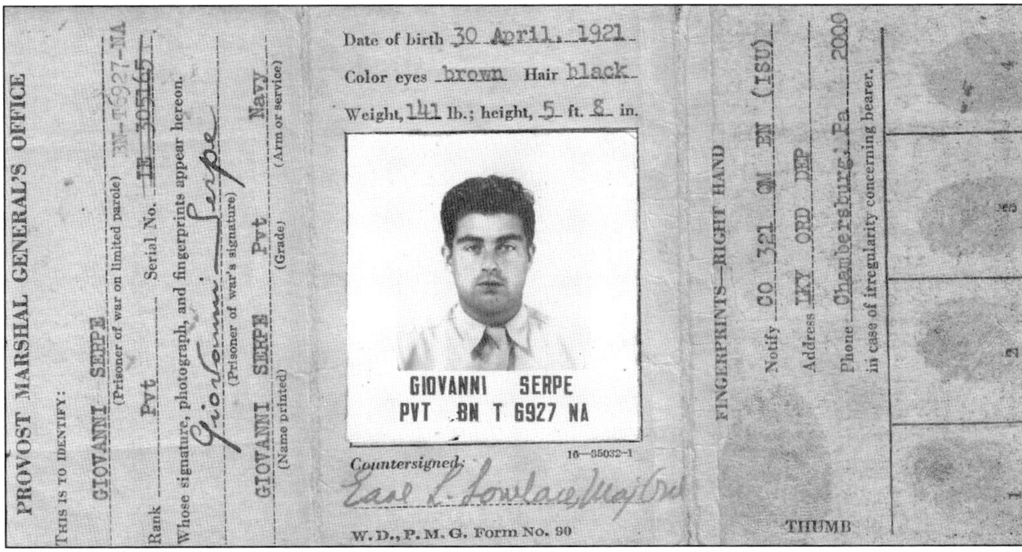

Pictured is POW Giovanni Serpe's official ID card that was issued at Letterkenny. As an official government document, the ID card consists of a photograph and fingerprints, and indicates the POW's birth date, serial number, rank, and branch of service. A POW was required to carry it with him at all times. Serpe's serial number, assigned to him by the English, was kept by the Americans for the duration of the war. (Courtesy of Giovanni Serpe.)

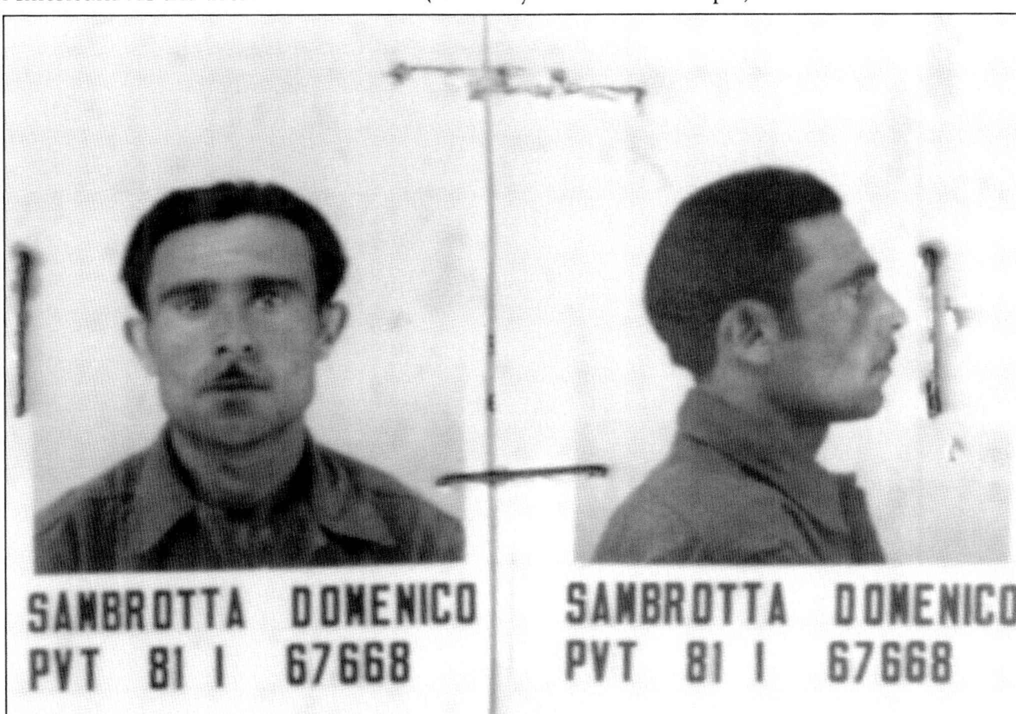

This is the identification photograph in the personnel file for Pvt. Domenico Sambrotta, taken at the Halloran General Hospital in New York. Sambrotta was first admitted here prior to being transferred to Letterkenny, where he was assigned to the 85th ISU, the same company to which his brother Luigi also belonged. (Courtesy of the MDDGCSGA, Rome, Domenico Sambrotta file.)

This identification photograph comes from the personnel file of Cpl. Luigi Sambrotta, Domenico's younger brother. He was also a POW with the 85th ISU at Letterkenny. The image was taken at the Scottsbluff, Nebraska, detention camp. The Sambrotta brothers were from a small town in the Abruzzi region—San Buono, near Chieti. (Courtesy of the MDDGCSGA, Rome, Luigi Sambrotta file.)

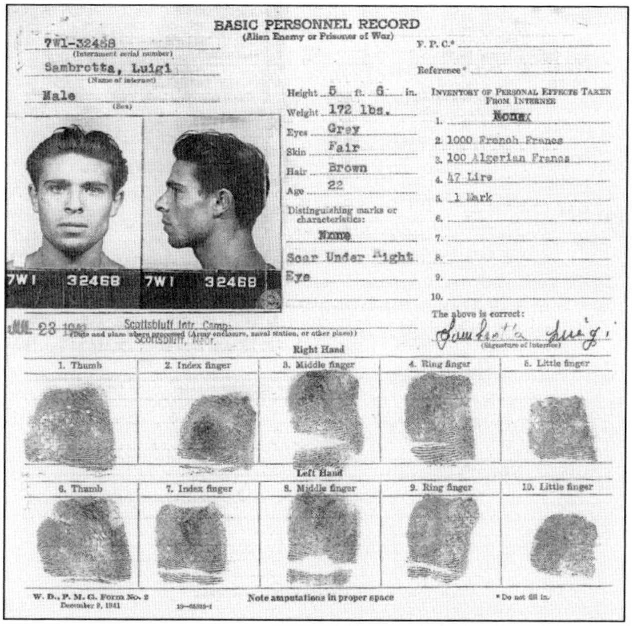
BASIC PERSONNEL RECORD
(Alien Enemy or Prisoner of War)

7WI-32468
(Internment serial number)
Sambrotta, Luigi
(Name of internee)
Male
(Sex)

F.P.C.*
Reference*

Height 5 ft. 6 in.
Weight 172 lbs.
Eyes Grey
Skin Fair
Hair Brown
Age 22
Distinguishing marks or characteristics:
None
Scar Under Right Eye

Inventory of Personal Effects Taken From Internee
1. None
2. 1000 French Francs
3. 100 Algerian Francs
4. 47 Lire
5. 1 Mark
6.
7.
8.
9.
10.
The above is correct:
(Signature of internee)

7WI 32468 7WI 32468

JUL 23 1943 Scottsbluff Intr. Camp.
(Date and place where processed (Army enclosure, naval station, or other place))

Right Hand
1. Thumb | 2. Index finger | 3. Middle finger | 4. Ring finger | 5. Little finger

Left Hand
6. Thumb | 7. Index finger | 8. Middle finger | 9. Ring finger | 10. Little finger

W. D., P. M. G. Form No. 2
December 9, 1941
Note amputations in proper space
*Do not fill in.

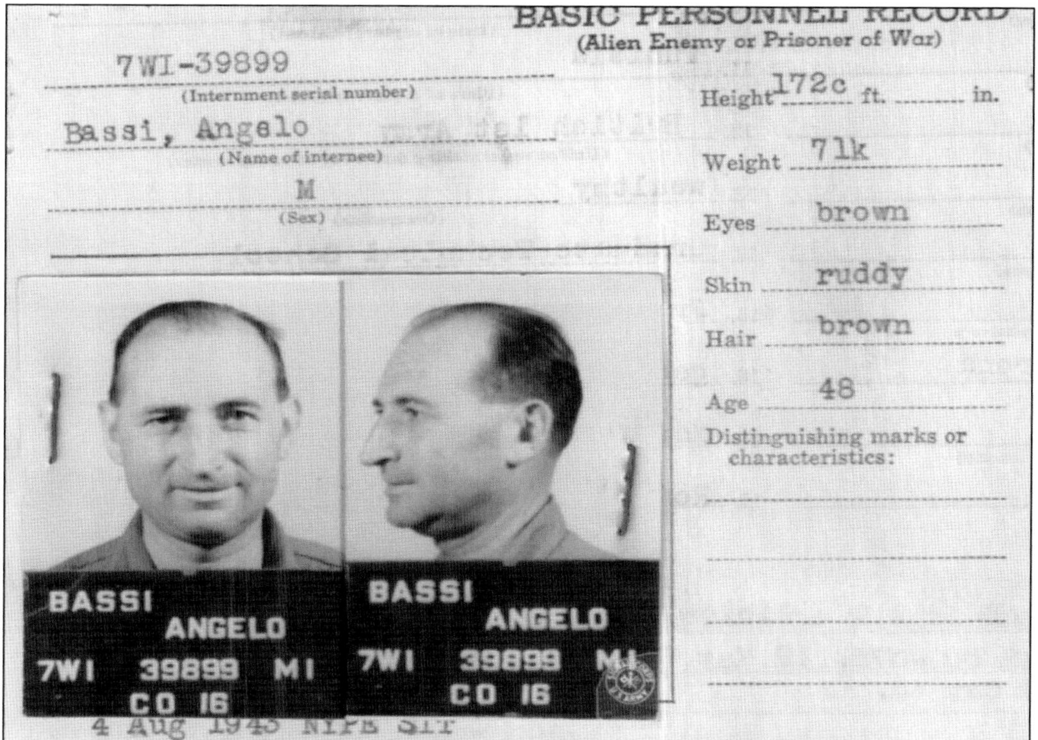
BASIC PERSONNEL RECORD
(Alien Enemy or Prisoner of War)

7WI-39899
(Internment serial number)
Bassi, Angelo
(Name of internee)
M
(Sex)

Height 172c ft. in.
Weight 71k
Eyes brown
Skin ruddy
Hair brown
Age 48
Distinguishing marks or characteristics:

BASSI ANGELO 7WI 39899 MI CO 16
BASSI ANGELO 7WI 39899 MI CO 16

4 Aug 1943 NYPE SIT
(Date and place where processed (Army enclosure, naval station, or other place))
RIGHT HAND

This is the identification photograph in the personnel file for Maj. Angelo Bassi, Italian commanding officer of Letterkenny's 321st Italian Quartermaster Battalion. As with several other Letterkenny POWs, Bassi was a bersagliere, an elite infantry soldier. He was captured in the spring of 1943 in North Africa. (Courtesy of the MDDGCSGA, Rome, Bassi file.)

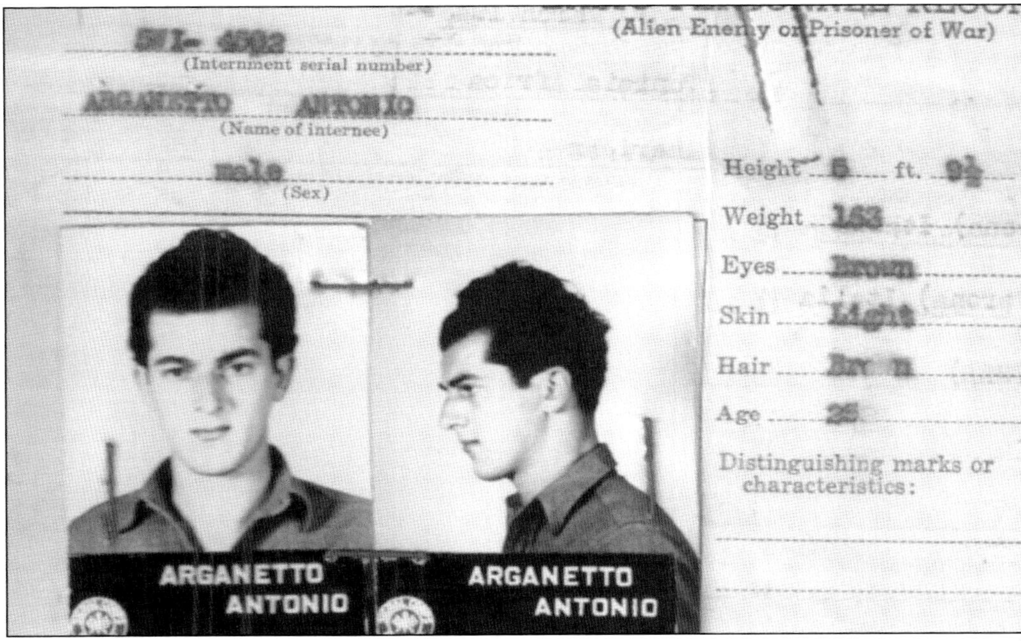

This is the identification photograph in the personnel file for Cpl. Antonio Arganetto. In North Africa, Arganetto served as his unit's barber, a trade that would come in very handy after the war. At Letterkenny, he met his future wife, Bruna D'Angelo, and they married in Italy before returning to the Philadelphia area to live in 1947. He set up his own barbershop and proudly practiced his trade well into the 1990s. His grandson treasures the first silver dollar Arganetto ever earned in the United States as a civilian. (Courtesy of the MDDGCSGA, Rome, Arganetto file.)

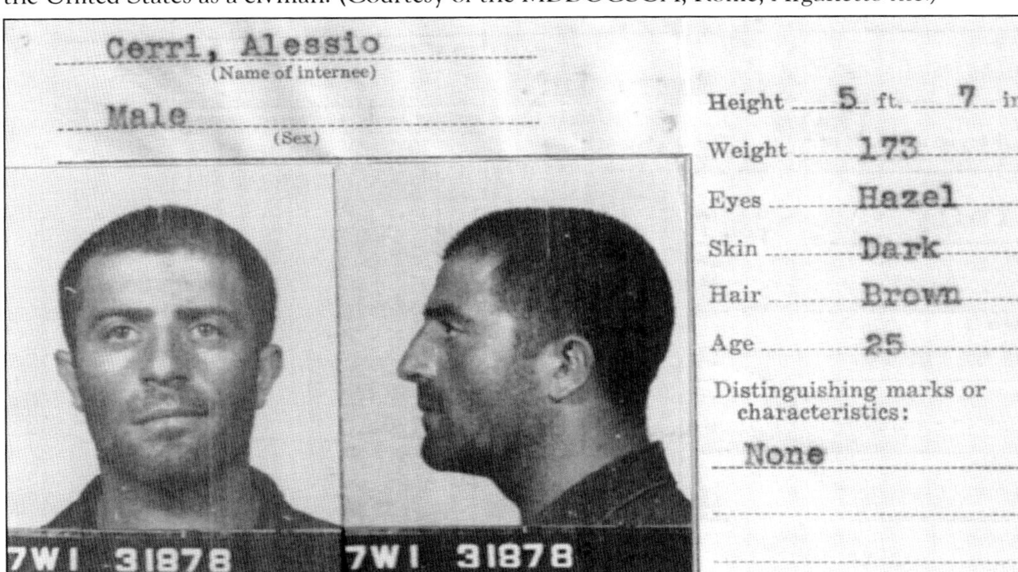

This is Sgt. Alessio Cerri's official identification photograph that was in his personnel file. Shortly after his arrival, Cerri met his future wife, Bette Rickroad. They married in Italy on November 11, 1946, and returned to the United States to settle eventually in Bette's hometown of Chambersburg, Pennsylvania. Cerri worked as baker in town and she as a civilian computer programmer at Letterkenny. They had one son, Tony. (Courtesy of the MDDGCSGA, Rome, Cerri file.)

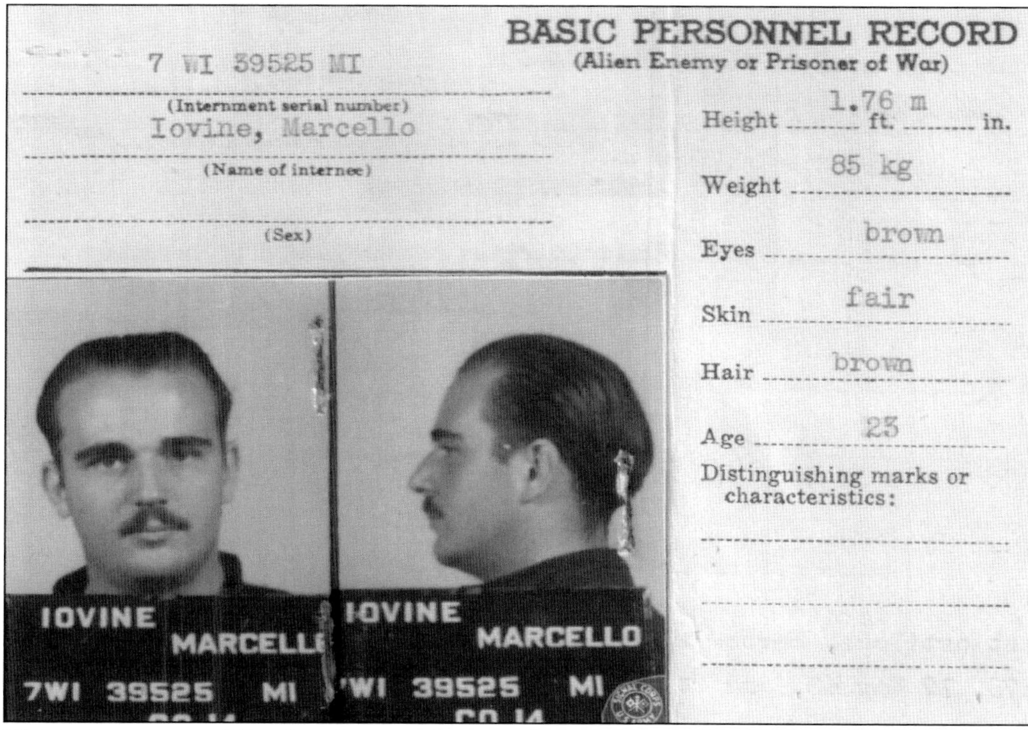
BASIC PERSONNEL RECORD
(Alien Enemy or Prisoner of War)

7 WI 39525 MI
(Internment serial number)
Iovine, Marcello
(Name of internee)
(Sex)

Height 1.76 m ft. in.
Weight 85 kg
Eyes brown
Skin fair
Hair brown
Age 23
Distinguishing marks or characteristics:

This is the personnel-file identification photograph for 2nd Lt. Marcello Iovine, who was assigned to the 82nd ISU at Letterkenny. Iovine returned to the United States and married Angela D'Oro, whom he had met as a POW. They had two daughters, Marcia and Andrea. Iovine had a very successful career, first as a toy engineer—among his creations was the Visible Man—and then as a coin and medallion designer. (Courtesy of the MDDGCSGA, Rome, Iovine file.)

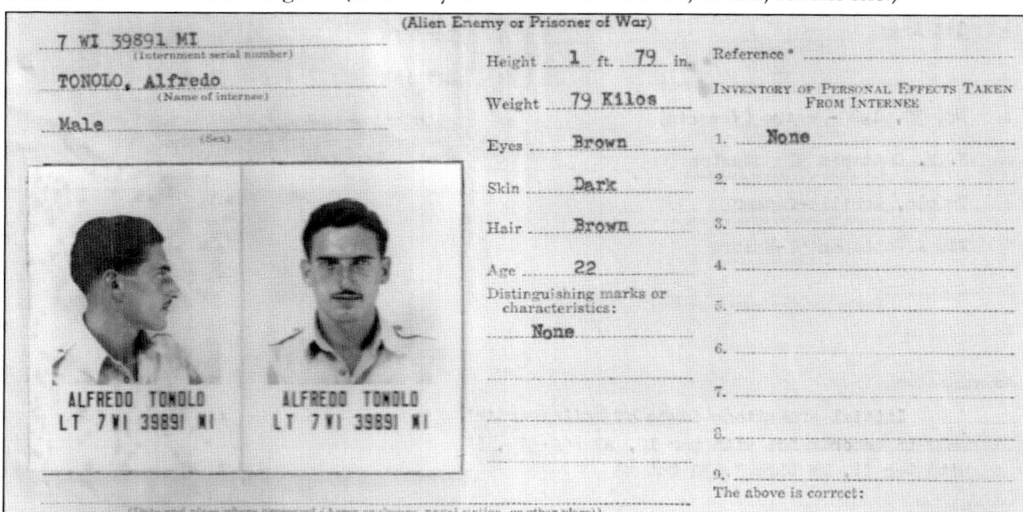
(Alien Enemy or Prisoner of War)

7 WI 39891 MI
(Internment serial number)
TONOLO, Alfredo
(Name of internee)
Male
(Sex)

Height 1 ft. 79 in.
Weight 79 Kilos
Eyes Brown
Skin Dark
Hair Brown
Age 22
Distinguishing marks or characteristics:
None

Reference*

INVENTORY OF PERSONAL EFFECTS TAKEN FROM INTERNEE

1. None
2.
3.
4.
5.
6.
7.
8.
9.

The above is correct:

(Date and place where processed (Army enclosure, naval station, or other place))

This is the identification photograph in the personnel file for 2nd Lt. Alfredo Tonolo, who was assigned to the 84th ISU at Letterkenny. Tonolo returned to the United States after marrying his Letterkenny sweetheart, Tina Norce, in Mestre, near Venice. He had a long career in education, earning his doctorate from the Universidad de Madrid. From 1963 until 1990, he served on the faculty of Bloomsburg University. (Courtesy of the MDDGCSGA, Rome, Tonolo file.)

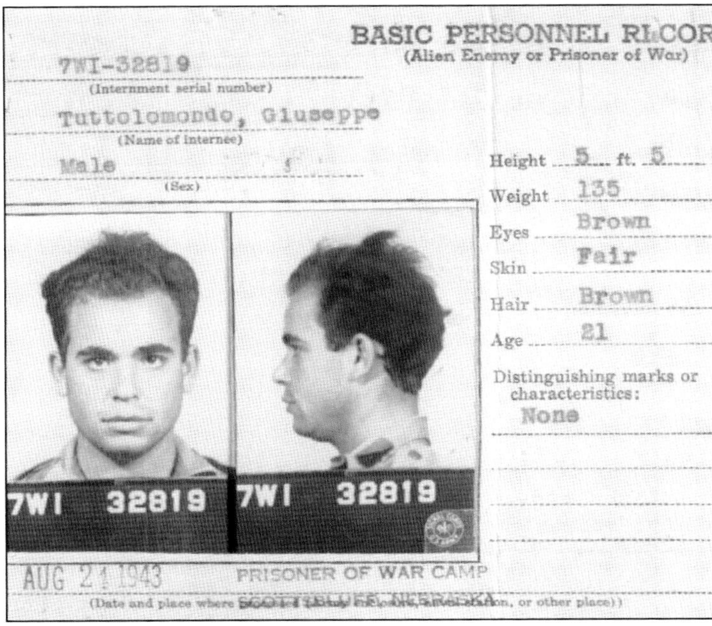

This is the identification photograph in the personnel file for Pvt. Giuseppe Tuttolomondo, who was assigned to the 84th ISU at Letterkenny. After the war, Giuseppe returned to the United States and lived in New York City, where he had relatives who had emigrated years earlier. He found work in the garment industry and retired some 20 years later because of a heart condition. He married and had a son and daughter. (Courtesy of the MDDGCSGA, Rome, Tuttolomondo file.)

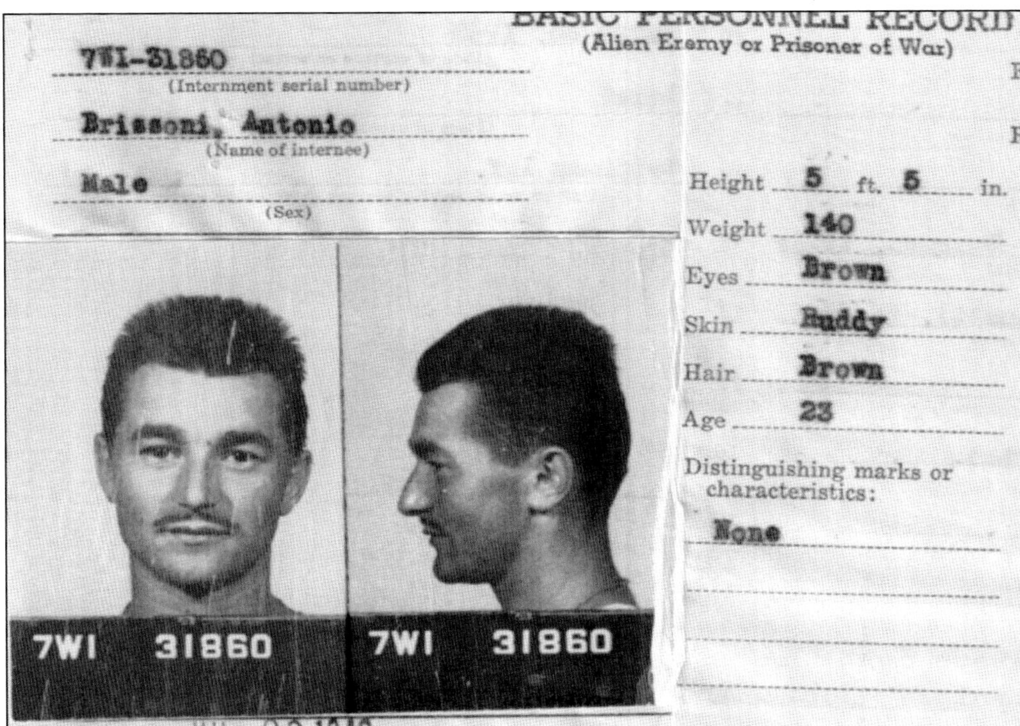

This is the identification photograph in the personnel file for Cpl. Maj. Antonio Brissoni, who was assigned to the 86th ISU at Letterkenny. While at Letterkenny, Antonio met and dated Portia Macchioni of Hershey, Pennsylvania. They corresponded by letter and eventually married in Grosseto, Italy, on May 5, 1947. They returned to America and had two girls. Toni was born in 1948, and four years later Karla was born in 1952. (Courtesy of the MDDGCSGA, Rome, Brissoni file.)

Two

Correspondence

The 1929 Geneva Convention Accords sanctioned the right of POWs to communicate with their families in their home countries. American authorities, however, had difficulty administering the free flow of mail, especially incoming correspondence, for the duration of the war. The ISU soldiers could send one letter and one postcard each week, and they obviously tried to take every advantage of this right. But return mail rarely arrived in a timely fashion, if at all.

The letters and postcards were standard-issue military forms, and the letters had space for 24 lines. The Catholic Church, through the Vatican's apostolic delegation in Washington, also facilitated the transmission of messages between family members, and its standard form consisted of 25 lines. All correspondence of this type was subject to censorship. In effect, the high number of POWs gave rise to more robust correspondence, and this situation overwhelmed censorship authorities who checked the mail; by October 1944, therefore, more than one million pieces of correspondence had been kept from arriving to their addressees.

When the program of cooperation began in the spring of 1944, all outgoing mail for each and every POW noted this location: Italian Postal Unit, Prisoner of War, Camp George G. Meade, Maryland, Box 20, G.P.O. New York, NY. Authorities used a single address to keep occupying German forces in Italy, should they intercept letters, from knowing that the POWs were interned at different camps, segregated as cooperators and noncooperators, so as to avoid potential reprisals wielded upon families of collaborators.

Mail call was, without a doubt, one of the most meaningful activities that the POWs undertook on a weekly basis, and they were truly despondent when they did not receive mail. The ISU members, especially those that were married and had children, were constantly fretting about life in Italy, as loved ones faced the Allied bombardment of cities, German retributions, and health and sanitary problems. Only after the end of the war in Europe did letters travel more freely, bringing great emotional relief to the soldiers.

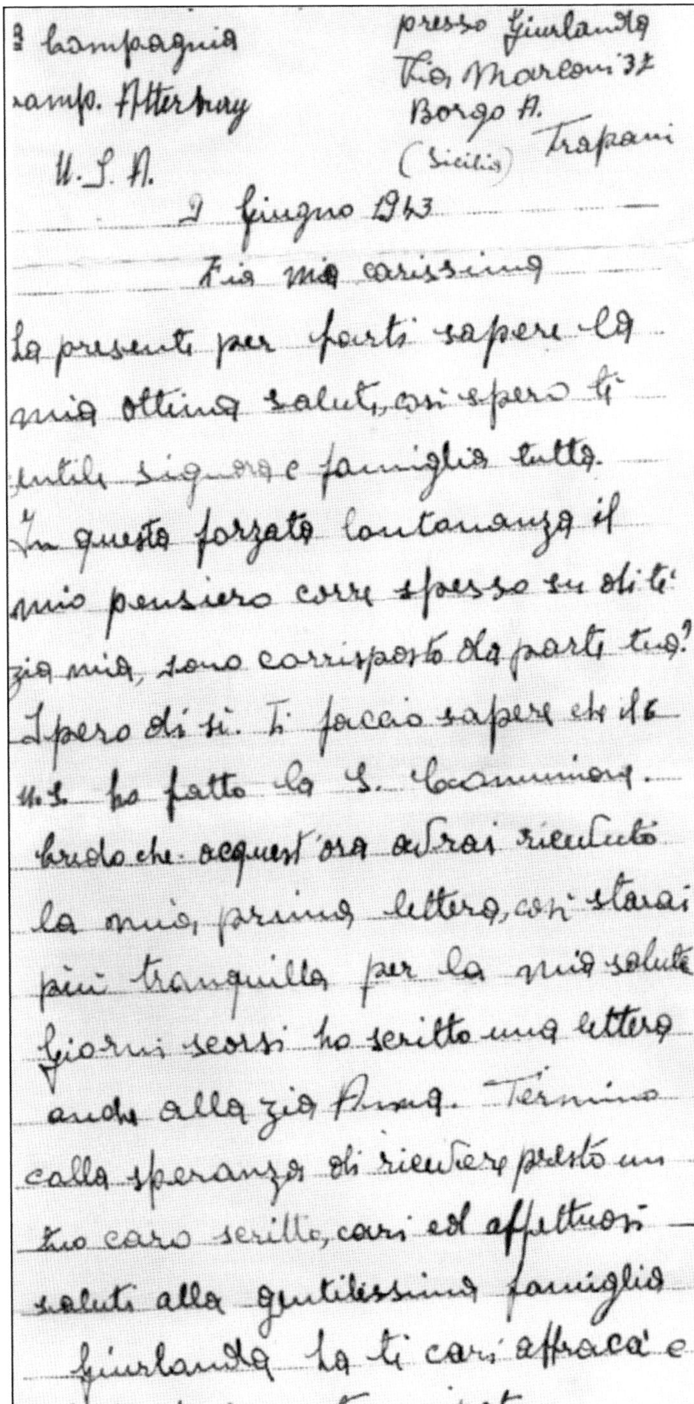

3 Compagnia
campo Atterbury
U.S.A.

presso Giurlanda
Via Marconi 37
Borgo A. Trapani
(Sicilia)

9 giugno 1943

Zia mia carissima

La presente per farti sapere la mia ottima salute, così spero di te, gentile signora e famiglia tutta. In questa forzata lontananza il mio pensiero corre spesso su di te zia mia, sono corrisposto da parte tua? Spero di sì. Ti faccio sapere che il 6 u.s. ho fatto la S. Comunione. Credo che a quest'ora avrai ricevuto la mia prima lettera, così starai più tranquilla per la mia salute. Giorni scorsi ho scritto una lettera anche alla zia Anna. Termino colla speranza di ricevere presto un tuo caro scritto, cari ed affettuosi saluti alla gentilissima famiglia Giurlanda la ti cari abbraccio e [illegible] tuo nipote

This is Pvt. Michele Allotta's letter, dated June 9, 1943, to his aunt Bartola Caruso in Trapani, Sicily. Allotta sent the letter from Camp Atterbury, Indiana. He assures her that his health is excellent, he was able to write to another aunt, Anna, and that on June 6 he received Holy Communion. (Courtesy of Antonina Allotta.)

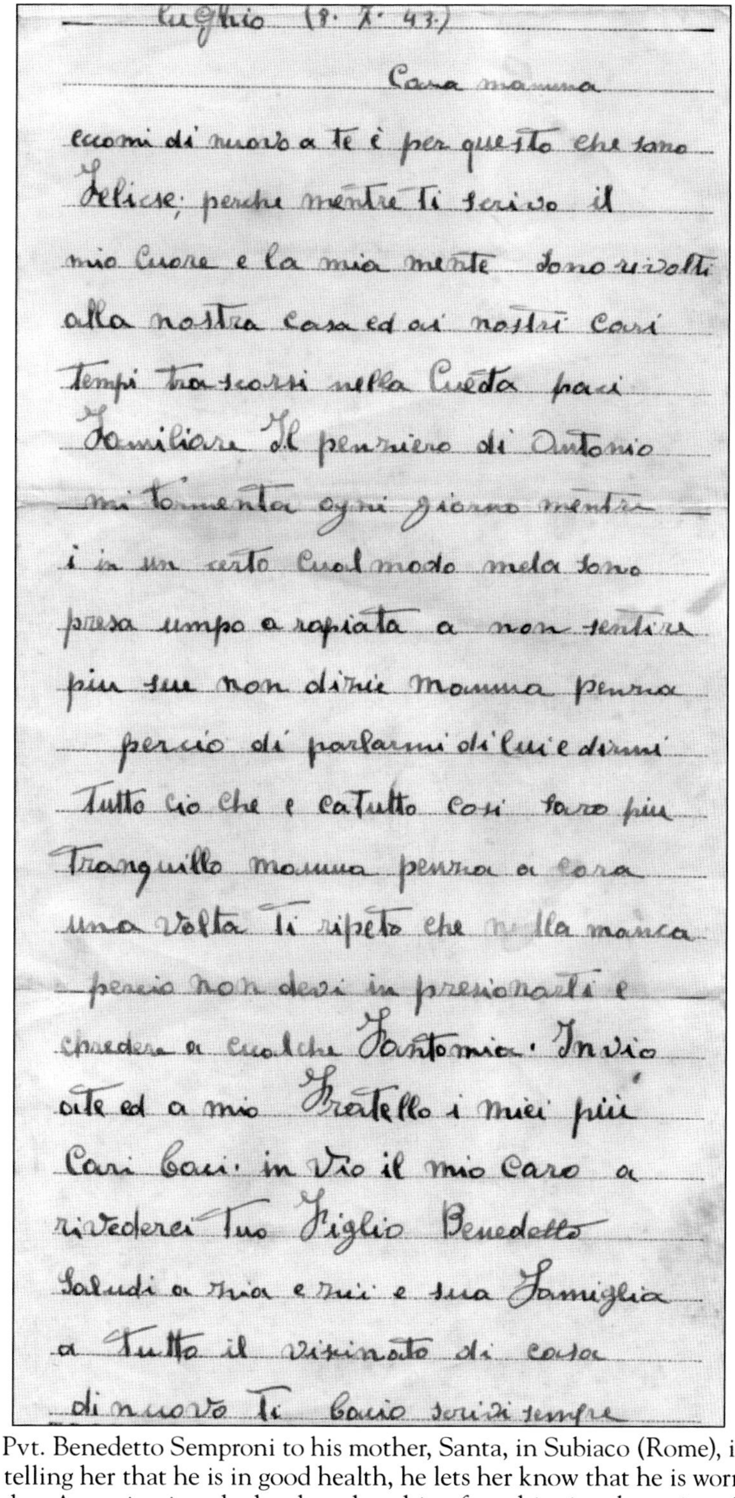

Luglio (8. 7. 43.)

Cara mamma

eccomi di nuovo a te è per questo che sono
felicse; perche mentre ti scrivo il
mio Cuore e la mia mente sono rivolti
alla nostra casa ed ai nostri cari
tempi trascorsi nella Cueta pace
familiare Il pensiero di Antonio
mi tormenta ogni giorno mentre
i in un certo Cual modo mela sono
presa umpo a rapiata a non sentire
piu sue non dirsie mamma pensa
percio di parlarmi di lui e dirmi
tutto cio che e catutto cosi saro piu
tranquillo mamma pensa a cora
una volta ti ripeto che nulla manca
percio non devi impresionarti e
credere a cualche fantomia. Invio
ate ed a mio fratello i miei più
cari baci. invio il mio Caro a
rivederci Tuo figlio Benedetto
Saludi a zia e zii e sua famiglia
a tutto il vicinato di casa
di nuovo ti bacio scrivi sempre

A letter from Pvt. Benedetto Semproni to his mother, Santa, in Subiaco (Rome), is dated July 8, 1943. Beyond telling her that he is in good health, he lets her know that he is worried about the fate of his brother Antonio, since he has heard nothing from him in a long time. Semproni was a member of the 86th ISU at Letterkenny. (Courtesy of Alberto Semproni.)

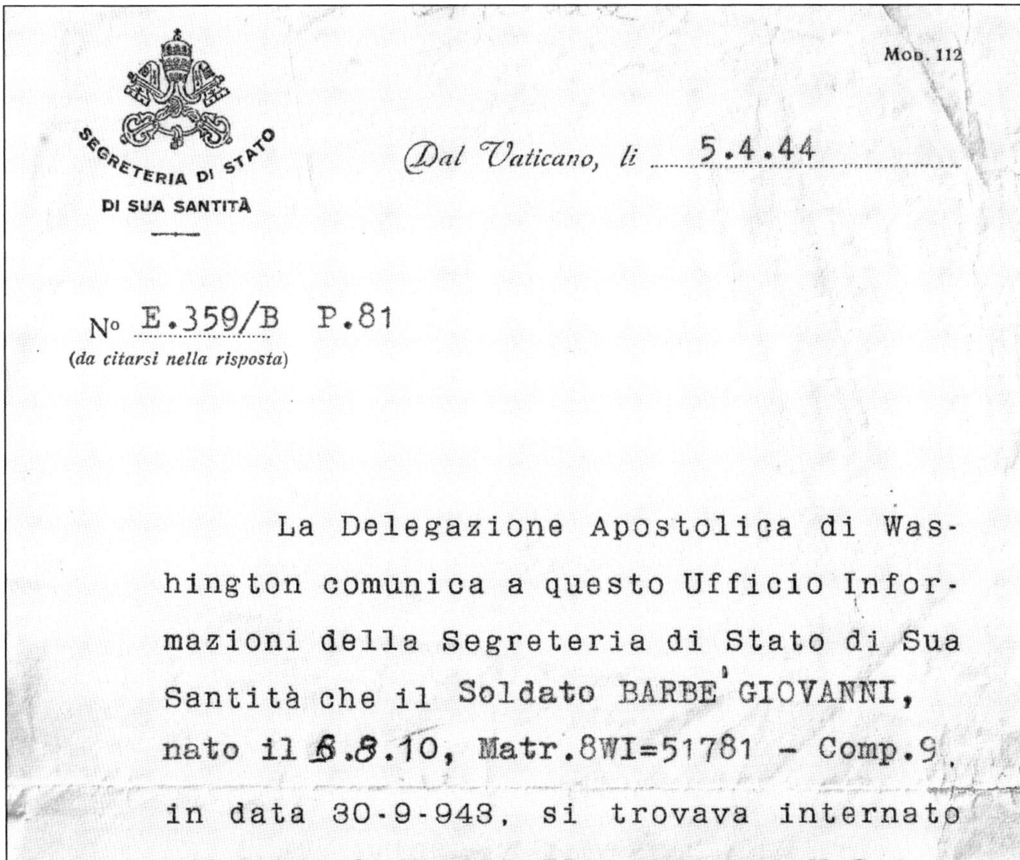

SEGRETERIA DI STATO
DI SUA SANTITÀ

MOD. 112

Dal Vaticano, li 5.4.44

No E.359/B P.81
(da citarsi nella risposta)

La Delegazione Apostolica di Washington comunica a questo Ufficio Informazioni della Segreteria di Stato di Sua Santità che il Soldato BARBE' GIOVANNI, nato il 6.8.10, Matr.8WI=51781 - Comp.9, in data 30-9-943, si trovava internato nel Campo di Monticello, Arizona – U.S.A. –, stava bene e mandava affettuosi ricordi alla famiglia.

This official notice from the Vatican secretary of state, dated April 5, 1943, announces that Cpl. Giovanni Barbè had been taken prisoner and was doing well in the United States. Note that in the communiqué, Camp Monticello is erroneously reported to be in Arizona instead of Arkansas. At Letterkenny, Barbè was assigned to the 82nd ISU. (Courtesy of Giancarla Barbè Biandrate.)

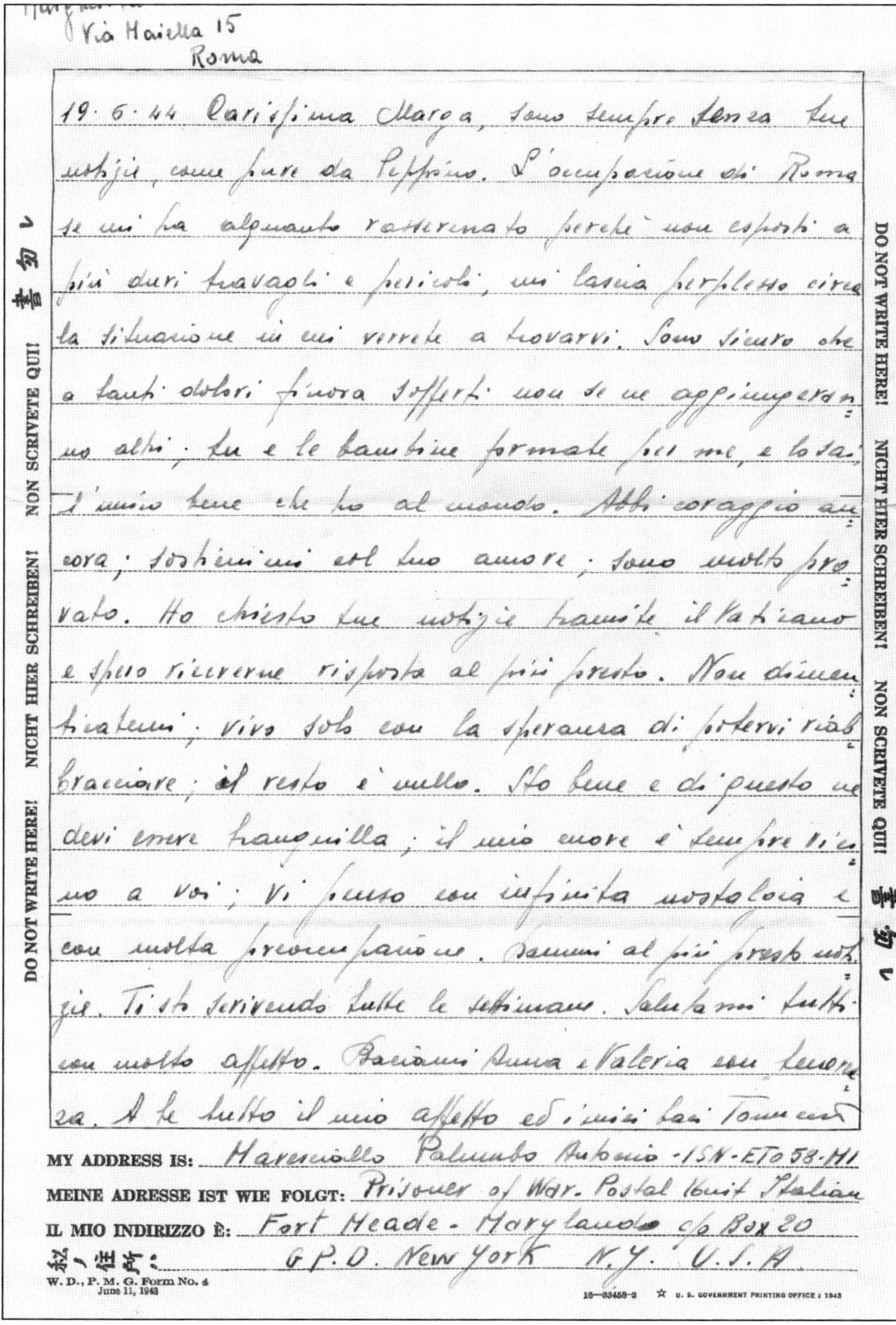

Via Maiella 15
Roma

19.6.44 Carissima Marga, sono sempre senza tue notizie, come pure da Peppino. L'occupazione di Roma se mi ha alquanto rasserenato perchè non esposti a più duri travagli e pericoli, mi lascia perplesso circa la situazione in cui verrete a trovarvi. Sono sicuro che a tanti dolori finora sofferti non se ne aggiungeranno altri; tu e le bambine formate per me, e lo sai, l'unico bene che ho al mondo. Abbi coraggio ancora; sostienimi col tuo amore; sono molto provato. Ho chiesto tue notizie tramite il Vaticano e spero riceverne risposta al più presto. Non dimenticatemi; vivo solo con la speranza di potervi riabbracciare; il resto è nullo. Sto bene e di questo ne devi essere tranquilla; il mio cuore è sempre vicino a voi; vi penso con infinita nostalgia e con molta preoccupazione. Dammi al più presto notizie. Ti sto scrivendo tutte le settimane. Salutami tutti con molto affetto. Baciami Anna e Valeria con tenerezza. A te tutto il mio affetto ed i miei baci Tonino

DO NOT WRITE HERE! NICHT HIER SCHREIBEN! NON SCRIVETE QUI! 書クナ

MY ADDRESS IS: Maresciallo Palumbo Antonio - ISN - ETO 58 - MI
MEINE ADRESSE IST WIE FOLGT: Prisoner of War - Postal Unit Italian
IL MIO INDIRIZZO È: Fort Meade - Maryland c/o Box 20
私ノ住所: G.P.O. New York N.Y. U.S.A.

W. D., P. M. G. Form No. 4
June 11, 1943

16—33458-2 ☆ U. S. GOVERNMENT PRINTING OFFICE : 1943

This June 19, 1944, letter from Chief Warrant Officer Antonio Palumbo was posted to his wife, Margherita, in Rome. Palumbo is relieved to learn about the liberation of Rome but still worried for his wife and two young daughters. He implores them, "Non dimenticatemi, vivo solo con la speranza di potervi riabbracciare" (Don't forget me; I live only hoping to be able to hug you all once again). (Courtesy of Cinzia Robbiano.)

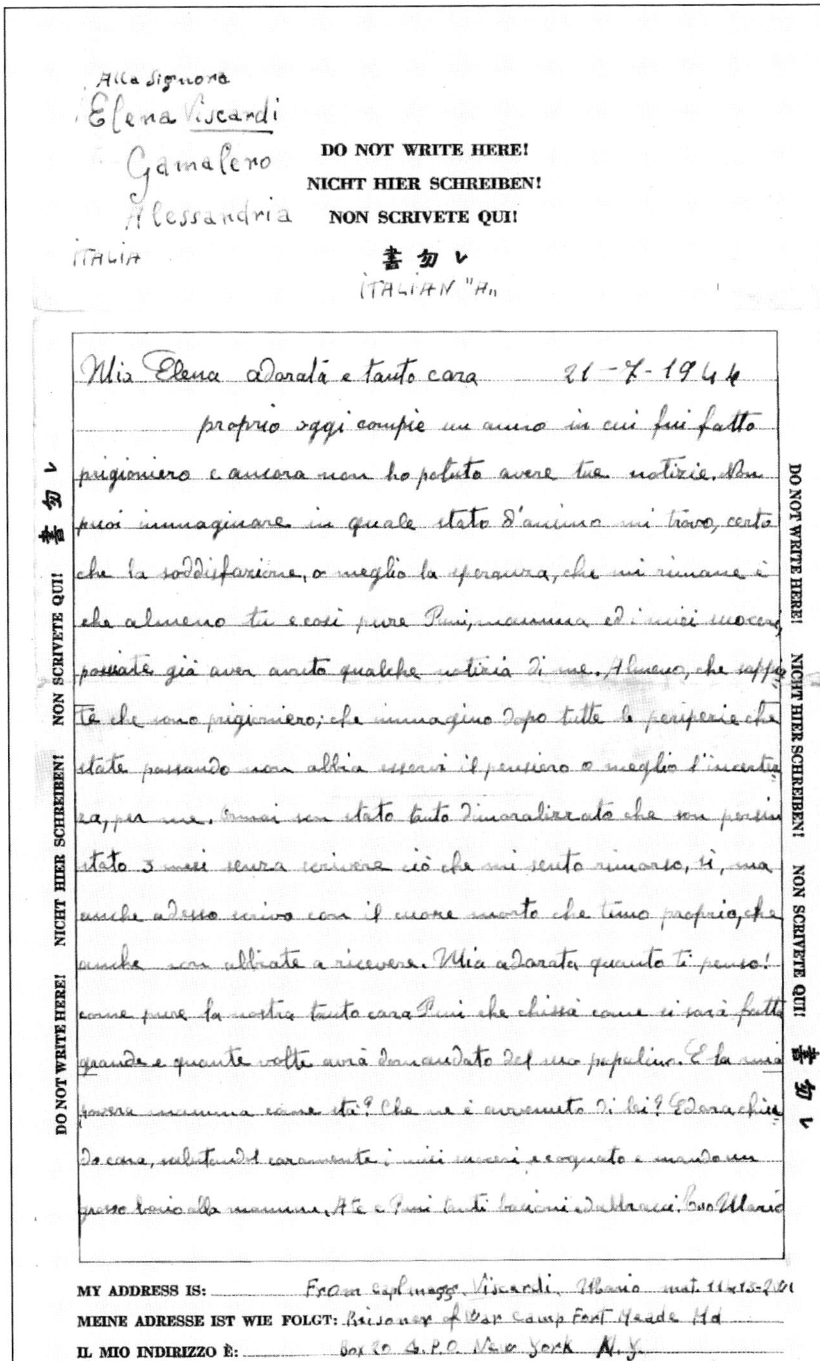

Alla Signora
Elena Viscardi
Gamalero
Alessandria
ITALIA

DO NOT WRITE HERE!
NICHT HIER SCHREIBEN!
NON SCRIVETE QUI!
書勿レ
ITALIAN "A"

Mia Elena adorata e tanto cara 21-7-1944
proprio oggi compie un anno in cui fui fatto prigioniero e ancora non ho potuto avere tue notizie. Non puoi immaginare in quale stato d'animo mi trovo, certo che la soddisfazione, o meglio la speranza, che mi rimane è che almeno tu e così pure Puni, mamma ed i miei suoceri possiate già aver avuto qualche notizia di me. Almeno, che sappiate che sono prigioniero; che immagino dopo tutte le peripezie che state passando non abbia essere il pensiero o meglio l'incertezza, per me. Ormai son stato tanto dimoralizzato che son persino stato 3 mesi senza scrivere ciò che mi sento rimorso, sì, ma anche adesso scrivo con il cuore morto che temo proprio, che anche non abbiate a ricevere. Mia adorata quanto ti penso! come pure la nostra tanto cara Puni che chissà come si sarà fatta grande e quante volte avrà domandato del suo papalino. E la mia povera mamma come sta? Che ne è avvenuto di lei? Ed ora chiudo cara, salutando caramente i miei suoceri e con questo ti mando un grosso bacio alla mamma, A te e Puni tanti baci e abbracci. tuo Mario

DO NOT WRITE HERE! NICHT HIER SCHREIBEN! NON SCRIVETE QUI! 書勿レ

MY ADDRESS IS: From cap. magg. Viscardi Mario mat. 11413-2101
MEINE ADRESSE IST WIE FOLGT: Prisoner of War Camp Fort Meade Md
IL MIO INDIRIZZO È: Box 20 A.P.O. New York N.Y.

Mario Viscardi's letter dated July 21, 1944, was sent to his wife, Elena. After exactly one year after being taken as a POW, Viscardi was very disheartened. He was not getting mail from home, but he nevertheless wrote regularly with the hope that perhaps at least his family members could receive his correspondence. He says that he continuously thinks about his wife and young daughter, nicknamed "Puni." (Courtesy of Carlo Viscardi.)

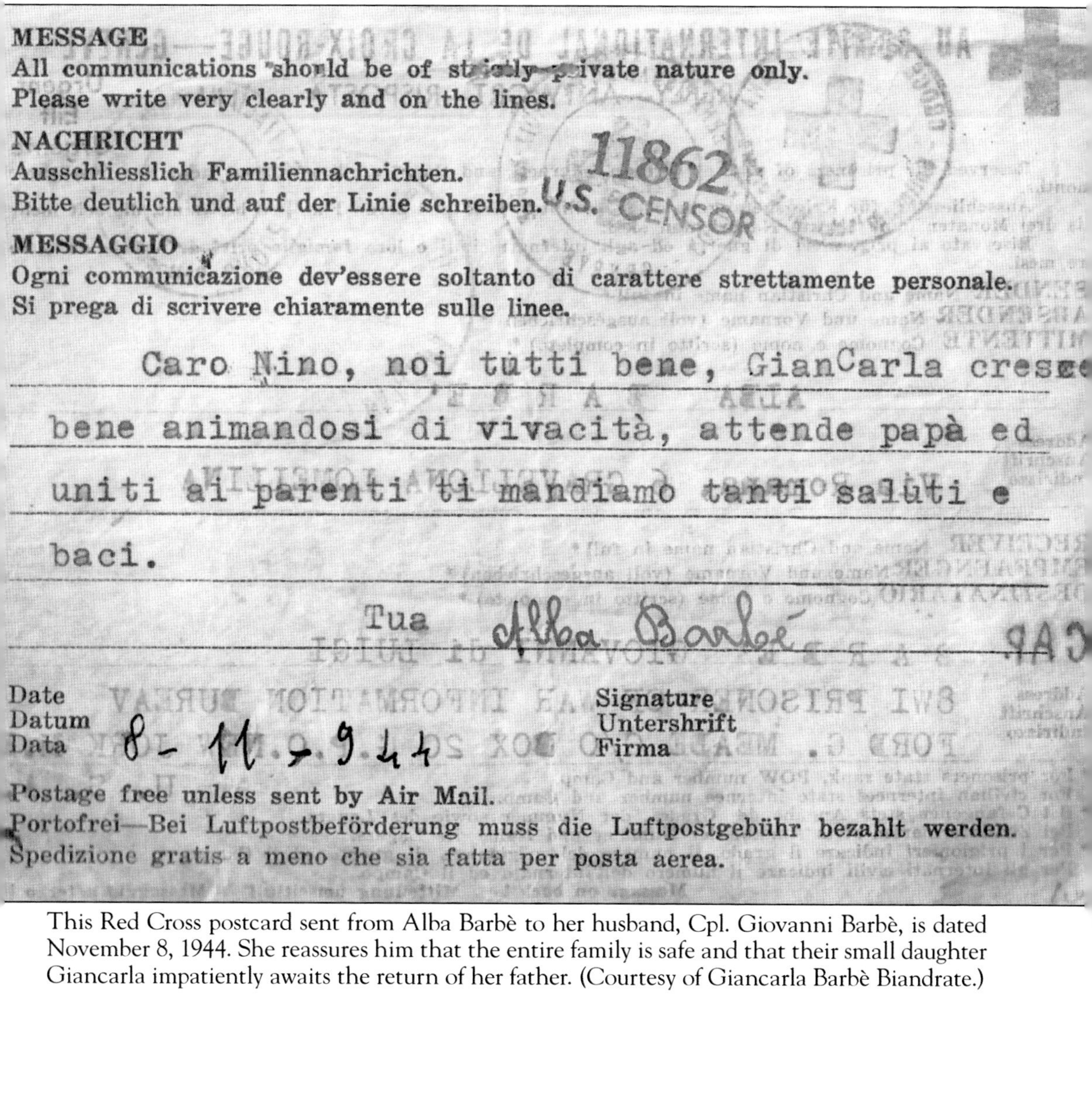

MESSAGE
All communications should be of strictly private nature only.
Please write very clearly and on the lines.

NACHRICHT
Ausschliesslich Familiennachrichten.
Bitte deutlich und auf der Linie schreiben.

11862
U.S. CENSOR

MESSAGGIO
Ogni communicazione dev'essere soltanto di carattere strettamente personale.
Si prega di scrivere chiaramente sulle linee.

Caro Nino, noi tutti bene, GianCarla cresce bene animandosi di vivacità, attende papà ed uniti ai parenti ti mandiamo tanti saluti e baci.

Tua Alba Barbè

Date
Datum
Data 8-11-944

Signature
Untershrift
Firma

Postage free unless sent by Air Mail.
Portofrei—Bei Luftpostbeförderung muss die Luftpostgebühr bezahlt werden.
Spedizione gratis a meno che sia fatta per posta aerea.

This Red Cross postcard sent from Alba Barbè to her husband, Cpl. Giovanni Barbè, is dated November 8, 1944. She reassures him that the entire family is safe and that their small daughter Giancarla impatiently awaits the return of her father. (Courtesy of Giancarla Barbè Biandrate.)

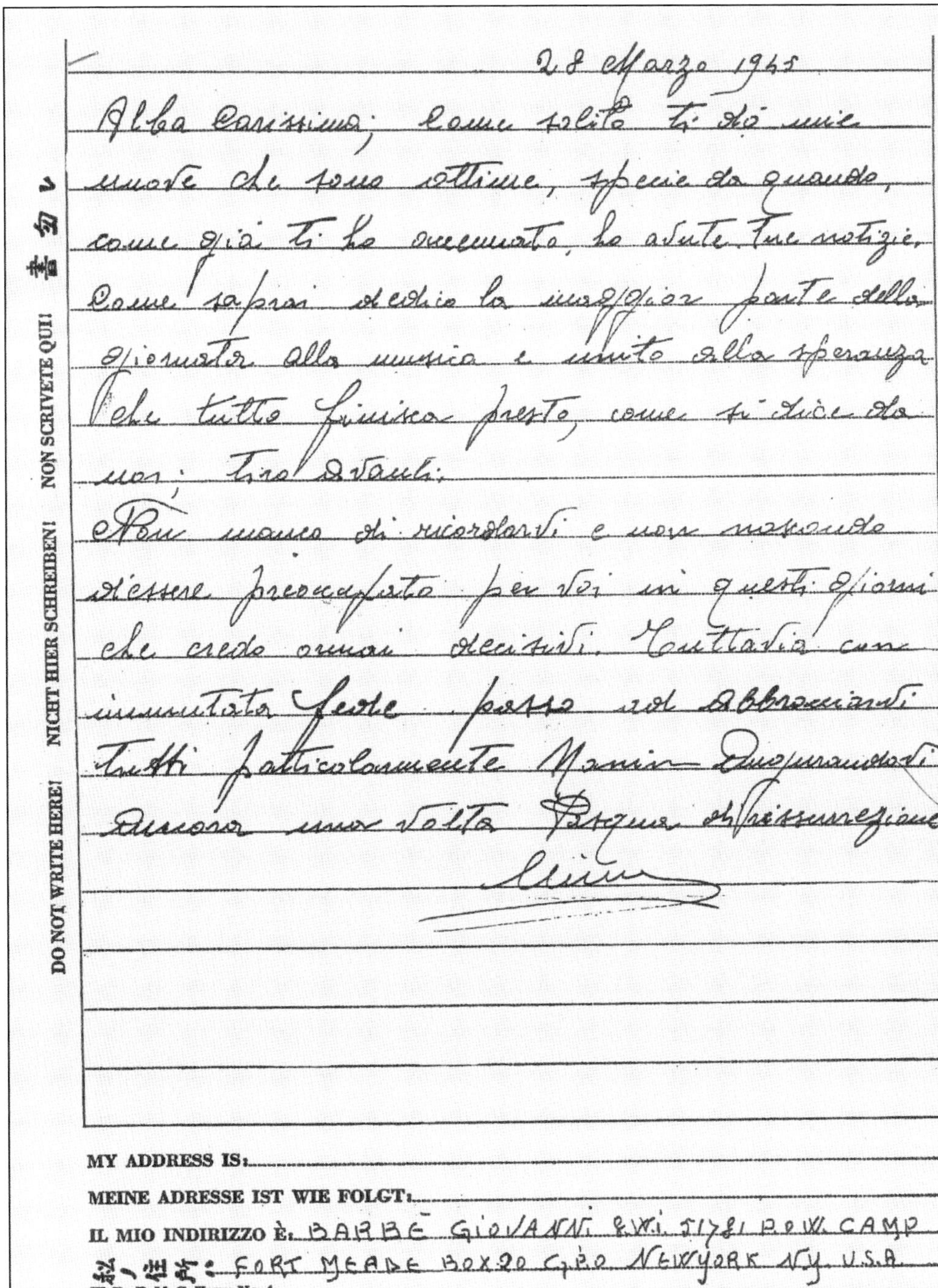

DO NOT WRITE HERE! NICHT HIER SCHREIBEN! NON SCRIVETE QUI! 書クナ

28 Marzo 1945

Alba Carissima; come solito ti do mie nuove che sono ottime, specie da quando, come già ti ho accennato, ho avute tue notizie. Come saprai dedico la maggior parte della giornata alla musica e unito alla speranza che tutto finisca presto, come si dice da noi; tira avanti.

Non manco di ricordarvi e non nascondo d'essere preoccupato per voi in questi giorni che credo ormai decisivi. Tuttavia con immutata fede posso sol abbracciarvi tutti particolarmente Mamma augurandovi ancora una volta Pasqua di Risurrezione

MY ADDRESS IS:

MEINE ADRESSE IST WIE FOLGT:

IL MIO INDIRIZZO È: BARBÈ GIOVANNI 8WI 51781 P.O.W. CAMP

私ノ住所: FORT MEADE BOX 20 G.P.O. NEW YORK N.Y. U.S.A.

W.D., P.M.G. Form No. 4 June 11, 1943

16—83458-3 U.S. GOVERNMENT PRINTING OFFICE 1943

Pvt. Giovanni Barbè's letter to his wife, Alba, is dated March 28, 1945. His health conditions, he says, are excellent, especially since he has recently heard from her. He spends most of his time focused on playing music, he relates, but reports that he is worried for his family members in Italy given the crucial war events playing out there. (Courtesy of Giancarla Barbè Biandrate.)

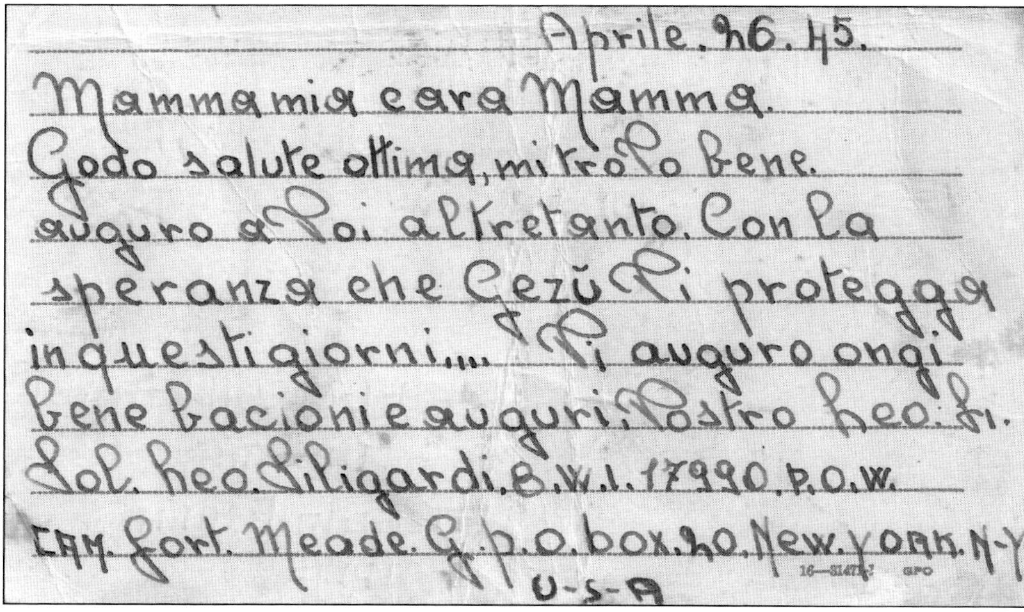
Aprile. 26. 45.
Mammamia cara Mamma.
Godo salute ottima, mi trovo bene.
auguro a voi altretanto. Con la
speranza che Gezù vi protegga
in questi giorni.... & vi auguro ongi
bene bacioni e auguri. Vostro Leo. fi.
Sol. Leo Siligardi. 8.W.I. 17990. P.O.W.
CAM. Fort. Meade. G. p.o. box. 20. New. YORK. N-Y.
U-S-A
16—81471-1 GPO

Pvt. Leo Siligardi, born on December 8, 1922, wrote this POW postcard on April 26, 1945, to his parents who lived in the Emilia Romagna region. Addressing his mother, he lets her know that he is in good health, is doing well, and prays that Jesus protects them in Italy as the war rages on. Evidently, Siligardi was unaware that Italy had been liberated from the Nazis on April 25. (Courtesy of Sandra Siligardi.)

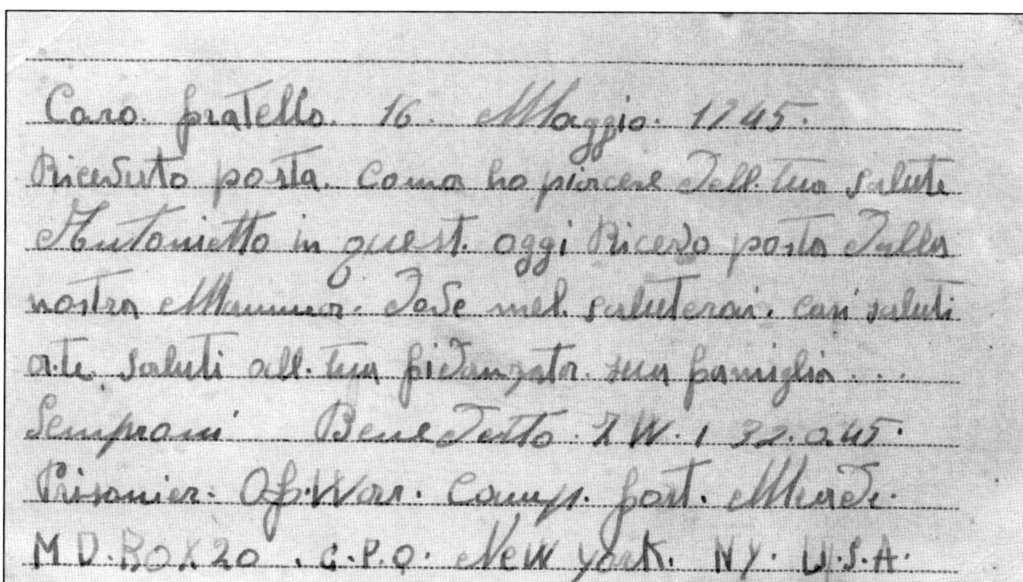
Caro fratello. 16. Maggio. 1945.
Ricevuto posta. Come ho piacere dell tuo salute
Antonietto in quest. oggi Ricevo posta dalla
nostra Mamma. Dose mel. saluterai. cari saluti
a te. saluti all. tua fidanzata. sua famiglia...
Semproni Benedetto 8W.I 32.245.
Prisonier. Of. War. Camp. fort. Meade.
M.D. BOX 20. C.P.O. New York. NY. U.S.A.
16—81471-1 GPO

Pvt. Benedetto Semproni sent this POW postcard, dated May 16, 1945, to his brother Antonio. He says that he did indeed receive his letter and wants him to say hello to his girlfriend and their mother. At this point in time, the war in Europe had concluded and Allied forces in Italy had liberated the entire country. (Courtesy of Alberto Semproni.)

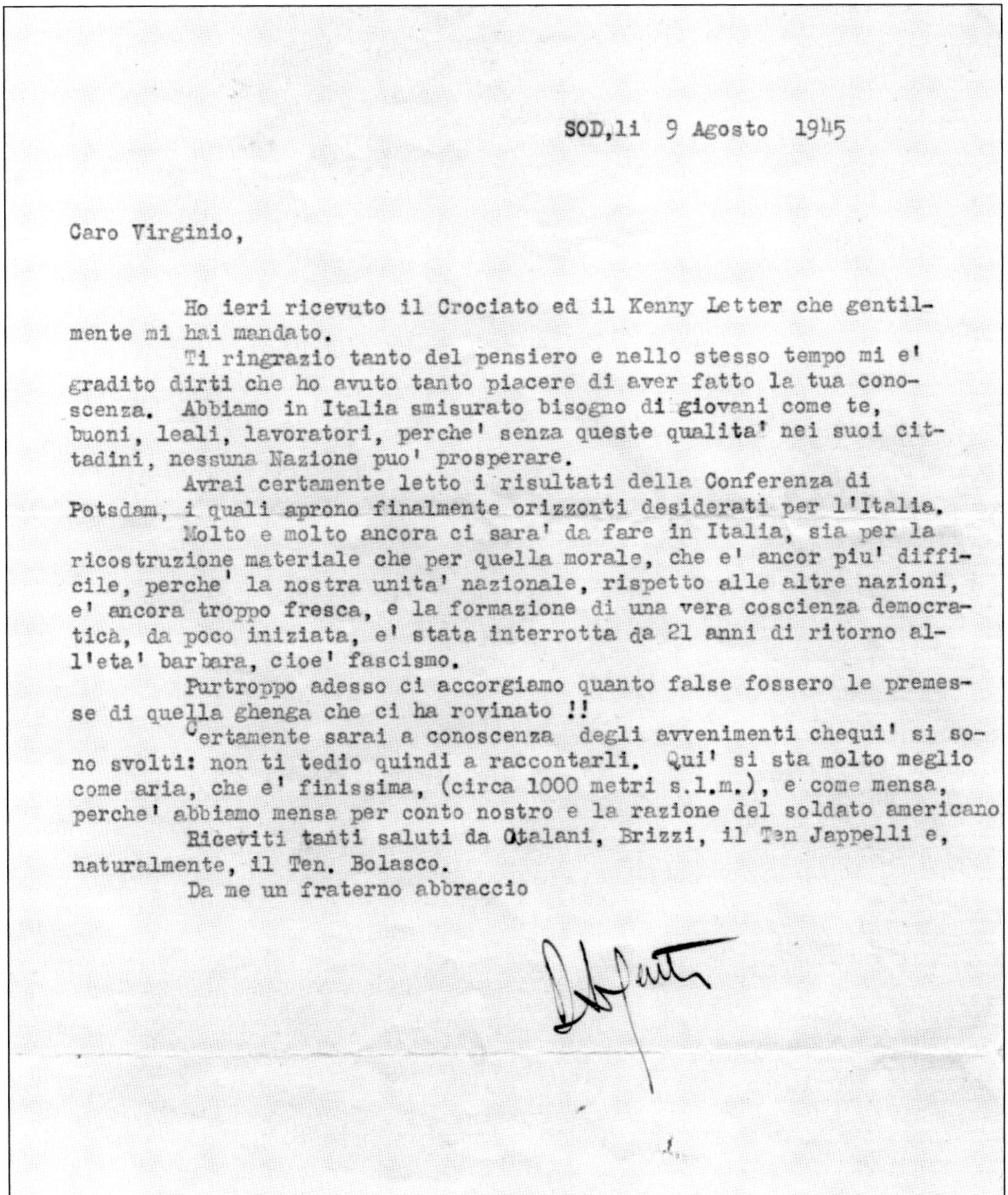

SOD,li 9 Agosto 1945

Caro Virginio,

Ho ieri ricevuto il Crociato ed il Kenny Letter che gentilmente mi hai mandato.

Ti ringrazio tanto del pensiero e nello stesso tempo mi e' gradito dirti che ho avuto tanto piacere di aver fatto la tua conoscenza. Abbiamo in Italia smisurato bisogno di giovani come te, buoni, leali, lavoratori, perche' senza queste qualita' nei suoi cittadini, nessuna Nazione puo' prosperare.

Avrai certamente letto i risultati della Conferenza di Potsdam, i quali aprono finalmente orizzonti desiderati per l'Italia.

Molto e molto ancora ci sara' da fare in Italia, sia per la ricostruzione materiale che per quella morale, che e' ancor piu' difficile, perche' la nostra unita' nazionale, rispetto alle altre nazioni, e' ancora troppo fresca, e la formazione di una vera coscienza democraticà, da poco iniziata, e' stata interrotta da 21 anni di ritorno all'eta' barbara, cioe' fascismo.

Purtroppo adesso ci accorgiamo quanto false fossero le premesse di quella ghenga che ci ha rovinato !!

Certamente sarai a conoscenza degli avvenimenti chequi' si sono svolti: non ti tedio quindi a raccontarli. Qui' si sta molto meglio come aria, che e' finissima, (circa 1000 metri s.l.m.), e come mensa, perche' abbiamo mensa per conto nostro e la razione del soldato americano

Riceviti tanti saluti da Catalani, Brizzi, il Ten Jappelli e, naturalmente, il Ten. Bolasco.

Da me un fraterno abbraccio

Capt. Domenico Argento, former commander of the 83rd ISU, writes to Cpl. Maj. Virginio Ranzoni from the Sioux Ordnance Depot in Sidney, Nebraska, where he and a contingent of 83rd soldiers were sent from Letterkenny in July 1945. He discusses the material-political reconstruction of Italy and the restoration of a democratic conscience after the "età barbara" (barbarous age) of fascism. Argento also passes along greetings from other soldiers. (Courtesy of Edoardo Ranzoni.)

Three

Prisoners Pose for Photographs

The Letterkenny cooperating POWs enjoyed greater freedoms than did normal prisoners of war detained in the United States. One of these privileges included taking pictures and having their images taken by others, a fact demonstrated by the incredible amount of photographs that family members possess today. The majority of images were taken during off-duty hours, both on post when they entertained guests and off the depot when they toured various American cities and visited friends and relatives. Often during these excursions, they had their pictures taken at professional studios.

The following photographs of Italian POWs easily demonstrate that they were treated well and had ample access to food. Indeed, all of them appear to be thriving, happy, and in good health. A few photographs show the prisoners on sightseeing trips or enjoying time at a swimming pool. They also cared for pets, especially dogs that often served as mascots.

The POWs wore US Army uniforms and would have been indistinguishable from US troops, save for the fact that they had an oval patch sewn on the left sleeve that read "Italy." At times when they had furloughs, they removed the patch and clearly wanted to be taken for American soldiers. The wearing of the uniform greatly bothered many Americans, both civilians and military alike, and it initially helped to foster negative perceptions of the ISU members and how they were treated. Not all American military personnel resented this uniform allowance; in particular, those that worked closely with the POWs could very much appreciate them as human beings and soldiers who joined them in the common fight against Hitler. Many US soldiers, in fact, posed with Italians as a sign of friendship and camaraderie.

These photographs also illustrate the architectural projects, both decorative and functional, that the POWs built—for example, the amphitheater where the orchestra played and dances took place on the weekend. Various photographs also show how the amphitheater's steps served as a perfect setting for individual and group pictures.

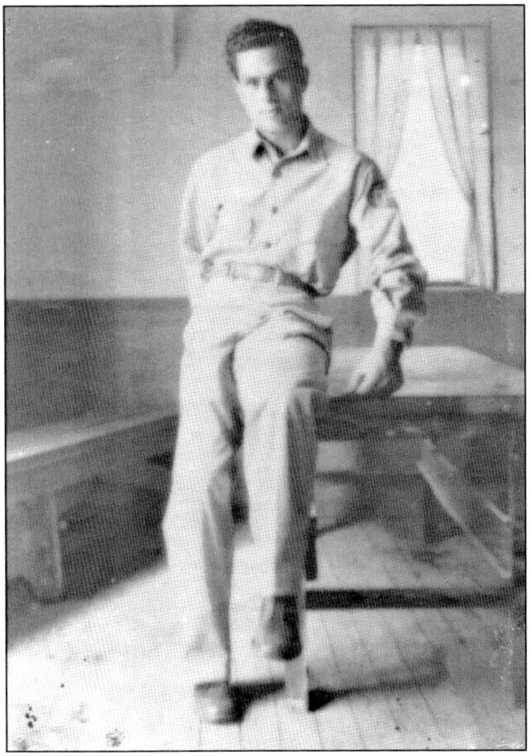

Antonio Falanga poses in a Letterkenny barracks room while wearing his cooperator uniform, sometime in 1944. Born in January 1922 in Paternò (Catania), Sicily, Falanga had been captured by American infantry in Gafsa, Tunisia, on March 30, 1943, and exactly one month later had already been shipped and interned at Camp Carson, Colorado. (Courtesy of Rosario Falanga.)

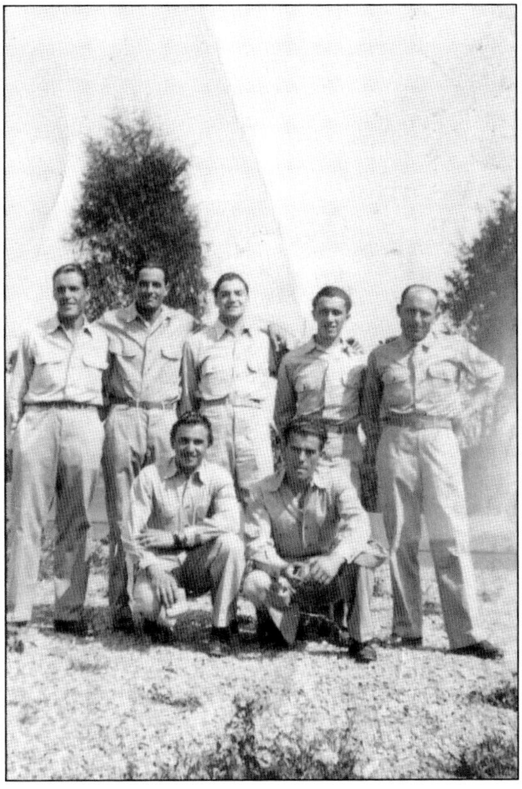

Renato Volpi stands third from the left, Luigi Brescianini at far right, and Renato Scattolini is crouching on the left. At Letterkenny, he was assigned to the 86th ISU and worked in a warehouse. Toward the end of the war, he kept a signature book and began to ask his fellow workers to jot down words of remembrance. This document is crucial for understanding the good relations that existed between American civilians and the Italian POWs on the depot. (Courtesy of Antonio Brescianini.)

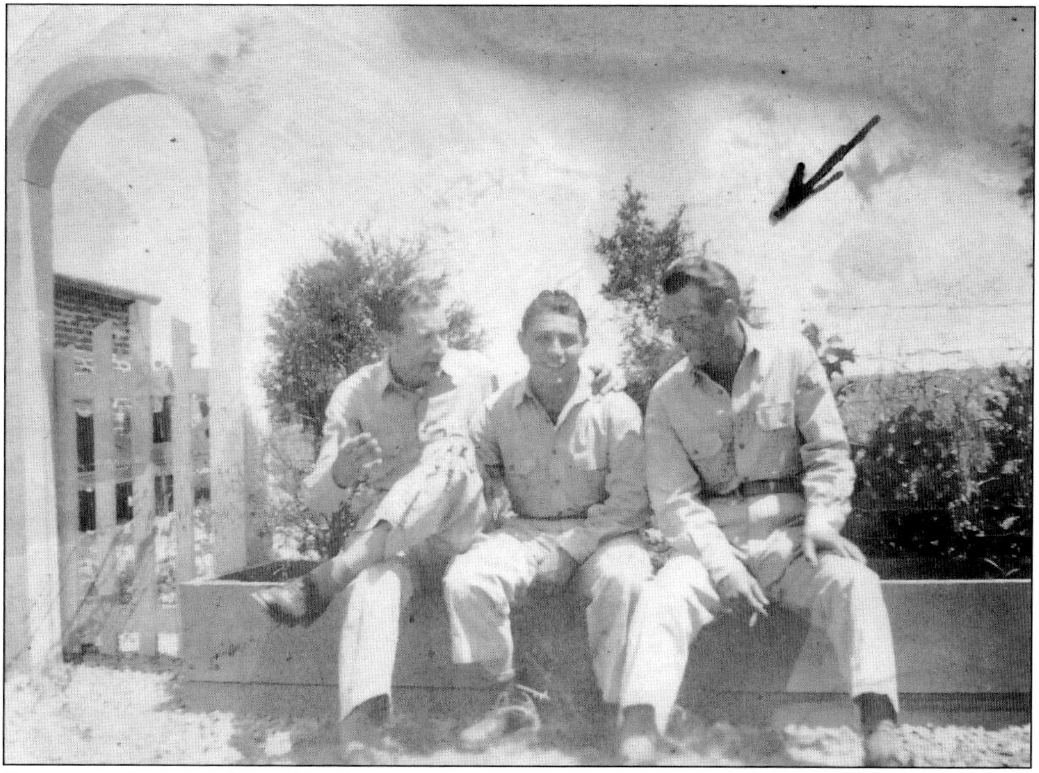

Domenico Censi, indicated by the arrow, along with two other POWs, sits in one of the preferred spots on the depot where POWs liked to take photographs. Domenico wrote to his parents on the back side of the photograph: "Su tutte le foto che ho fatto per mandarle a voi non mi è mai riuscito di sorridere—Baci Nino U.S.A. agosto 1945" (In all of the photos that I've made to send to you, I've never managed to smile—Kisses, Nino U.S.A, August 1945). (Courtesy of Claudio Censi.)

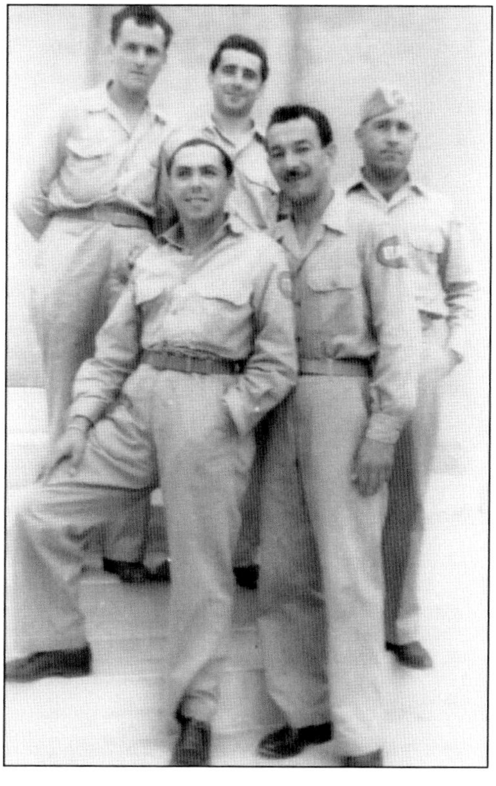

Cpl. Maj. Ettore Calizza, from Rome, stands with hand in pocket, first on the left in the front row together with other POWs, on the steps near the amphitheater, on August 5, 1945. Immediately to his left is Sgt. Maj. Arcisio Raccanello, from Padua. Calizza and Raccanello most likely became friends while at Letterkenny, because they often appear together in photographs. (Courtesy of Maurizio Calizza.)

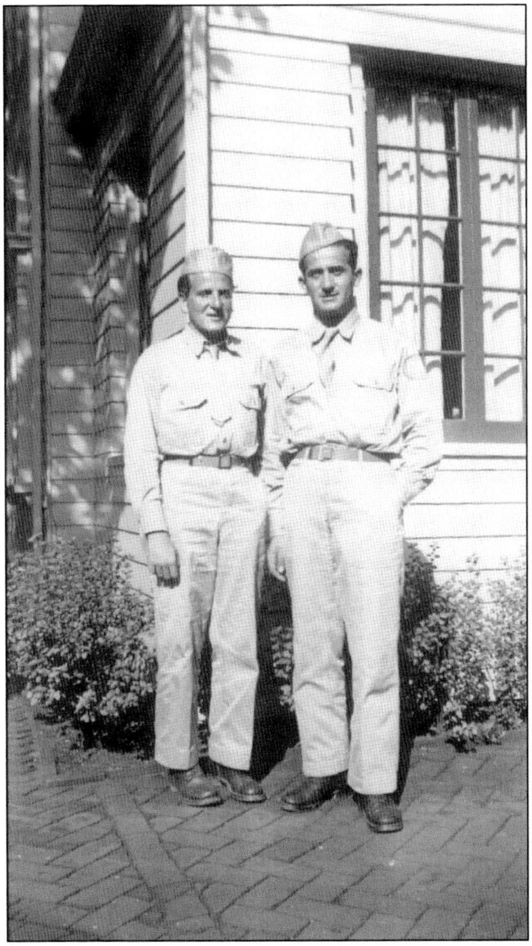

Federico Cavicchi (right) stands with another POW in front of a civilian home. Cavicchi was a sergeant in the Signal Corps assigned to the 85th ISU. Upon his repatriation and arrival at the port of Naples, thieves robbed Cavicchi of every cent he had—unfortunately not an uncommon experience, and it took him two full weeks to make his way back to his hometown of Bologna. (Courtesy of Sonia Cavicchi.)

Almerindo Briganti stands third from the left along with other ISU members. Silvio Mattia is also present, standing at far right. Note that all appear to be in full form and exuberant. Briganti was born on January 31, 1922, in Farnese (Viterbo), a town in the Lazio region. On May 12, 1943, US forces captured him in Tunisia, and he was first sent to Camp Monticello, Arkansas. Briganti died in 2015. (Courtesy of Alessandra Briganti.)

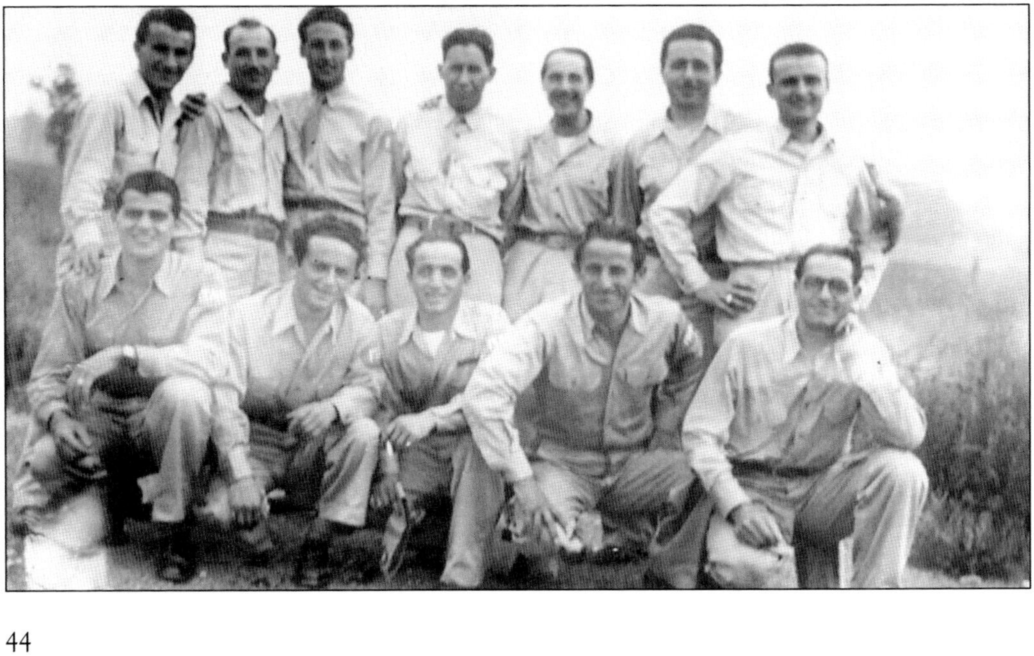

1st Lt. Giovanni Fresta (right) poses with an American, 2nd Lt. Harry C. Poulton, on June 24, 1945. Fresta and Poulton served, respectively, as the Italian and American commanders of the 159th ISU, a unit that arrived from Fort George G. Meade, Maryland, on February 26, 1945. 1st Lieutenant Poulton was part of an American military contingent that accompanied Italian POWs back to Italy upon their repatriation. (Courtesy of Isidoro Fresta.)

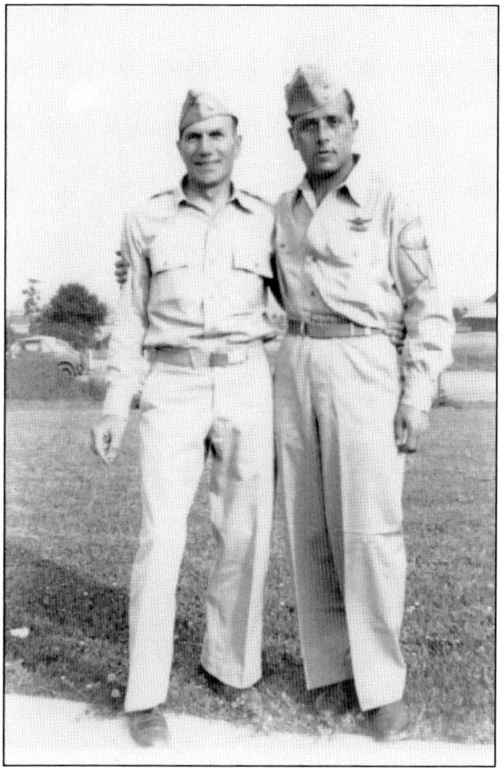

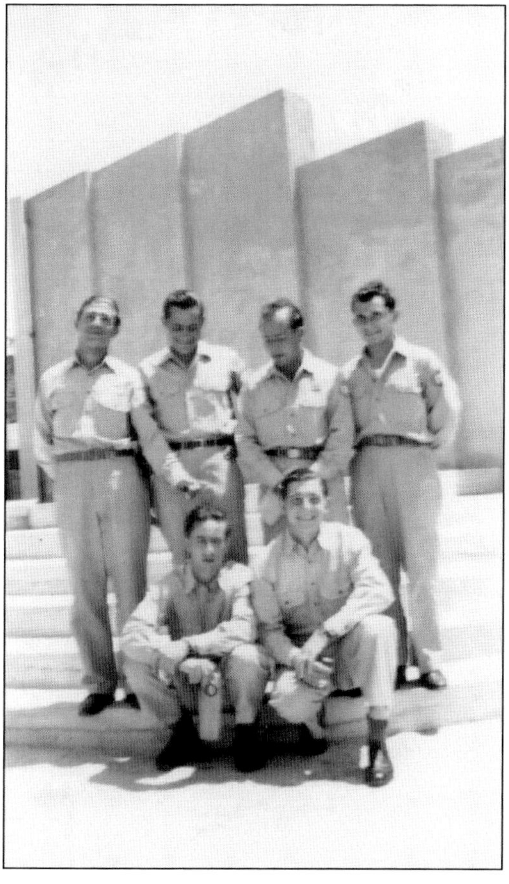

Along with other POWs in May 1945, 1st Lt. Giovanni Fresta stands third from the left on the steps of a set of walls that the POWs had built near the amphitheater. This spot was one of the most preferred by the POWs in picture taking. On the garrison cap held in the hand of the seated soldier is the round "Italy" patch. (Courtesy of Isidoro Fresta.)

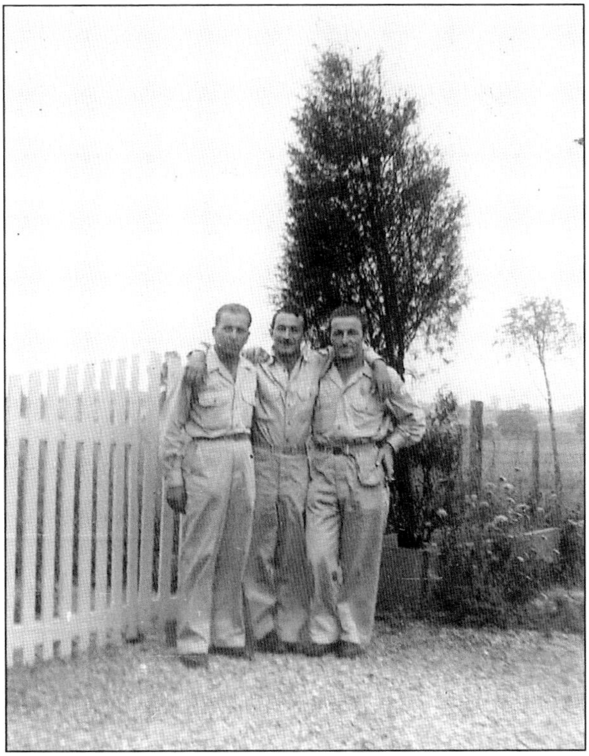

Sgt. Giovanni Lucchi of the 86th ISU, from San Mauro Pascoli (Forli), left, Sgt. Maj. Arcisio Raccanello of the 86th ISU, from Padua, center, and Sgt. Maj. Luciano Boneschi of the 82nd ISU, from Vidigulfo (Pavia) pose relaxed in one of the favorite spots the POWs had for taking pictures. (Courtesy of Valeria Conconi.)

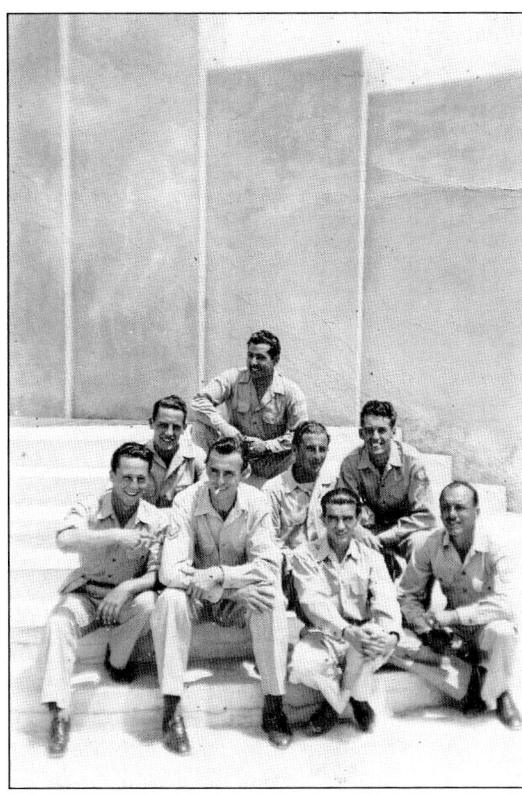

Sgt. Maj. Mario Luigini, from Pescara, a city in Abruzzo region, was the director of the prisoner orchestra. He is pictured here in 1945 sitting at top, above other prisoners who pose on the steps near the amphitheater. As with almost all the other photographs, the prisoners are smiling, relaxed, and in good health—verification of their excellent treatment and high standard of living in the depot. (Courtesy of Mario Luigini [grandson].)

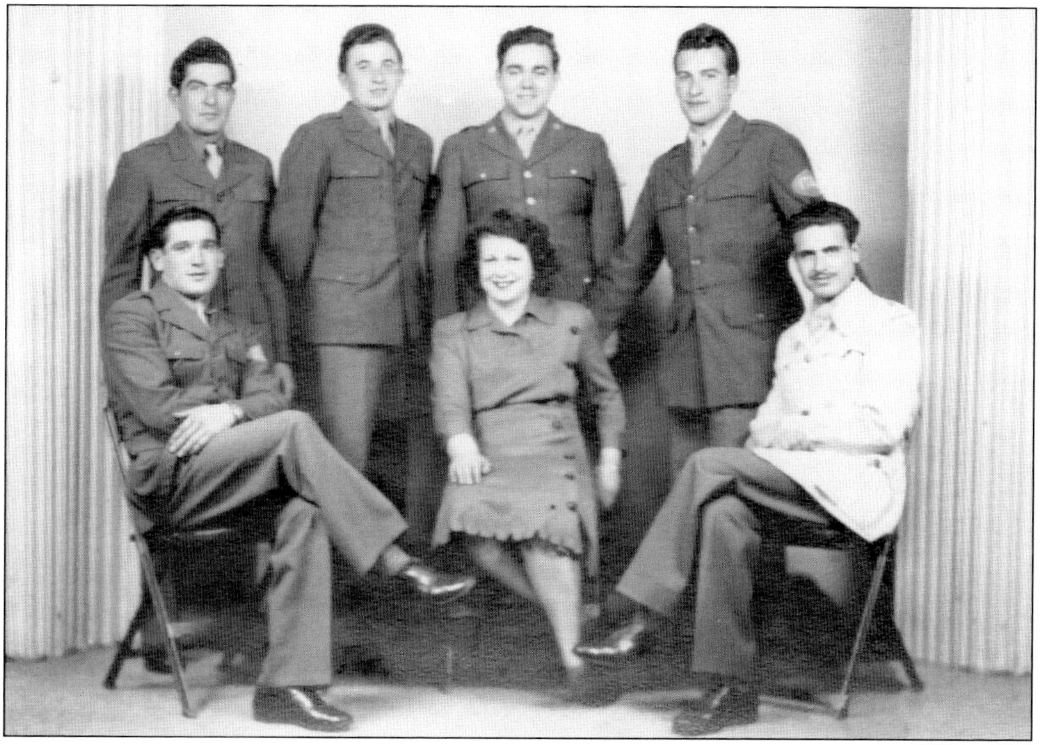

Renato Scattolini stands second from the left with other POWs and an American woman. The third from the left, standing, is a US soldier who often appears in other POW photographs. Scattolini, assigned to the 159th ISU, was originally from a town near Verona. At Letterkenny, he often participated in choral activities and sang for Monsignor Cicognani when he came to the depot in October 1944 and May 1945. (Courtesy of Marta Scattolini.)

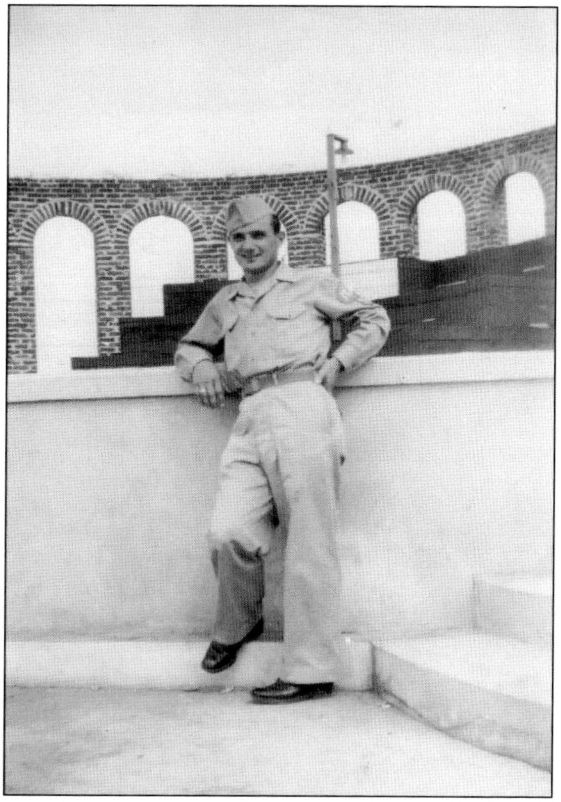

This 1945 photograph shows Virginio Ramella, from Gaggiano (Milan) in front of the amphitheater that Letterkenny POWs built. The amphitheater provided prime entertainment space for the orchestra, and elaborate dance parties were held there most often on the weekend. Unfortunately, unlike the chapel, bell tower, and assembly hall, all monuments that the POWs also built, the amphitheater no longer exists. (Courtesy of Annamaria Ramella.)

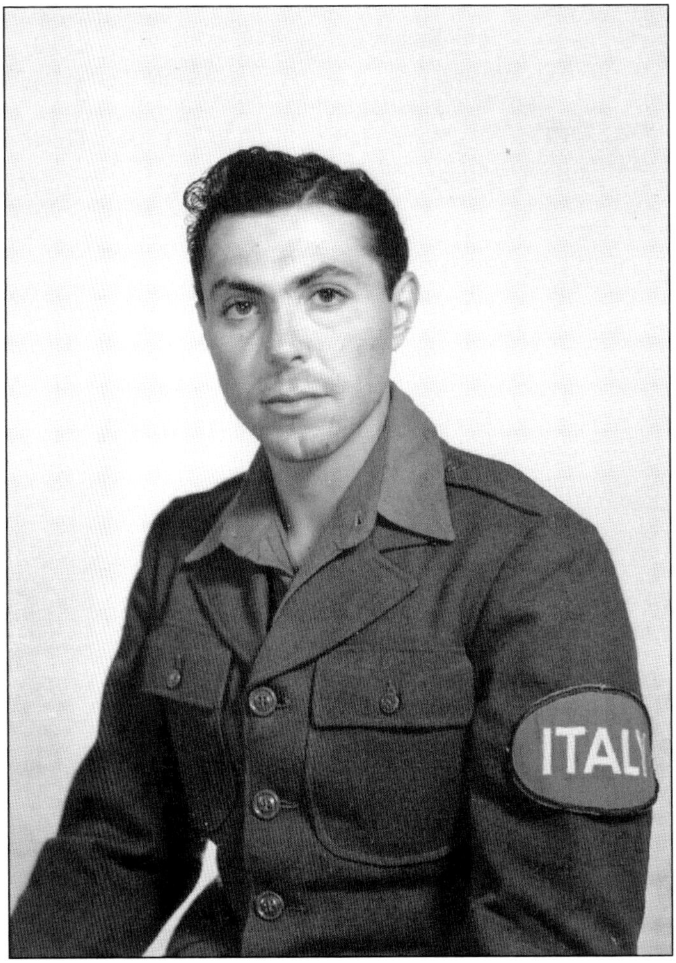

Ettore Calizza, from Rome, poses formally here in his cooperator's uniform on July 11, 1945. Calizza's large "Italy" patch is clearly visible on his left sleeve. This important emblem ensured that cooperators were distinguishable from other Italian prisoners who did not agree to collaborate with the United States. This image was most likely taken in a studio. (Courtesy of Maurizio Calizza.)

Pvt. Antonio Coin, first on the left, stands with three POW sergeants while visiting an Italian American neighborhood. Coin was born in Arzergrande (Padua), on August 2, 1922, and was captured by the English 8th Army on May 13, 1943, in Enfidaville, Tunisia. He arrived at Letterkenny on May 1, 1944, after having spent time at Fort Meade and Camp Ritchie, both in Maryland. (Courtesy of Fausta Coin.)

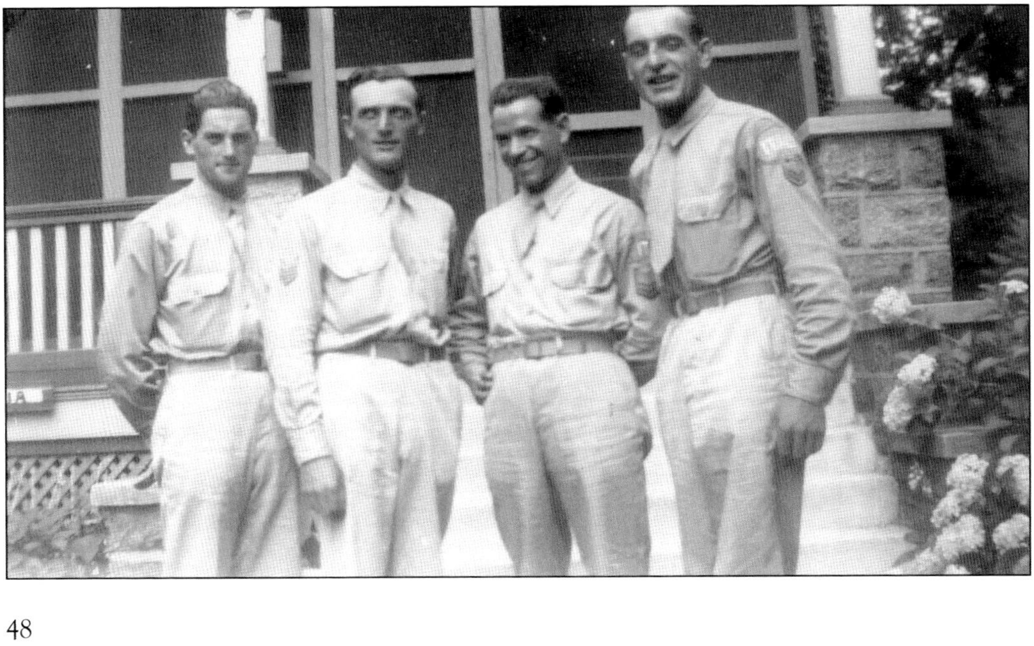

Paolo Muratore, from Borgomale (Cuneo), in the Piedmont region, left, stands next to the visiting area with another collaborating POW. The gesture of linked arms is typical of Italians, regardless of gender, and it signifies close friendship, nonsexualized affection, or a desire to be undisturbed in order to discuss important matters. Note also the common placement of the *bustina*, or garrison cap, as it was often tucked under one's belt. (Courtesy of Teresa Cometa.)

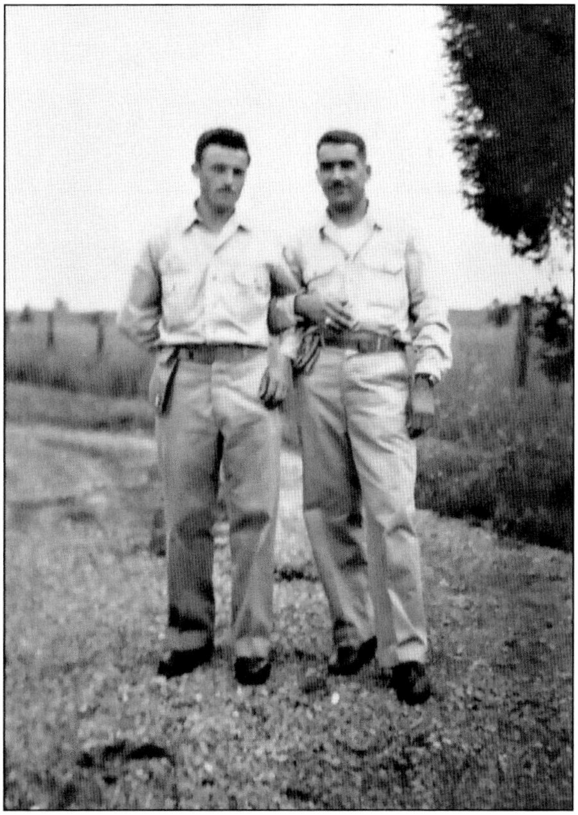

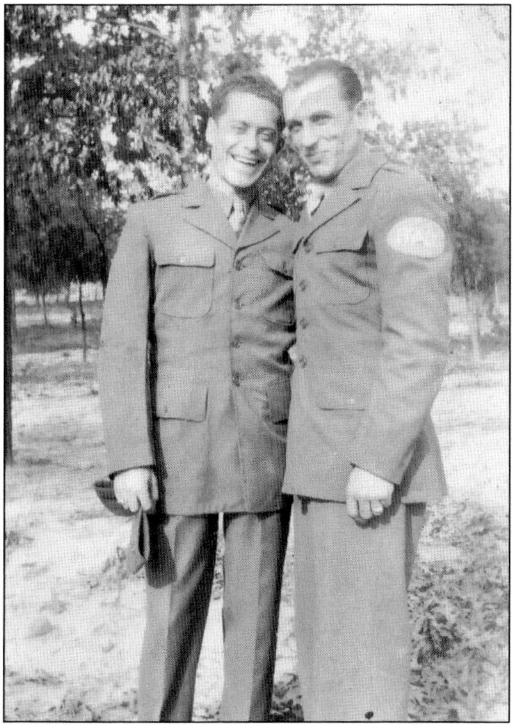

Antonio Santambrogio, on the right, poses with another unidentified ISU cooperator. The "Italy" patch is clearly visible on his left jacket sleeve, an emblem that authorities meant to distinguish Italian soldiers from American servicemen. Santambrogio was born in Seveso (Milan) on June 13, 1911, and was a wood-carver in civilian life. (Courtesy of Natale Santambrogio.)

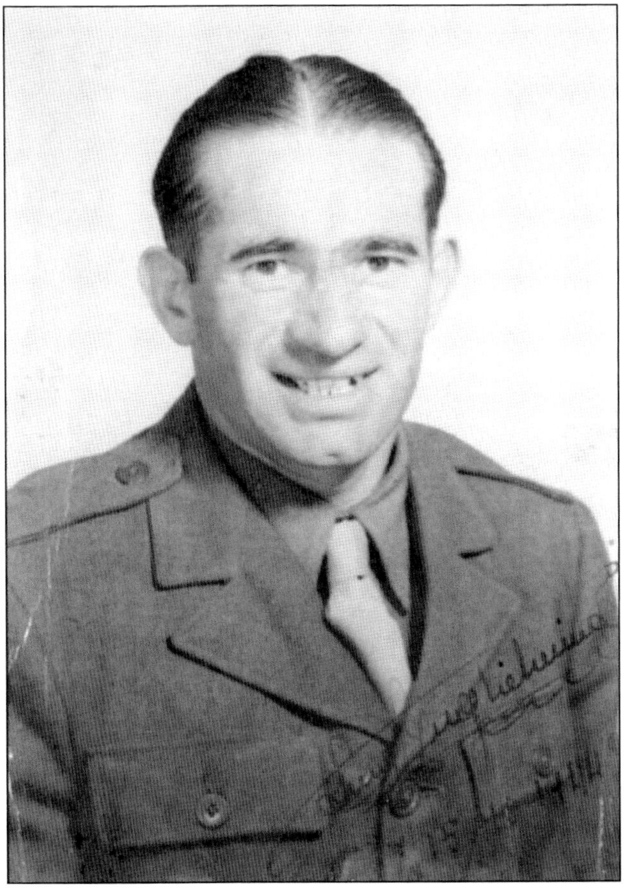

Luigi Guglielmino poses for this official photograph in his cooperator's uniform on October 15, 1944. Guglielmino, originally from Gassino (Turin), was an infantry private assigned to the 86th ISU. His daughter Carla moved in the 1980s with her ex-husband to the United States, where she and their two children still reside. (Courtesy of Carla Guglielmino.)

Ubaldo Salsa, on the right, along with two other POWs, is here seen visiting Italian Americans. Salsa was originally from Bellinzaga, a town in the province of Novara, in the Piedmont region. He often appears in photographs together with other ISU members who were from the same province. At Letterkenny, he was assigned to the 86th ISU. (Courtesy of Ornella Salsa.)

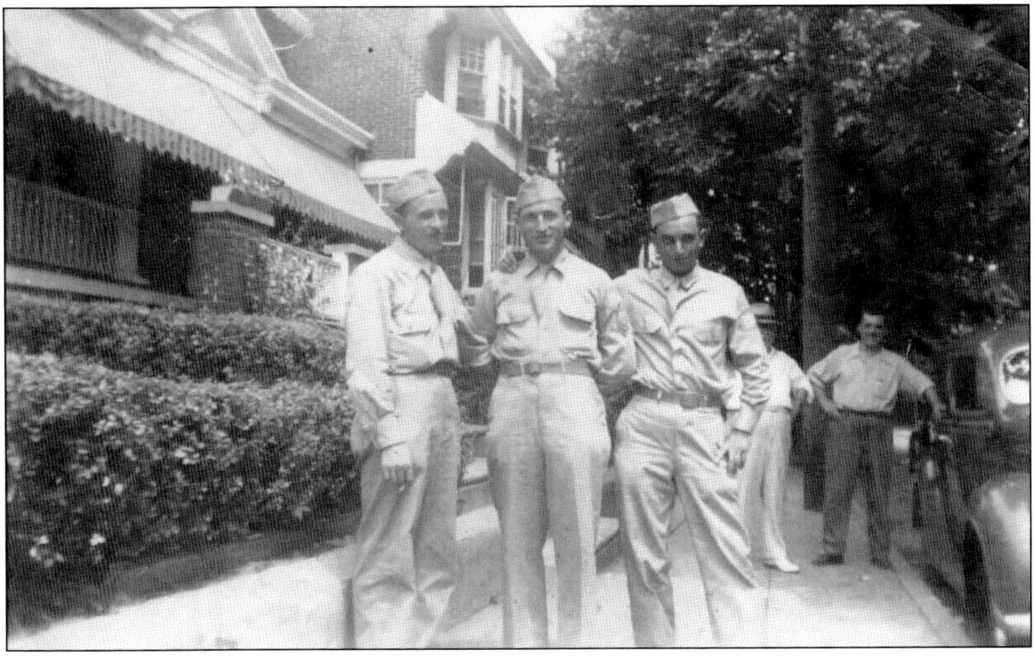

Capt. Roberto Cardinale, left, and Lt. Pietro Napoli, respectively the 85th ISU commander and executive officer, pose in James Fabiano's yard in Sharpsburg, Pennsylvania, on July 9, 1944. During the encounter, a few other relatives of Lieutenant Napoli were present. That same day, the two officers went to visit the Turano family in Vandergrift, Pennsylvania. (Courtesy of Giuseppe Grasso.)

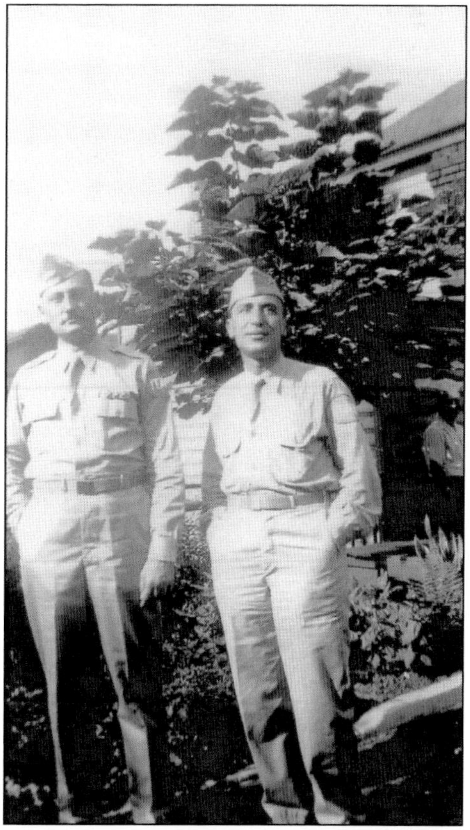

Innocente Salini stands second from the left along with several other POWs in front of the Letterkenny officer's club. All of them were most likely cooks at the facility. Salini was originally from Torre Pallavicina, near Bergamo, in the Lombardy region. At Letterkenny, as a cavalry private, he was assigned to the 86th ISU. (Courtesy of Mariantonia Salini.)

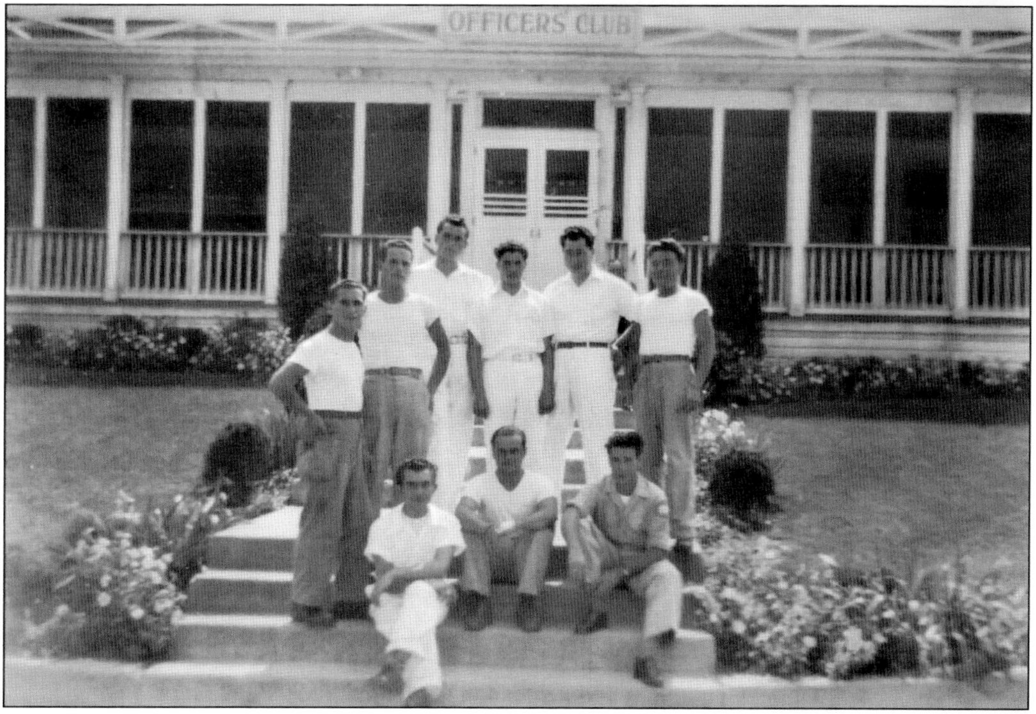

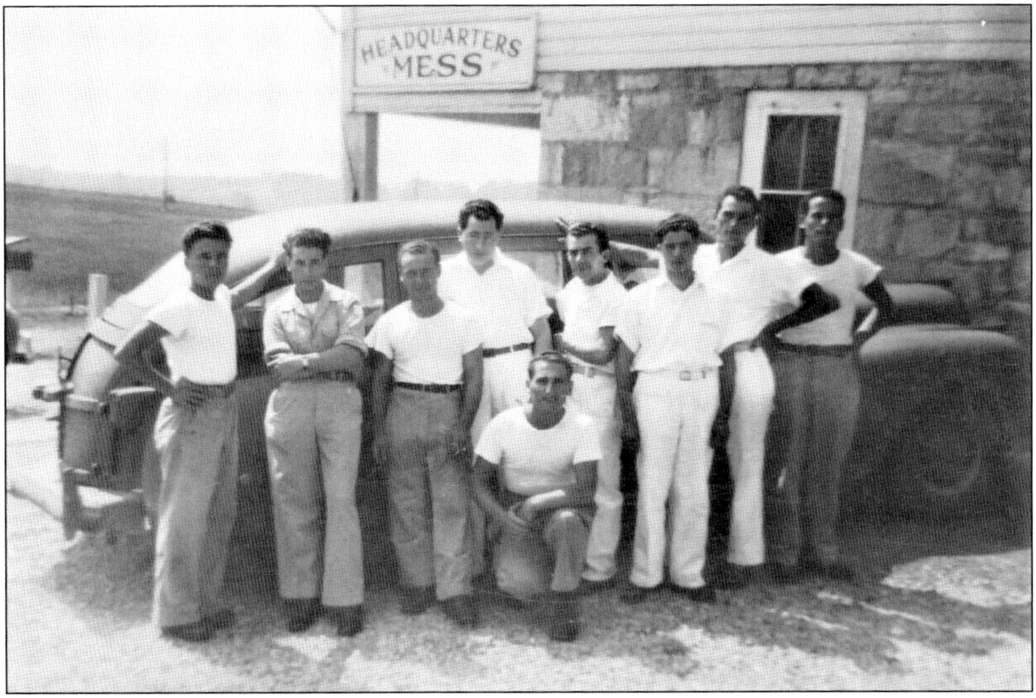

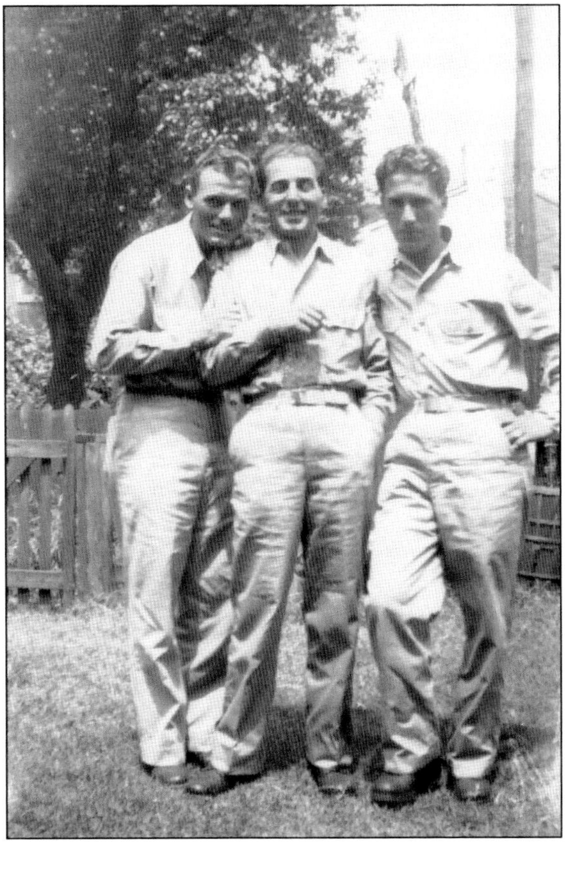

Innocente Salini stands eighth from the left, along with other POWs in front of Letterkenny's 321st Battalion headquarters mess hall. The Italian soldiers ate separately from US personnel in their own dining facilities and prepared their own food, but, as was often the case, US soldiers gravitated toward the fare that the Italians offered and would often join them in their own mess halls. (Courtesy of Mariantonia Salini.)

Vito Campanini poses in the center with two other POWs on July 21, 1944. Campanini was from Lungavilla (Pavia) in Lombardy. Note their informal military bearing. During formal formations and work hours, Italian soldiers, following US military regulations, could not put their hands into their pockets while relaxing or talking with superiors. Campanini died young at age 59 in 1968 in Milan. (Courtesy of Fabrizio Campanini.)

Standing, from left to right, are POWs Zefferino Trevisan, Innocente Salini, and Carlo Buffoni, and an unidentified Italian soldier, along with two kneeling. They are ready to socialize with civilians who visited them at the depot. From the prisoners' uniforms and the clothing worn by a civilian in the background, it is clear that the photograph was taken in the summer of either 1944 or 1945. (Courtesy of Vittoria Buffoni.)

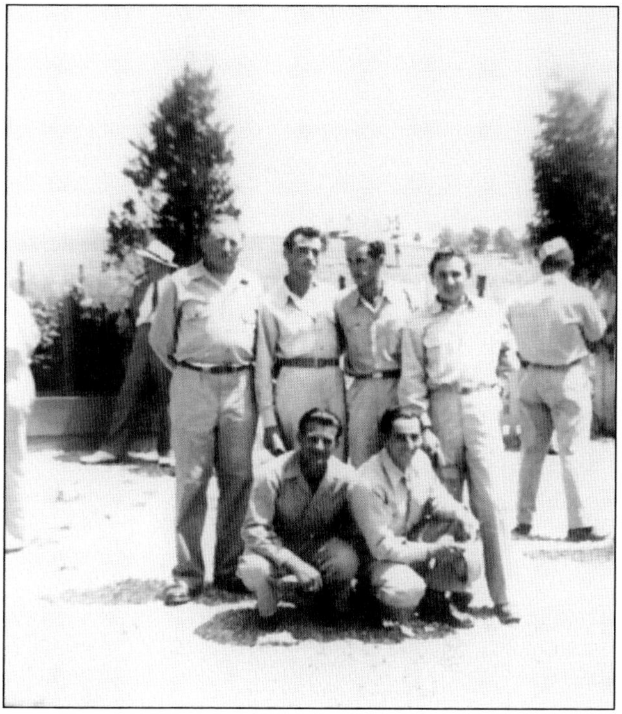

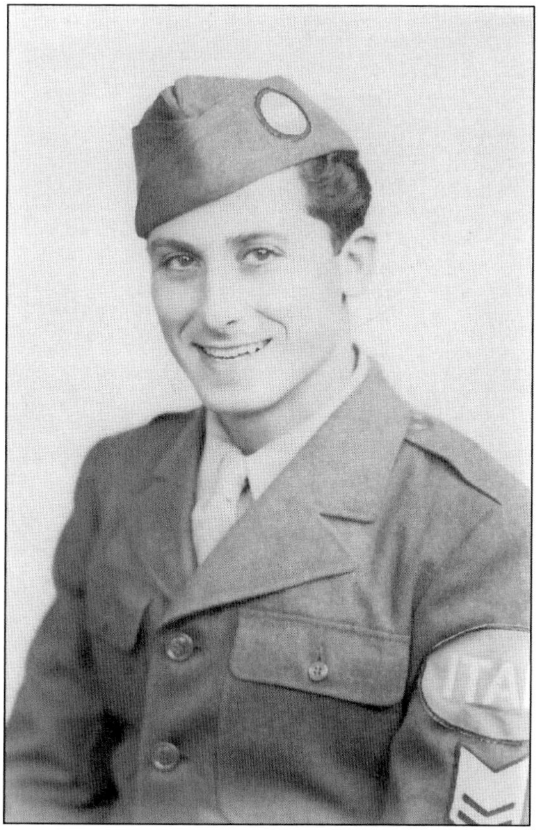

Francesco Maccione officially poses in his standard cooperator uniform with cover jacket. Note the "Italy" patches on his left sleeve and garrison cap and the Italian rank insignia of sergeant major. Originally from Milan, at Letterkenny he served in the 321st Battalion's headquarters. On June 28, 1945, Maccione asked to be repatriated because he was married, had a young daughter, and Allied bombings had destroyed his home in Italy. (Courtesy of Paola Maccione.)

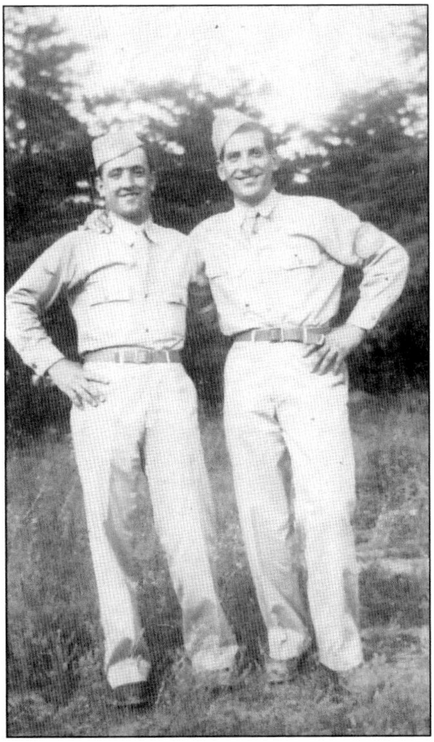

Pietro Spisni, left, stands with an unidentified POW. Born on January 31, 1922, in San Lazzaro di Savena (Bologna), Spisni was captured on July 21, 1943, in Sicily. At Letterkenny, he was assigned to the 159th ISU. Spisni lived to the age of 94 and passed away in November 2016 in Medicina, a town near Bologna where he had been living. (Courtesy of Guido Spisni.)

Alfredo Arienti, standing at center in the second row, poses in front of an orderly shack on the depot with Pasquale Cirillo, standing at far right in the same row. Arienti was a corporal originally from Desio (Milan). While traveling by Liberty ship to the United States, he fell 20 feet and broke a vertebra and foot bone. He arrived at Letterkenny from a hospital in Temple, Texas. (Courtesy of Pietro Arienti.)

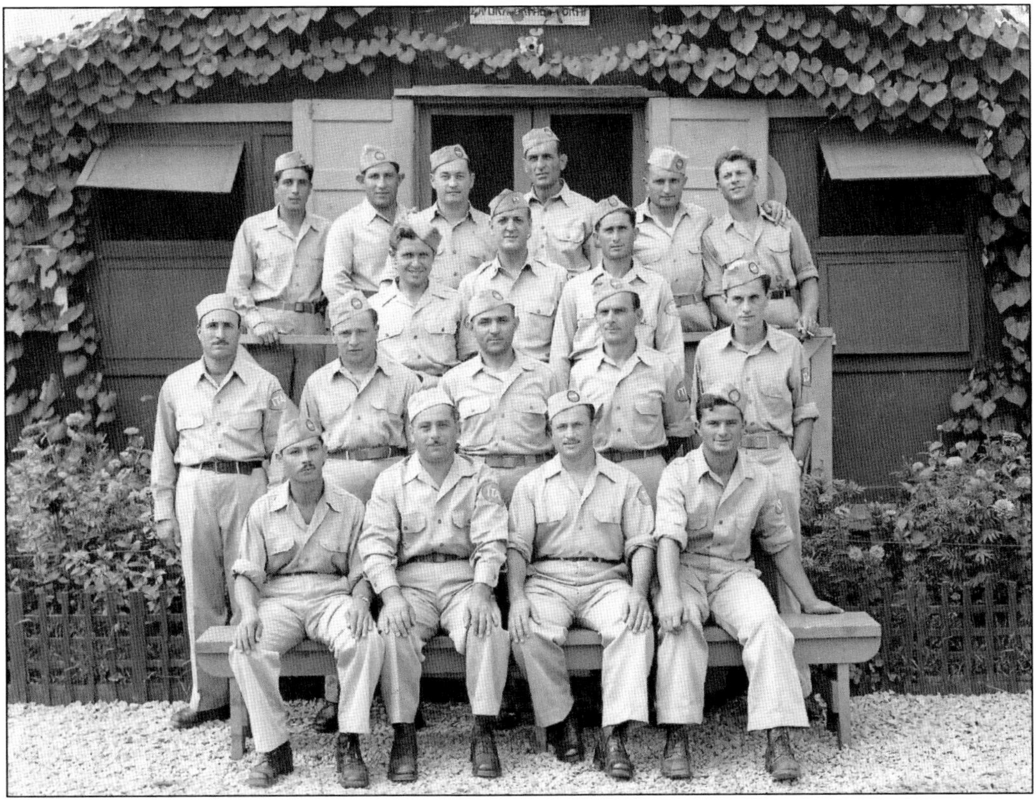

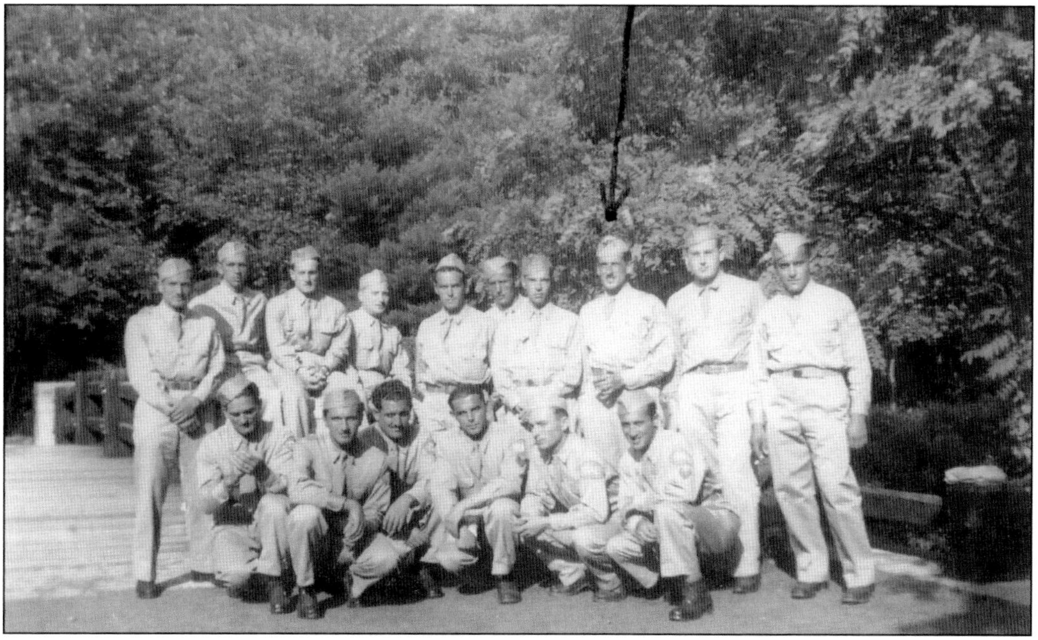

2nd Lt. Alfredo Tonolo, a bersagliere infantry officer, here indicated by the arrow, poses with other ISU officers and NCOs at the Caledonia State Park near the depot. Tonolo was from Mestre (Venice) and almost lost his life in a motorcycle accident in Tunisia. Maj. Angelo Bassi, the 321st Battalion commander, is fourth from the left, sitting in the back row. Cpl. Remo Cittadini is crouching, first on the left. (Courtesy of Frances Tonolo MacAvoy and Eva Cittadini.)

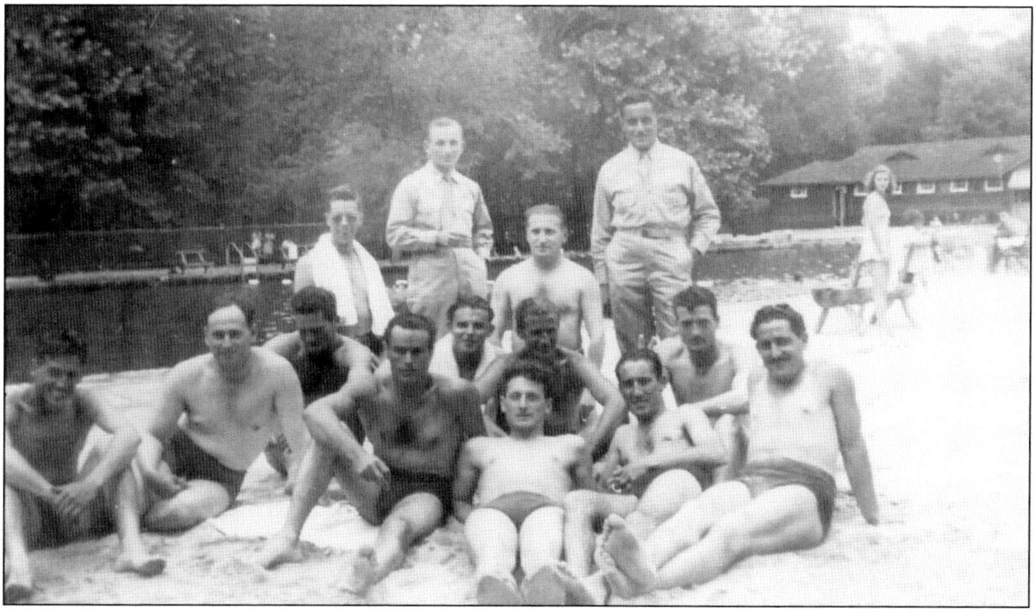

ISU soldiers enjoy a recreational trip to the Caledonia State Park swimming pool. 2nd Lt. Alfredo Tonolo, first on the left, seated, was an avid athlete and instrumental in receiving authorization from the Letterkenny Command to build athletic facilities at the depot. Cpl. Remo Cittadini, first on the left, second row, wrote on his copy, "Bella la vita. Poterla vivere." (Beautiful life. To be able to live it.) (Courtesy of Frances Tonolo MacAvoy and Eva Cittadini.)

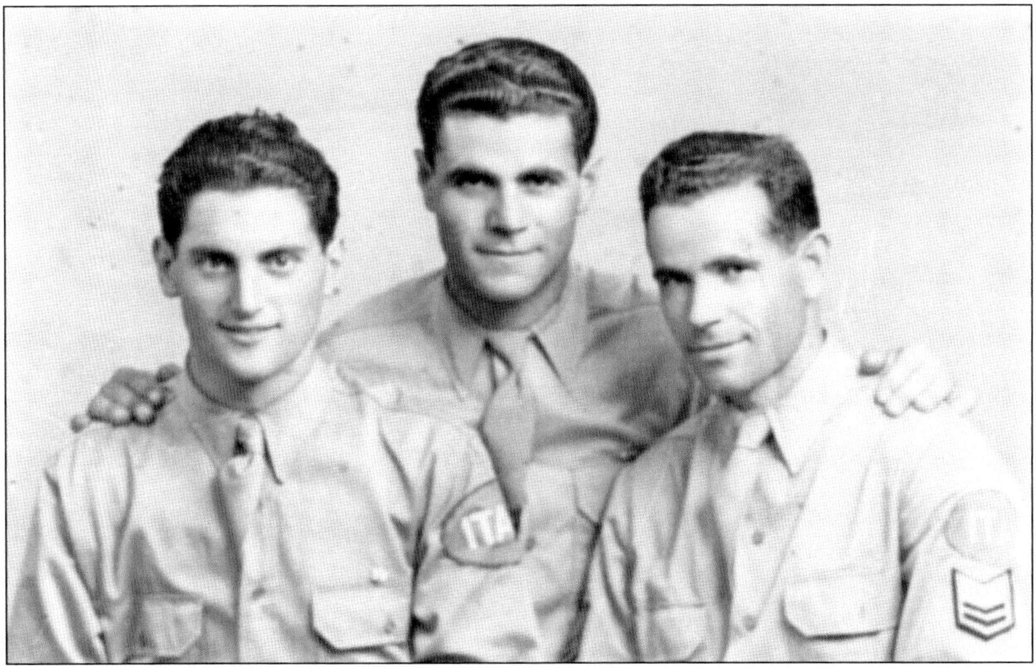

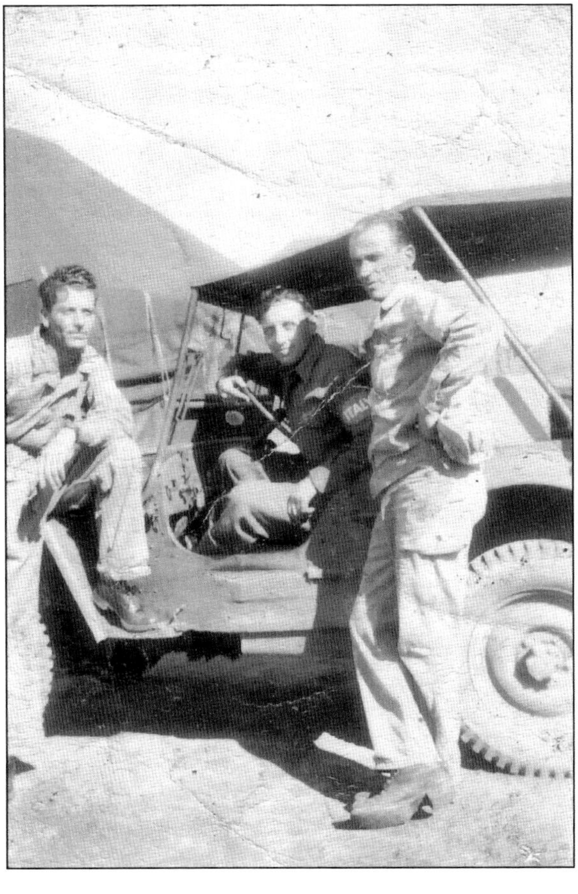

Pvt. Antonio Coin (left) hailed from the province of Padua, in the Veneto. Here, he poses with two other POWs, of whom the one on the right is a sergeant major. Coin had sworn allegiance as a cooperator on March 14, 1944, when he was at Camp Ritchie, Maryland. This photograph, as with several others, seems to have been taken in a professional studio. (Courtesy of Fausta Coin.)

Pvt. Antonio Santambrogio (right) poses beside a US jeep along with two other POWs. Many ISU soldiers obtained a driver's license at Letterkenny for automobiles, trucks, forklifts, and nail collectors. Santambrogio was one of the depot's accomplished artisans, and his specialty was woodcarving on inlaid pieces, since that had been his professional training before the war. (Courtesy of Natale Santambrogio.)

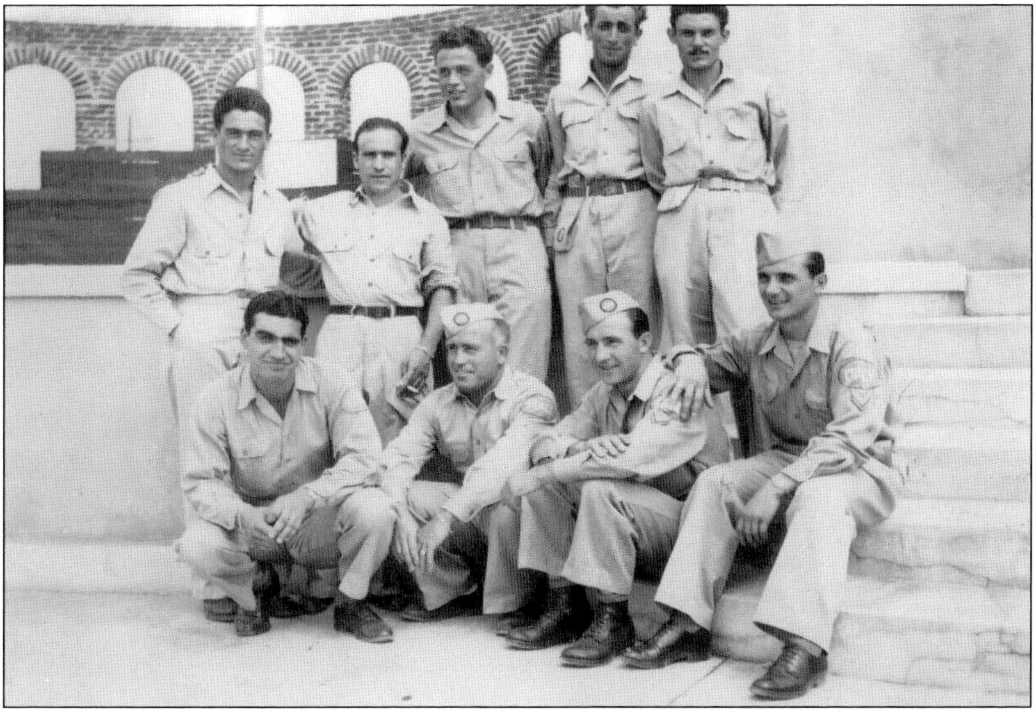

Pvt. Angelo Sala, born in Merate (Como), in the Lombardy region, on January 4, 1914, is standing third from the left. The fourth from the left, sitting, is Sgt. Virginio Ramella. The soldiers are posing on the steps located near the ISU-built amphitheater and arcade that is visible in the background. (Courtesy of Carlo Sala.)

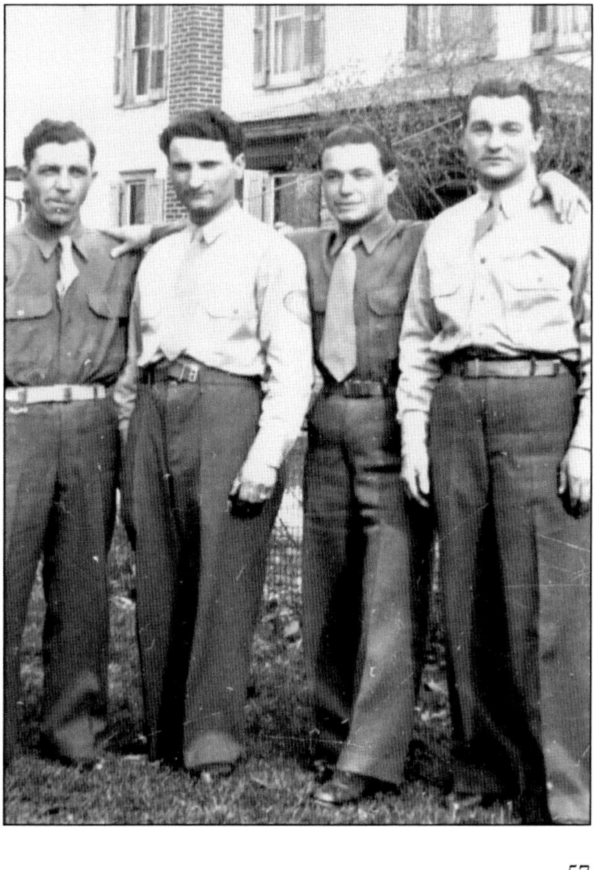

Antonio G. Brissoni, born on April 20, 1921, in Nembro (Bergamo) in the Lombardy region, stands on the right. He had been captured in Tunisia, and before coming to Letterkenny, he was detained in Camp Carson, Colorado, and then Pine Camp, New York. During his imprisonment, Brissoni underwent an appendectomy and had an inguinal hernia; nevertheless, he regularly played soccer. Brissoni died very young in 1959 at only 38 years of age in Hershey, Pennsylvania. (Courtesy of Karla Brissoni-Taylor.)

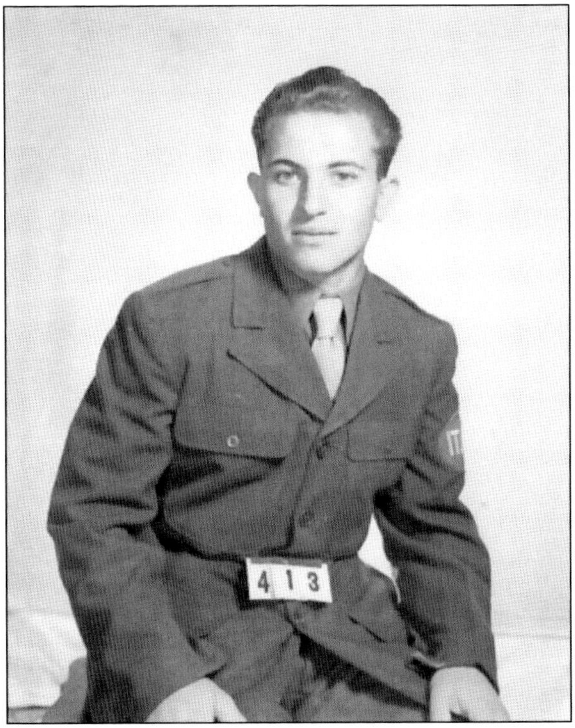

Pvt. Giuseppe Donatiello, born in Bisaccia (Avellino) in the Campania region, on September 14, 1920, is pictured here posing in his ISU cooperator's uniform. Before coming to Letterkenny on May 23, 1944, to serve with the 84th ISU, Donatiello had been at Camp Carson, Colorado, before being transferred to Camp Scottsbluff, Nebraska. (Courtesy of Antonio Gerardo Donatiello.)

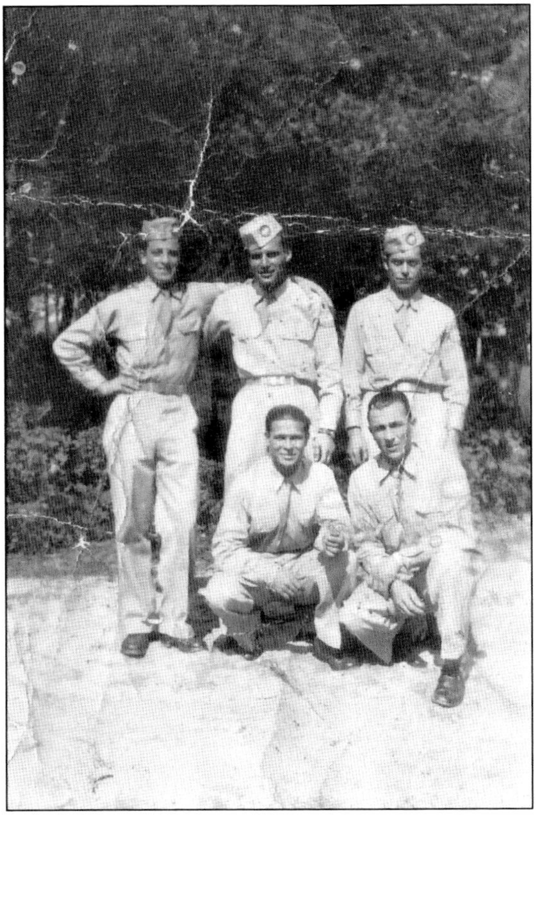

Pvt. Antonio Santambrogio is crouching at right. Captured in Sicily on July 10, 1943, during the initial phases of the Allied invasion of the island, he was shipped to the United States—first to Camp Butner, North Carolina, before going to Fort George G. Meade, Maryland. He served there with the 159th ISU until February 26, 1945, when he arrived with his entire unit at Letterkenny. (Courtesy of Natale Santambrogio.)

Three ISU cooperators smile while posing on the steps in front of the amphitheater in the summer of 1944 or 1945. On the left is Angelo Sala, born in Merate (Como), in the Lombardy region, on January 4, 1914. Note that here, as in many photographs, the POWs are smoking. After months of not having cigarettes in combat, they liberally lit them up in detention. (Courtesy of Carlo Sala.)

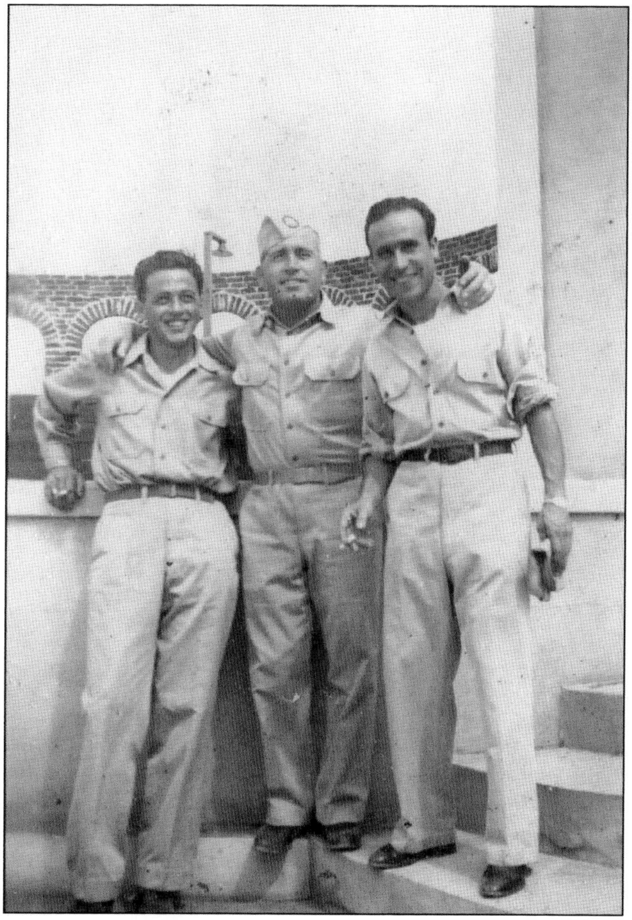

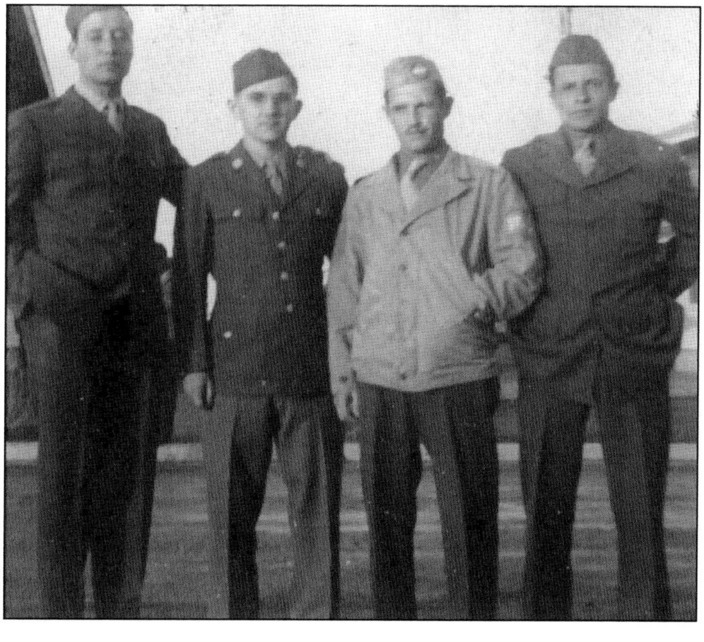

Pictured here are Guglielmo Rovida, on the right with other POWs, and American Warren Dolby, second from the left. The appearance of American soldiers together with Italian POWs in many photographs attests how warm friendships occurred on the depot between enemies that had once fought each other in North Africa and Europe, and on the seas earlier in the war. (Courtesy of Ettore Rovida.)

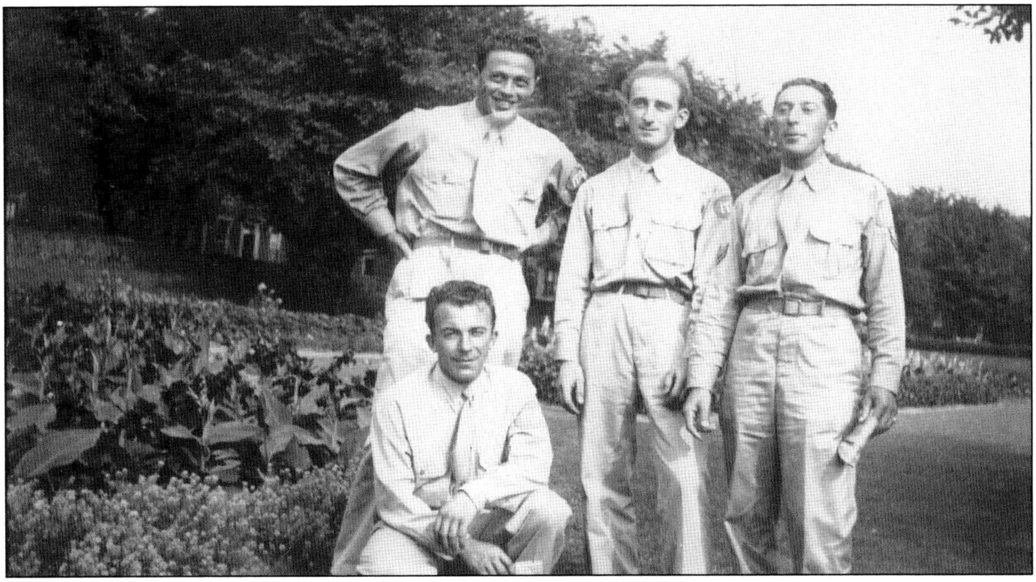

Angelo Sala, standing on the left, poses with three other cooperating soldiers in what appears to be a park or large lawn most likely during a visit to an Italian American community in a Pennsylvania town or city. Sala always appears smiling for the camera. (Courtesy of Carlo Sala.)

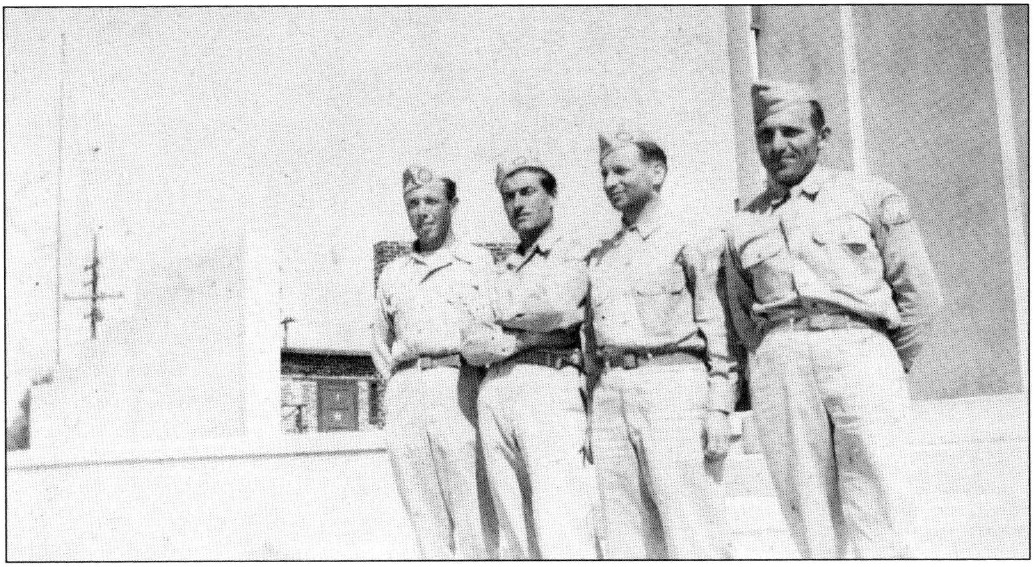

Cpl. Aldo Lorenzi from Mozzecane (Verona), second from the left; Cpl. Giovanni Barbè from Gravellona Lomellina (Pavia), third; Pvt. Luigi Brescianini from Barbata (Bergamo), fourth; and an unidentified prisoner pose on the steps near the amphitheater, most likely in summer 1945. The photograph's background, near the area where the chapel and bell tower were also built, shows either a warehouse or POW barracks. (Courtesy of Keti Melotto.)

Four

POWs, Italian Americans, and Women

Approximately five million Italian Americans lived in the United States in 1940, and this demographic meant that many Letterkenny ISU members had relatives and friends that could come to visit them from as far away as New York City and Boston. Saturday evenings and Sundays were the two days of the week when most visits took place. These guests brought food of every type, but it was their simple presence that greatly helped to raise morale. For their part, the POWs often repaid these family visits by traveling to cities both near and far.

The prisoners tended to conglomerate according to their regional, provincial, and even township provenience. In this way, they could share news from home that might very well involve extended family of the other POWs they associated with as ISU members. Norman Kogan, a future political scientist who had a stellar career at the University of Connecticut, served as a US Army sergeant at Letterkenny, and one Sunday he accompanied six cooperators to a club in Philadelphia. There, he realized that all of the Italian American civilians originally hailed from Piedmont, just as did the prisoners he chaperoned. Often, by finding a common identity through geographical grouping, the POWs could communicate with each other in their local dialects instead of standard Italian, a powerful way of helping to reinforce emotional ties to their home and loved ones.

Several young women, either of Italian extraction or not, usually accompanied by parents, came to parties organized on the depot. These occasions, as one can readily understand, helped to foster many romances with the POWs, and after the war, several women traveled to Italy to marry their sweethearts. Beyond this experience, there are four known cases in which unmarried American women gave birth to a son or daughter from a liaison with an ISU soldier. Such is the case with Betty Gilbert and the POW Elio De Angelis.

After the war, many POWs kept in touch with Italian Americans they had met at Letterkenny and on a few occasions even hosted them in their homes in Italy.

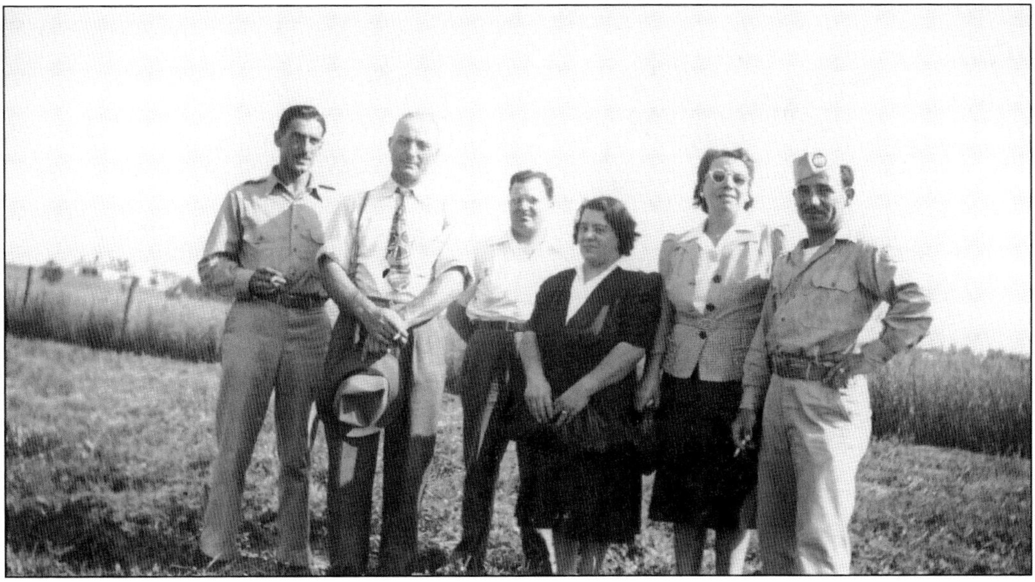

2nd Lt. Alfredo Tonolo stands on the left with another POW and Italian American civilians who are visiting Letterkenny, most likely in the summer of 1945. Note that both POWs are smoking cigarettes. ISU members actually received a standard weekly ration of them, and both cigarettes and other tobacco products, such as cut tobacco for pipes, were sold at the depot's post exchange. (Courtesy of Frances Tonolo MacAvoy.)

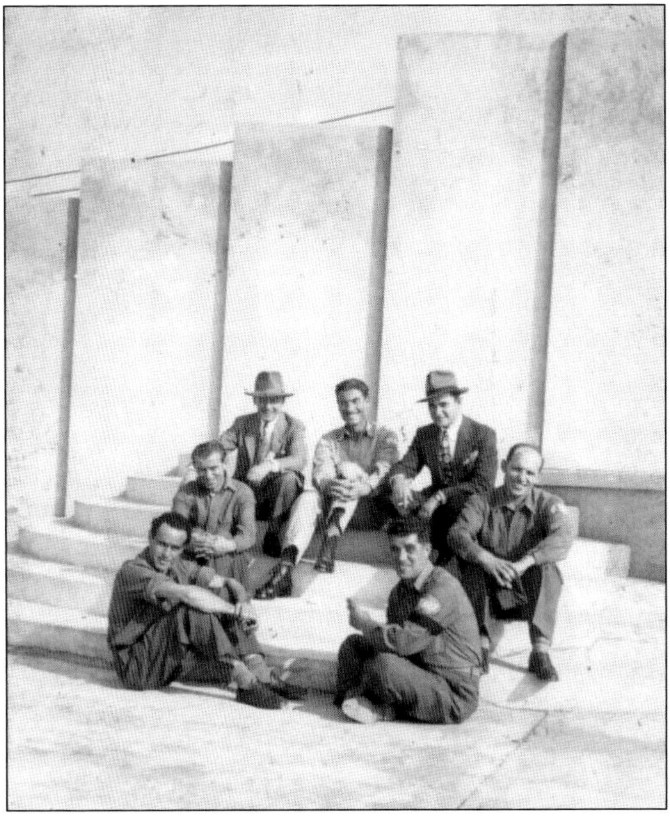

Luigi Brescianini, right; Aldo Lorenzi, center; other prisoners; and two Italian American civilians wearing fedoras relax together on the steps in front of the amphitheater walls at Letterkenny in 1945. Brescianini and Lorenzi were good friends and remained in touch long after repatriation, often visiting each other during holidays to reminisce. They often appear together in photographs. (Courtesy of Antonio Brescianini.)

Pictured from left to right are ISU soldiers Emilio Pizzetti, from Olgiate Comasco (Como); Angelo Milanesi, from Offanengo (Cremona); and Luigi Brescianini, from Barbata (Bergamo). Two Italian Americans pose with them on the steps near the amphitheater, most likely in the summer of 1945. The hometowns of these ISU members were in the Lombardy region, a point that confirms how most prisoners tended to group together according to geographical origins. (Courtesy of Antonio Brescianini.)

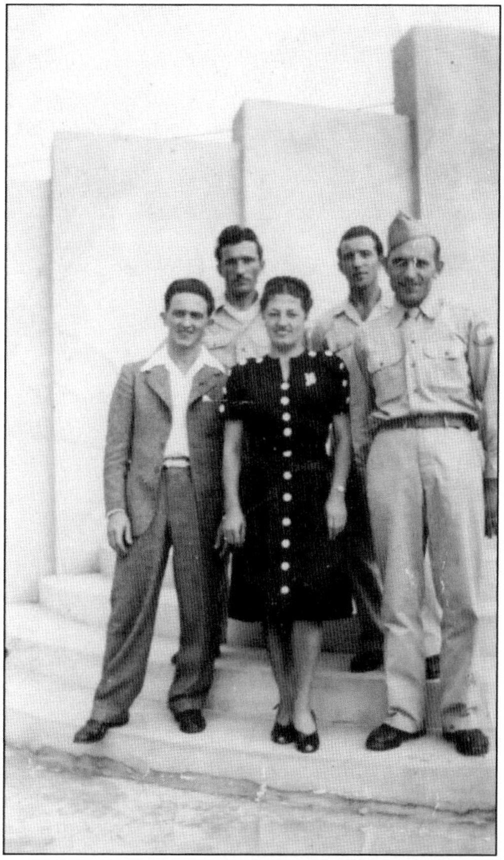

Domenico Censi, from Ancona, sits on the right together with another POW and an Italian American woman who is visiting Letterkenny. Everyone seems to be enjoying the reciprocal company, in particular the POWs, many of whom felt lonely being so far away from their own wives and girlfriends in Italy. The chance to spend time with American and Italian American women was a great source of comfort to them. (Courtesy of Claudio Censi.)

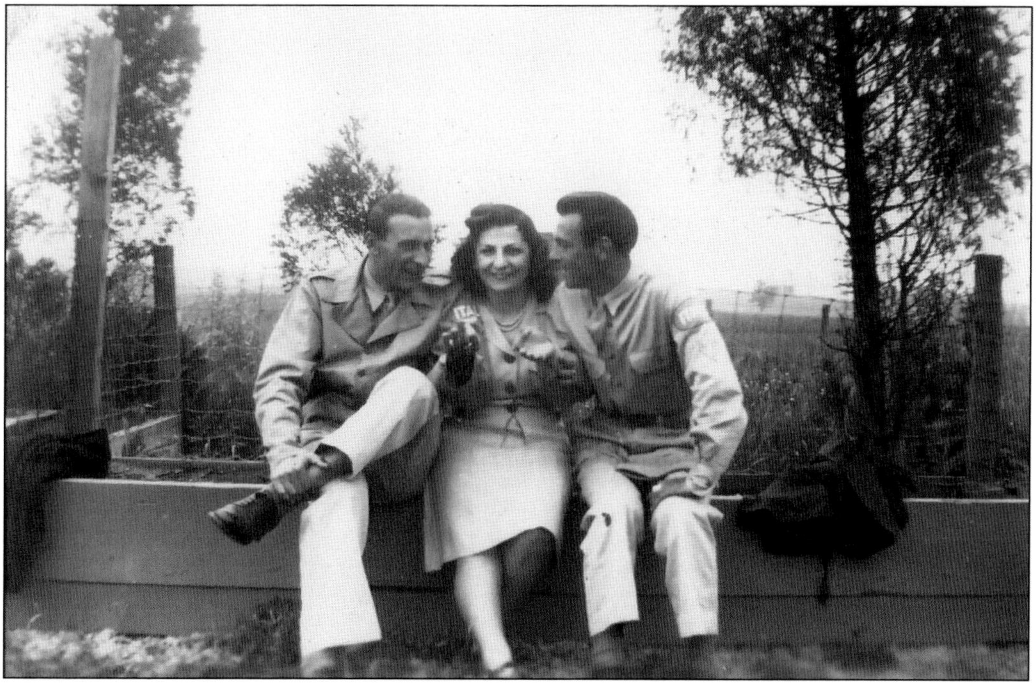

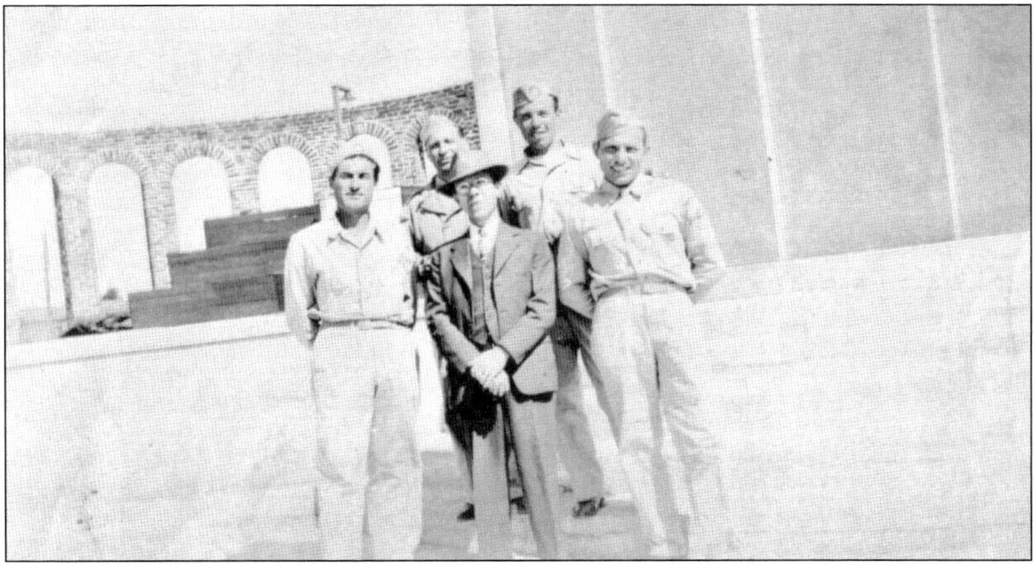

Ettore Cardellini, a resident of Blairsville, Pennsylvania, is seen here in his fedora as he visits Letterkenny on August 26, 1945. Cardellini was very dedicated to keeping company with the ISU members. Aldo Lorenzi is first from the left; Giovanni Barbè, second; and Luigi Brescianini, fourth. In the background is the amphitheater constructed by the POWs where they would host dances and festivities on the weekend. (Courtesy of Giancarla Barbè Biandrate.)

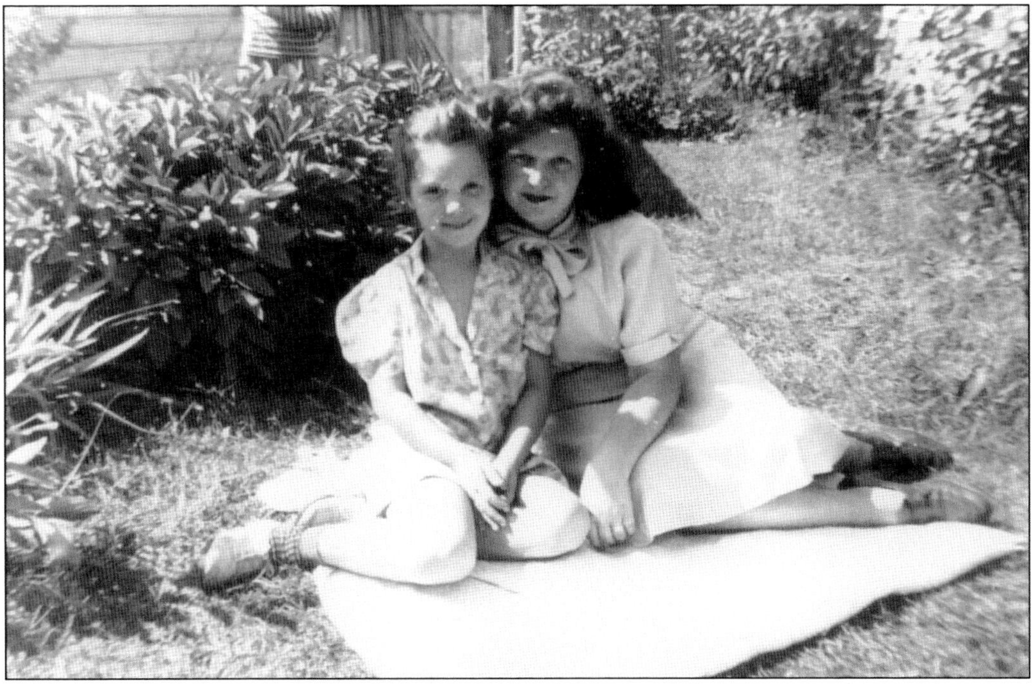

Jenny, a friend of Ettore Calizza, poses for him with her niece in her sister's yard in August 1944. On the back of the photograph, she wrote the following: "With all my love your Jenny, xxxx." Jenny hoped that one day Ettore could come see her sister's house for himself, and evidently she nurtured feelings for him that went beyond mere friendship. (Courtesy of Maurizio Calizza.)

In a photograph dated May 25, 1945, Giovanni Serpe, from Gaeta, crouches on the left, with Giovanni Molfesi, from Naples, in front of two American women who worked at the depot. Many POWs went out with young women who worked on the depot. Serpe himself recounted later in life that the women themselves would put secret messages in their pockets and even make wolf whistles as the POWs walked in front of them. (Courtesy of Giovanni Serpe.)

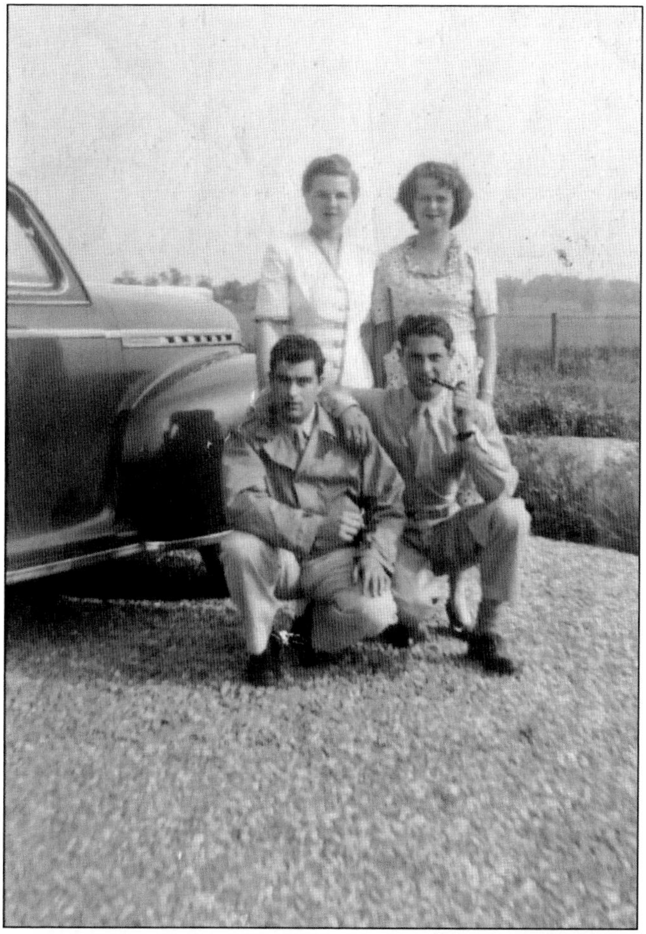

Mario Viscardi, first row, second from the left; Luigi Guglelmino, upper back row, far left; Luigi Sorisio, far right; unidentified children; and an Italian American couple are all gathered during a POW visit to an Italian American community in May 1945. Despite a few restrictions in late 1944 and early 1945, the cooperating ISU soldiers could visit friends and relatives off base if chaperoned by an American soldier. (Courtesy of Rosi Sorisio.)

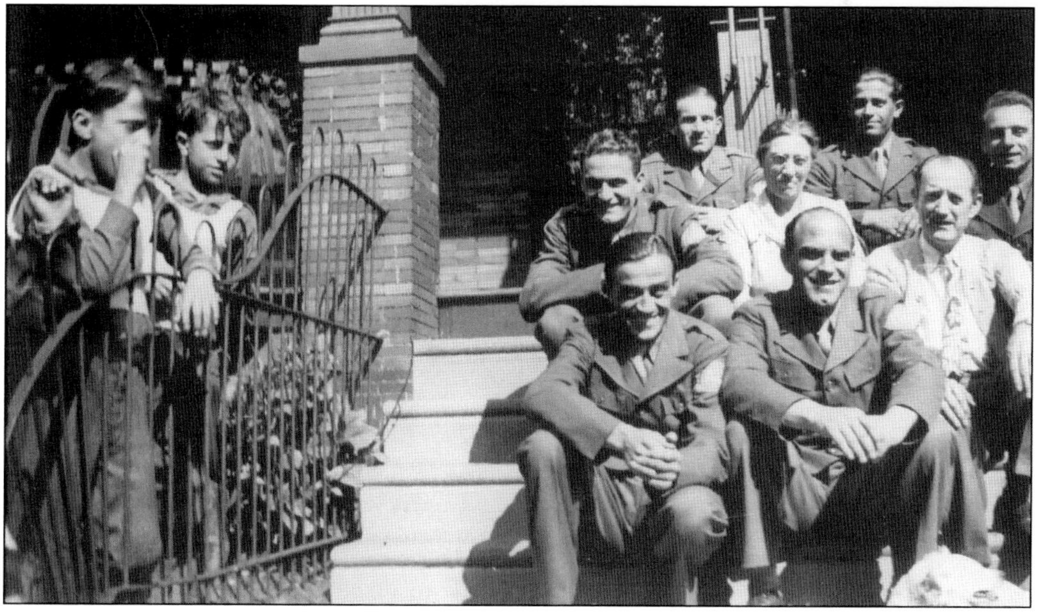

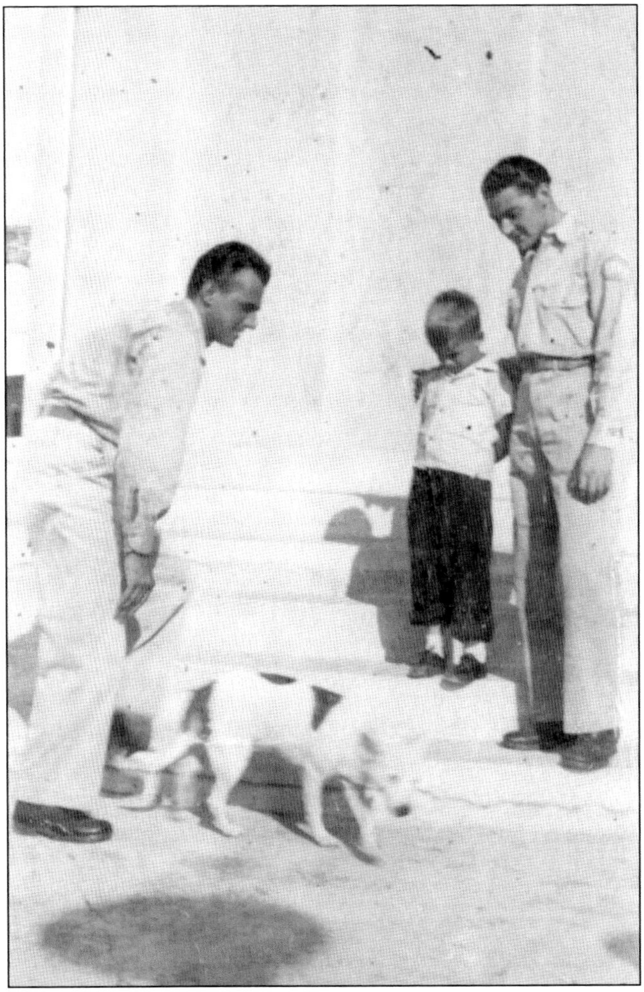

Mario Garbagnati stands on the left with Renato Volpi and a boy who had come with his family to visit the POWs at Letterkenny. His attention is focused on one the mascot dogs that roamed the depot and kept the POWs in great company. The same dog appears in other photographs with the prisoners. There were so many dogs, in fact, that the POWs built a penned in area for the canines where they could be kept sheltered overnight. (Courtesy of Ferdinando Garbagnati.)

Angelo Sala is fourth from the left with two other ISU members and an Italian American couple who is visiting the depot either in the summer of 1944 or 1945. The Americans captured Sala on March 23, 1943, in North Africa. (Courtesy of Carlo Sala.)

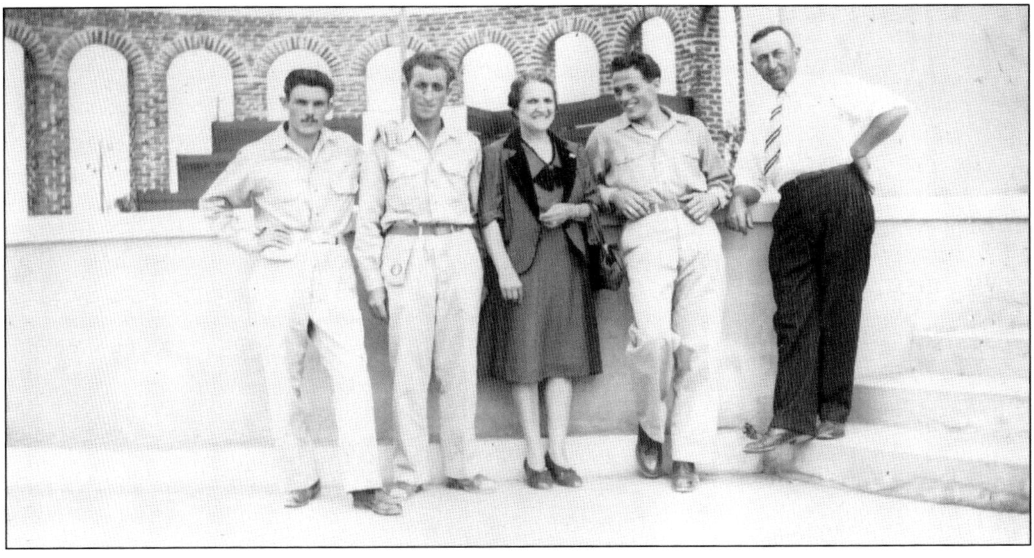

Giovannni Serpe is pictured here with his cousin Civitina Pirro. Civitina and her sister Clotilde lived with their family in Malden, near Boston, and the two went to visit Giovanni twice during his detention at Letterkenny, a long trip of 450 miles. Serpe recalled that Civitina seemed to be a little too fond of him, but he always treated her as the cousin that she was. (Courtesy of Giovanni Serpe.)

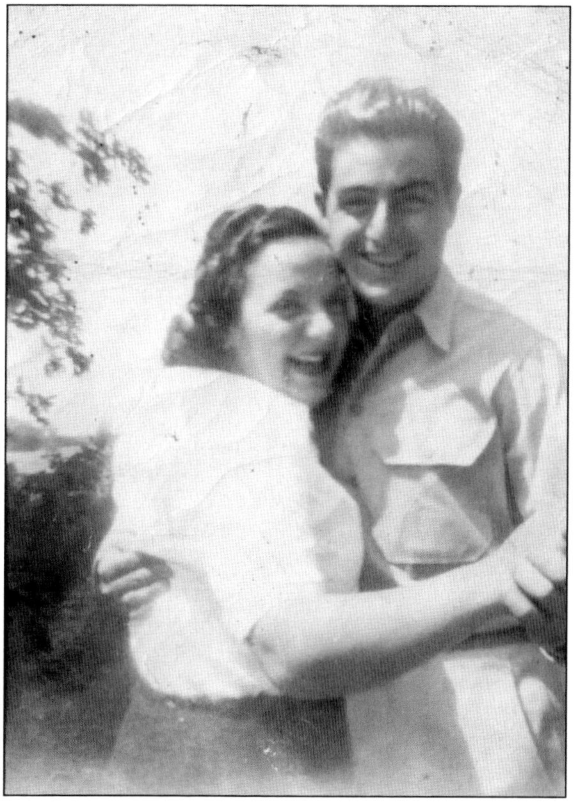

POWs gather with Italian American women who were visiting the depot. Ettore Calizza is standing, fourth from the left, and has his arms around two women. Sgt. Arcisio Raccanello, crouching in the first row, is hugging another. Clearly, in general terms, there was an excellent rapport between the POWs and women. (Courtesy of Maurizio Calizza.)

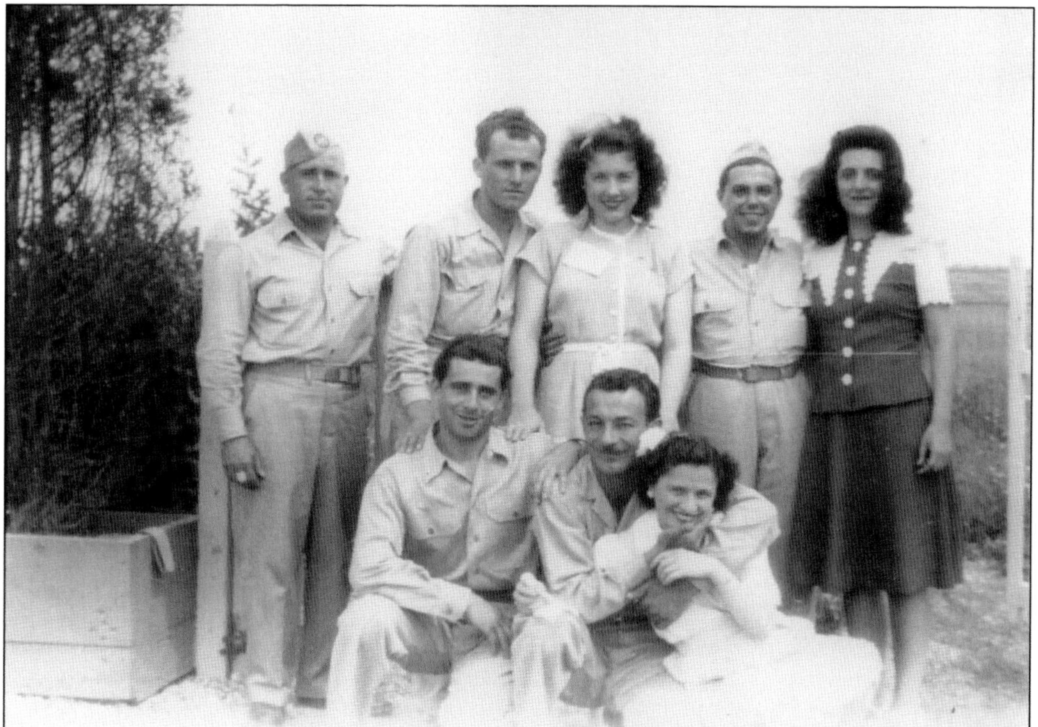

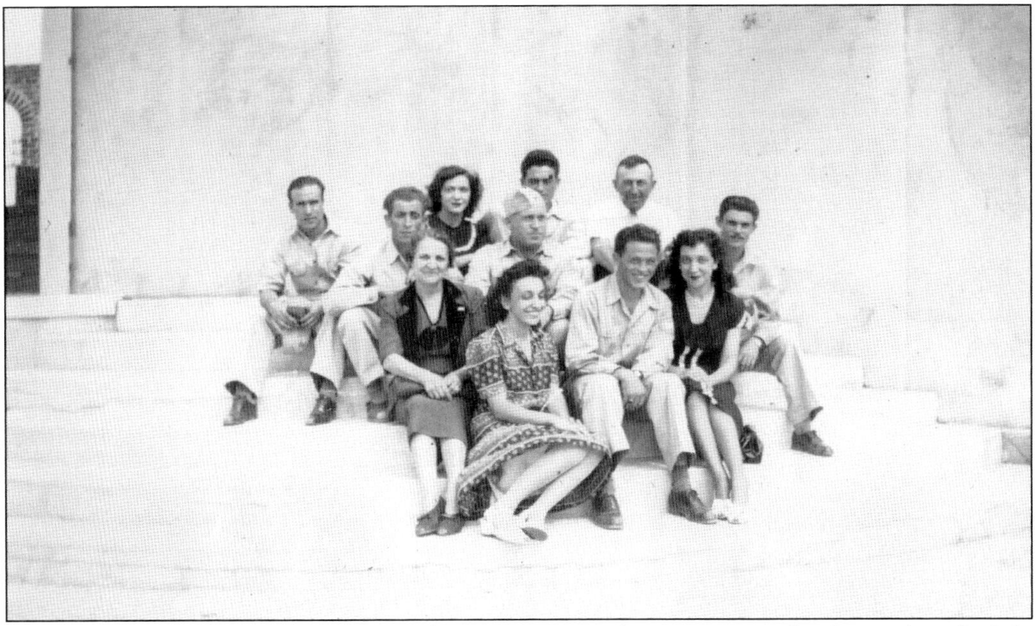

A group of Italian POWs poses with Italian Americans who are visiting the depot. Angelo Sala is smiling and sitting third from the left in the first row. These civilians are evidently one large family—a fact that can be surmised by how much the three young women resemble each other. (Courtesy of Carlo Sala.)

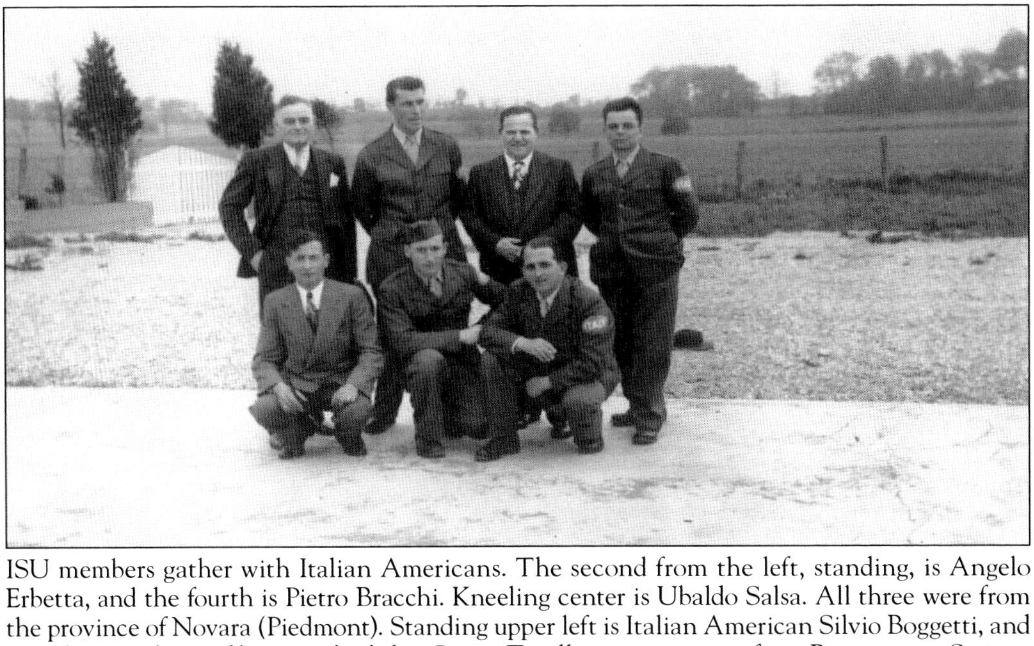

ISU members gather with Italian Americans. The second from the left, standing, is Angelo Erbetta, and the fourth is Pietro Bracchi. Kneeling center is Ubaldo Salsa. All three were from the province of Novara (Piedmont). Standing upper left is Italian American Silvio Boggetti, and crouching in front of him on the left is Pietro Tinelli, an immigrant from Romagnano Sesia, a town located in the same province of Novara. (Courtesy of Silvana Erbetta and Ornella Salsa.)

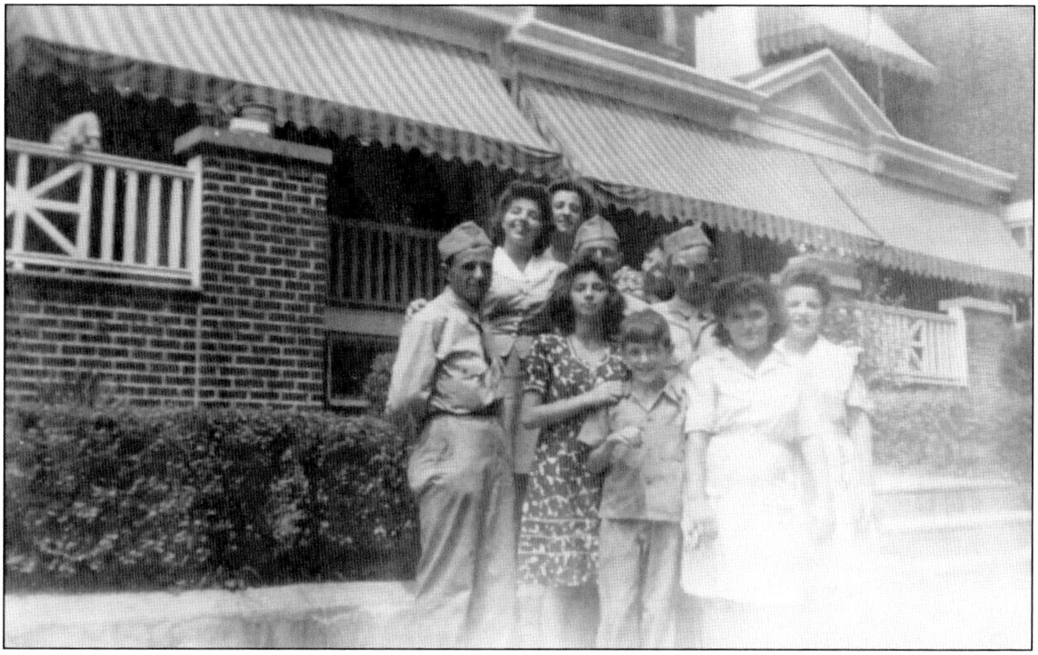

Sgt. Maj. Ubaldo Salsa, from Bellinzago, Novara, is on the far right and stands with two other Letterkenny POWs who are visiting Italian American families, either in the summer of 1944 or 1945. At Letterkenny, Salsa was assigned to the 86th ISU as one of the highest-ranking NCOs in the outfit. (Courtesy of Ornella Salsa.)

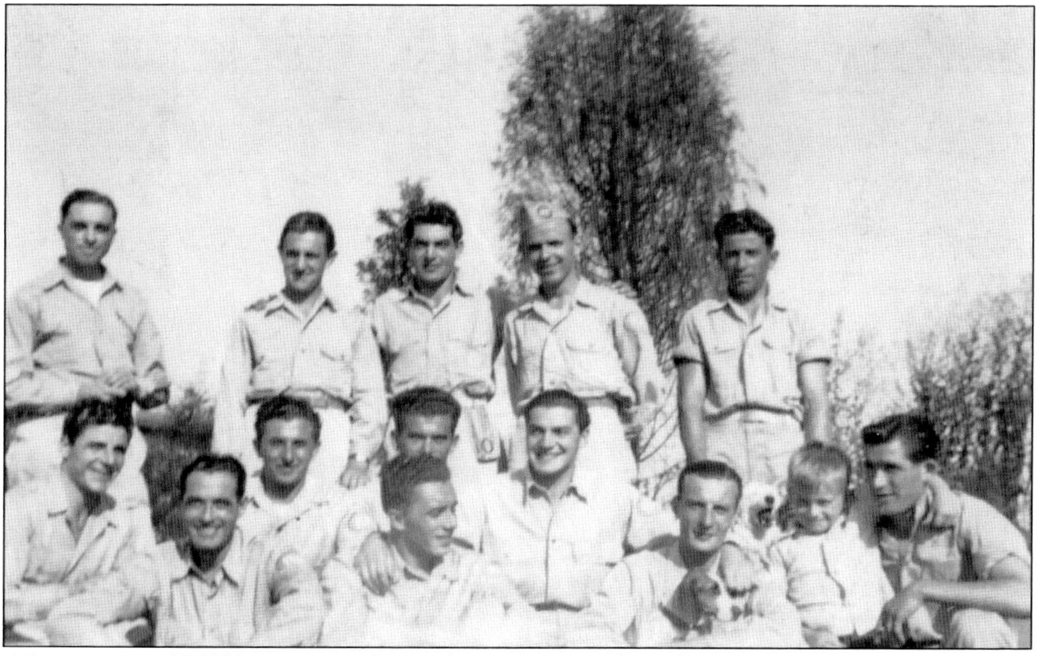

A large group of POWs poses together with an American boy who, most assuredly, came with his family during a weekend visit to the depot. Note that the boy has his arm around a possible POW relative. Mario Garbagnati, to boy's left, cradles a beagle, and to his left is a radiant Renato Volpi. A second dog, held by his front paws, is behind the boy. (Courtesy of Ferdinando Garbagnati.)

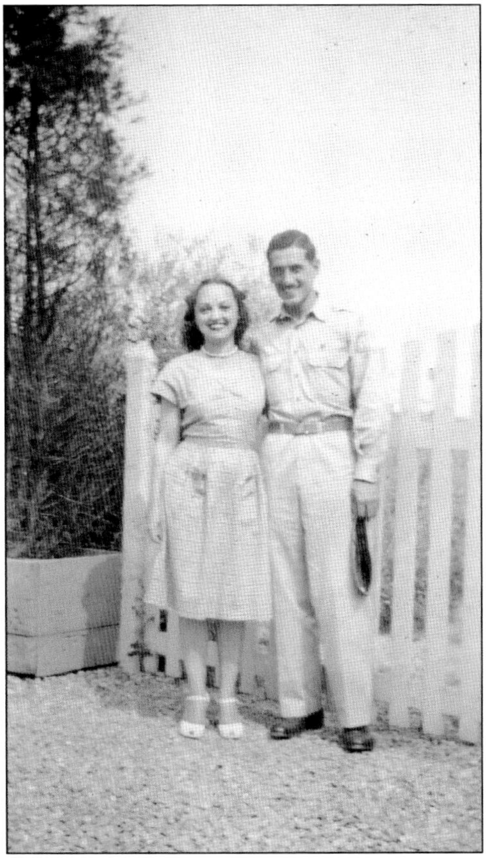

2nd Lt. Alfredo Tonolo and Tina Norce pose together in 1945. They met on a typical Sunday visit when Tina's family, residents of Berwick, Pennsylvania, had traveled to the depot. Tina immediately caught Alfredo's eye, and he tried to speak to her in Italian, broken English, and Latin. It worked. They corresponded for four years after the war, married in Italy in 1949, and returned to live in the United States. (Courtesy of Frances Tonolo MacAvoy.)

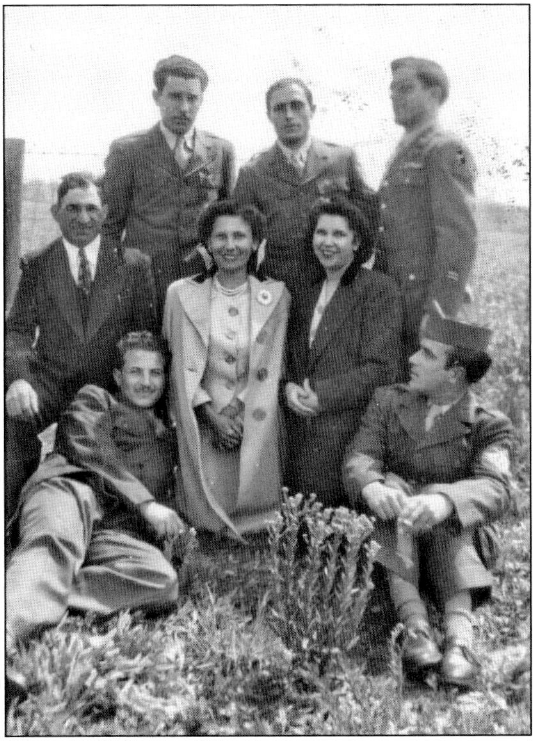

Giuseppe Imperiale stands on the left, while Giuseppe Donatiello reclines in front of him, both enjoying the company of their visitors. Judging from the civilians' dress clothes, it most likely is a Sunday, the day of the week when the highest numbers of Italian Americans came to visit the POWs at Letterkenny. On the back of the photo, Imperiale had written "dolci prigioni americane" (sweet American captivity). (Courtesy of Franca Imperiale.)

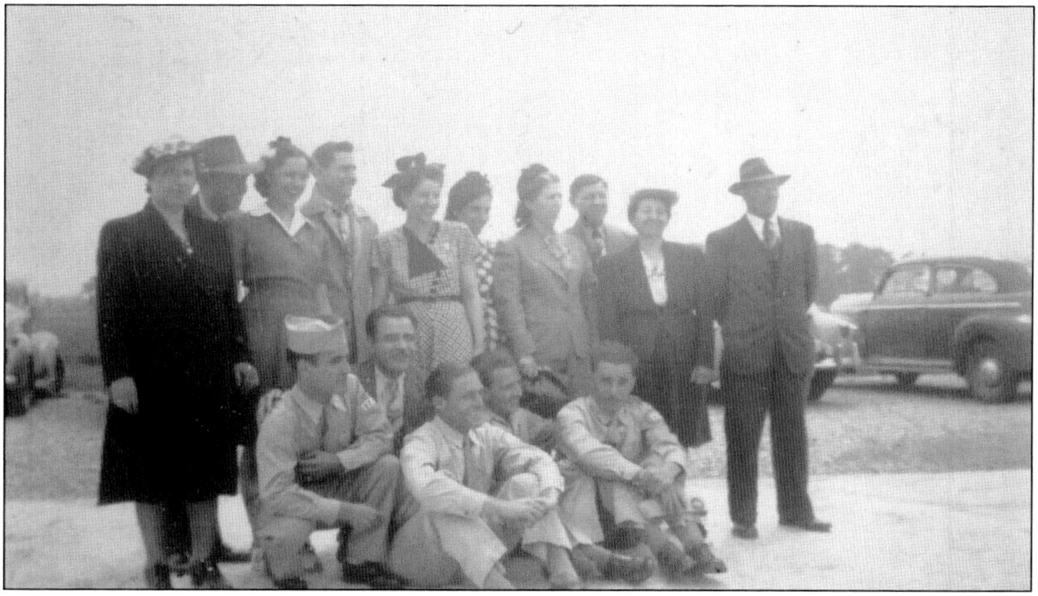

A large group of Italian Americans on a visit to Letterkenny poses together with four POWs. The fourth from the left, seated, is Giuseppe Donatiello and the fifth is Giuseppe Imperiale. Imperiale was originally from Bisaccia (Avellino) and served in the infantry. At Letterkenny, he was assigned to the 84th ISU. Donatiello was also assigned to the 84th ISU and, likewise, hailed from the same hometown. (Courtesy of Franca Imperiale.)

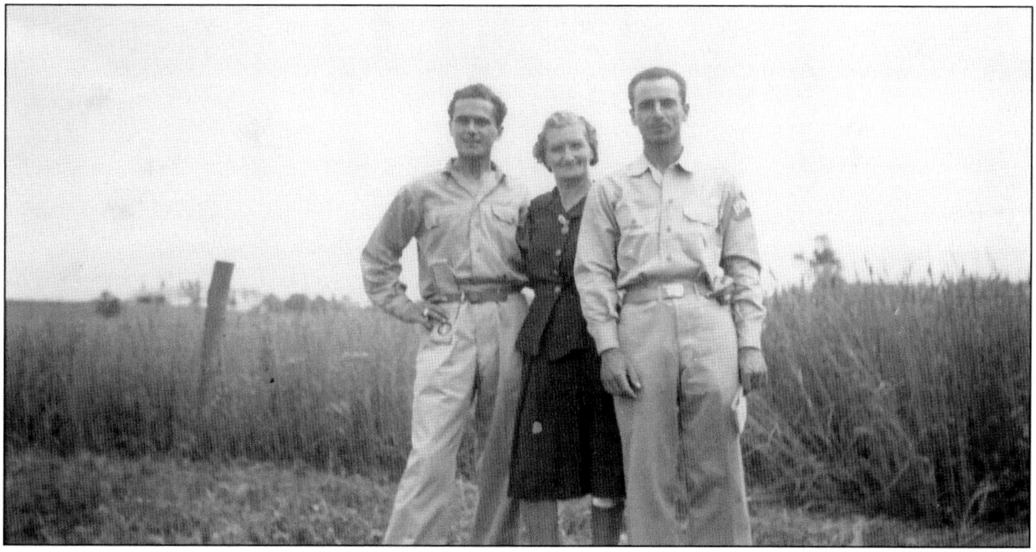

Luigi Sorisio, from Moncalvo Monferrato (Asti) in the Piedmont region, right, poses with an ISU soldier and an unidentified Italian American woman who appears in other photographs taken by prisoners. As at other detention camps, many visitors who came to spend time at Letterkenny were relatives—even parents or siblings—who had been separated because of immigration. (Courtesy of Rosi Sorisio.)

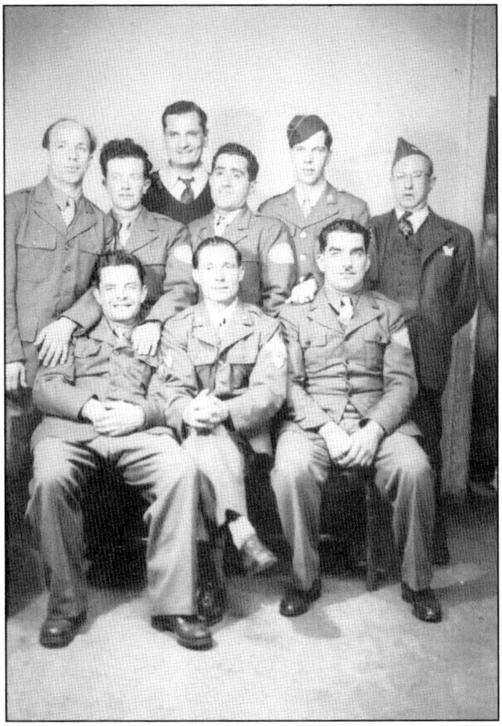

Pietro Bracchi, originally from Saluzzo (Cuneo), Piedmont, was taken prisoner on August 9, 1943, in Sicily. Here, he is seated on the far left with other prisoners and Italian Americans during a visit to Philadelphia on March 19, 1943. The fifth from the left, standing, is an American sergeant. The person who snapped the photograph wrote on the back, "Remember of Philadelphia." The grammatical error indicates that an immigrant was most likely the photographer. (Courtesy of Carmela Bracchi and Sara De Giorgis.)

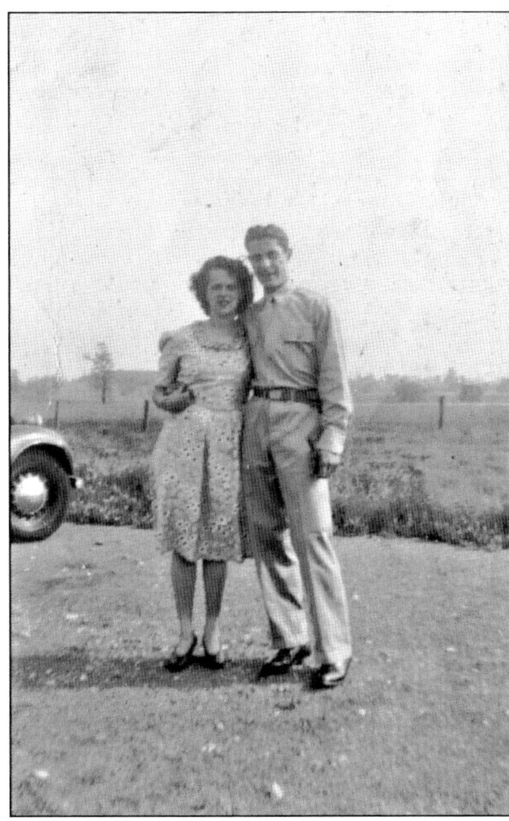

Gianni Molfesi hugs an American woman at the depot. The physical contact between POWs and American women was one of the principal behaviors that infuriated American civilians, and active duty and retired military members were especially offended. Indeed, in the summer of 1944 many of them wrote to American authorities to protest the perceived lenient treatment of the POWs who at one time had been their enemy. (Courtesy of Giovanni Serpe.)

A certain E. Baker cut this silhouette of Ettore Calizza on February 28, 1945. Calizza had several female admirers who often came to visit him at the depot. In a souvenir album of his POW experience in the United States, he kept at least 20 photographs of American women that he had met at Letterkenny. It is unclear whether E. Baker was one of them. (Courtesy of Maurizio Calizza.)

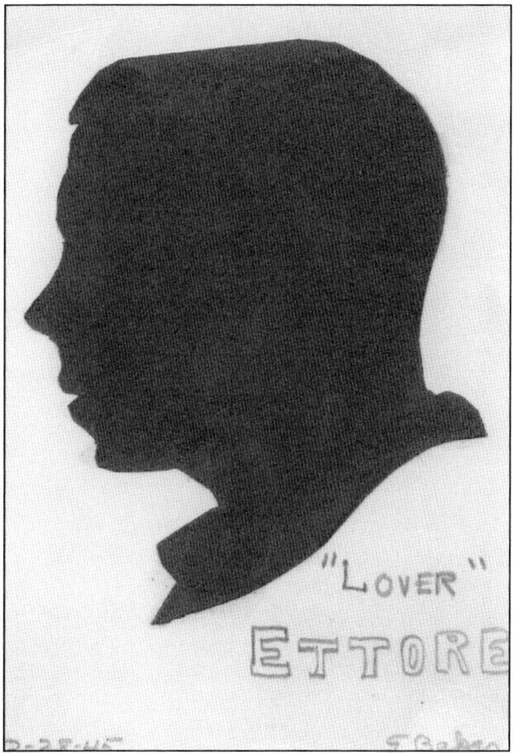

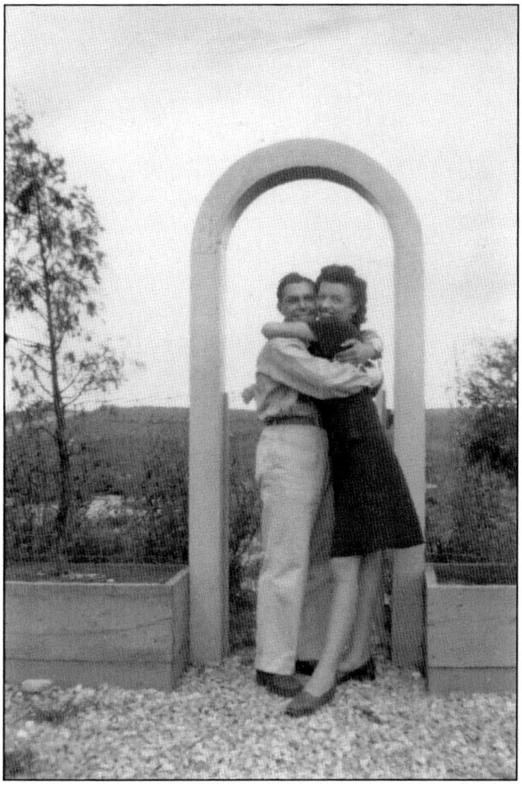

Ettore Calizza embraces one of his many female friends on September 18, 1945. Out of jealousy, many wives of the POWs later ripped up photographs of American women that their husbands had brought back with them to Italy. Fortunately, this was not Calizza's case, and his photographs provide ample documentation of the great friendliness that existed between the POWs and women, in particular, and the larger civilian populace, in general. (Courtesy of Maurizio Calizza.)

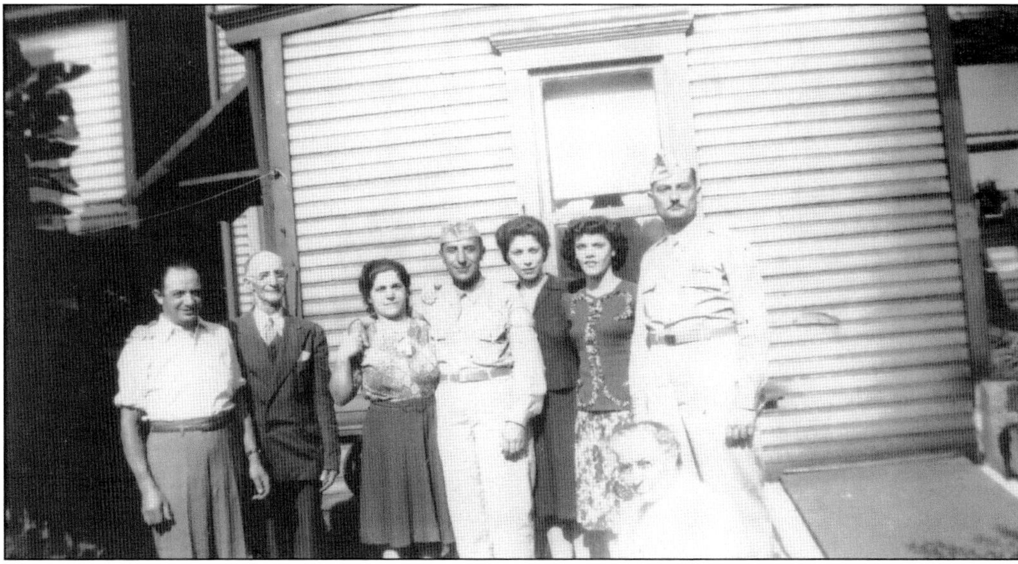

Capt. Roberto Cardinale stands on the far right with 1st Lt. Pietro Napoli, fourth from the left, on a visit to James Fabiano in Sharpsburg, Pennsylvania, on July 9, 1944. The second from the left is a Mr. Napoli, uncle of 1st Lieutenant Napoli, and on his left is Rosa Buccieri. Standing to Captain Cardinale's right is Lena Costanzo. Lieutenant Napoli's aunt is seated in front of Captain Cardinale. (Courtesy of Giuseppe Grasso.)

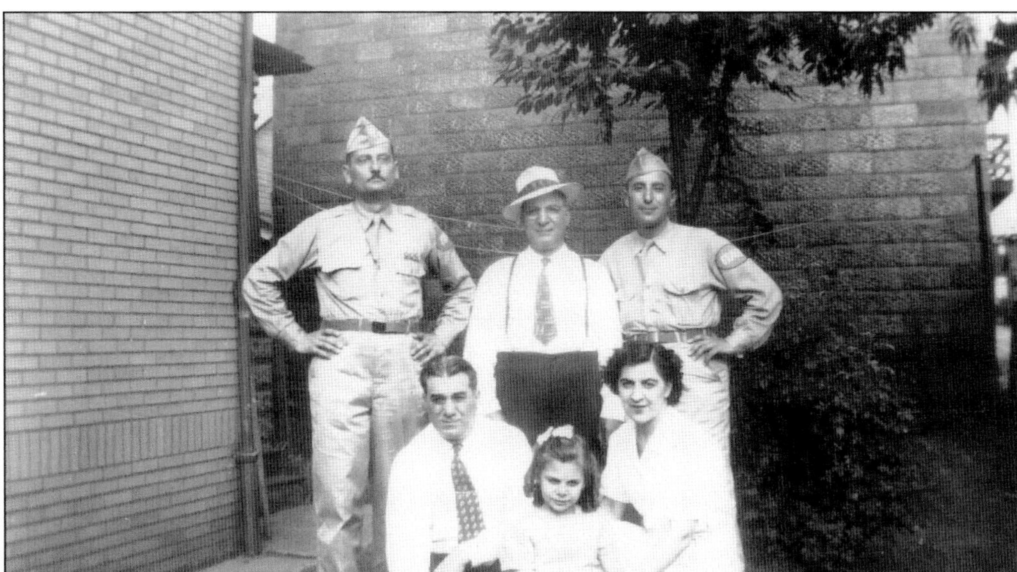

Capt. Roberto Cardinale poses in uniform, left, along with 1st Lt. Pietro Napoli, on the right. Cardinale and Napoli were, respectively, the Italian commander and executive officer of the 85th Italian Service Unit. This image was taken the same day that Cardinale and Napoli visited the Fabiano family in Sharpsburg. (Courtesy of Giuseppe Grasso.)

Pvt. Carlo Buffoni, from Besate (Milan), sits on the left together with another POW and an unidentified elderly Italian American couple who is visiting Letterkenny. Buffoni was assigned to the 83rd ISU on the depot. The location of the photograph, near Gate 17 and not too far from the POW barracks, was a common one since it was part of the usual gathering place of the visits. (Courtesy of Vittoria Buffoni.)

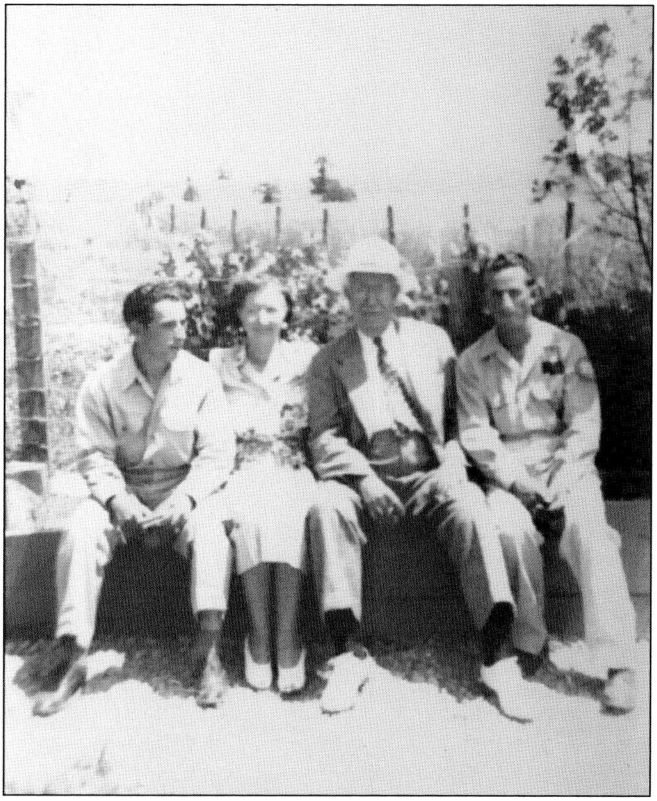

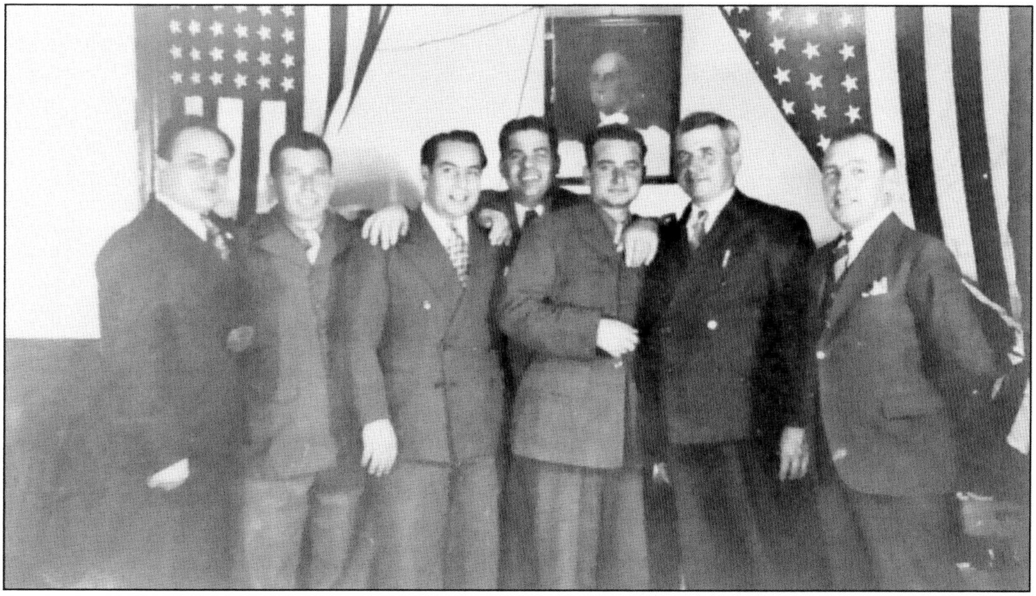

Antonio Torneo, fifth from left, stands with another prisoner, second from left. They are visiting a friend, Gaetano Farinella, first on the left, who lived in Hartford, Connecticut, a distance of about 340 miles from Letterkenny. Farinella, like Torneo, was originally from Floridia (Syracuse), Sicily. Note the American flags and the picture of George Washington that are intended to show Italian American allegiance to the United States. (Courtesy of Salvatore Torneo.)

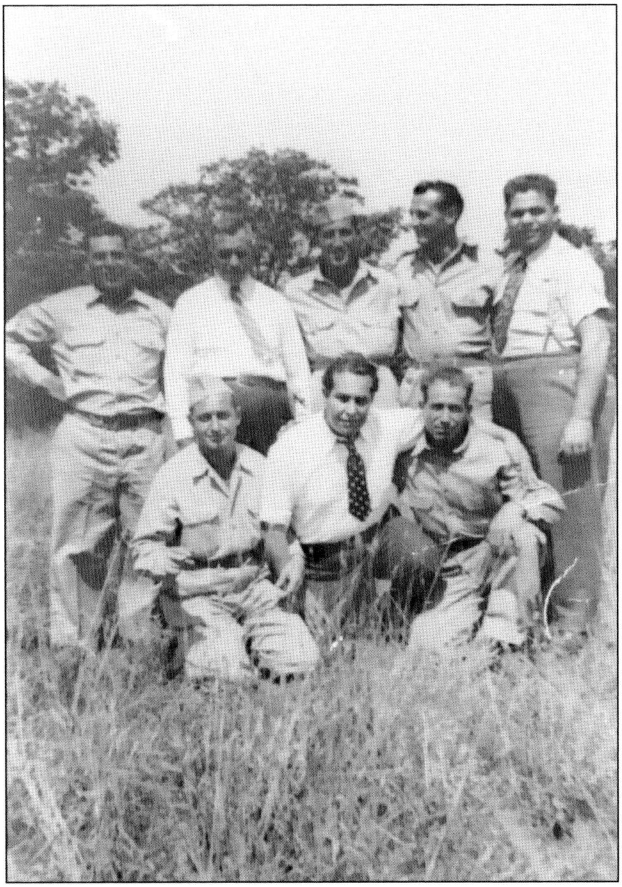

Kneeling in the first row from the left are POW Antonio Torneo, Italian American Sebastiano Privitera, and POW Salvatore Testa. Standing from the left are POW Gaetano Romano; an Italian American from Catania, Sicily; POW Vittorio Marcellino, from Catania; POW Gaetano Mazzarella; and Rosario, brother of the Italian American. Torneo, Testa, Romano and Mazzarella were all from Floridia (Syracuse). (Courtesy of Salvatore Torneo.)

Pvt. Almerindo Briganti, of Farnese (Viterbo) in the Lazio region, crouching on the right, is pictured with two other POWs and a family of Italian Americans who are visiting the depot. The surrounding flora and dress indicate that the picture was taken in the summer of 1944 or 1945. Briganti was a member of the 86th ISU. (Courtesy of Alessandra Briganti.)

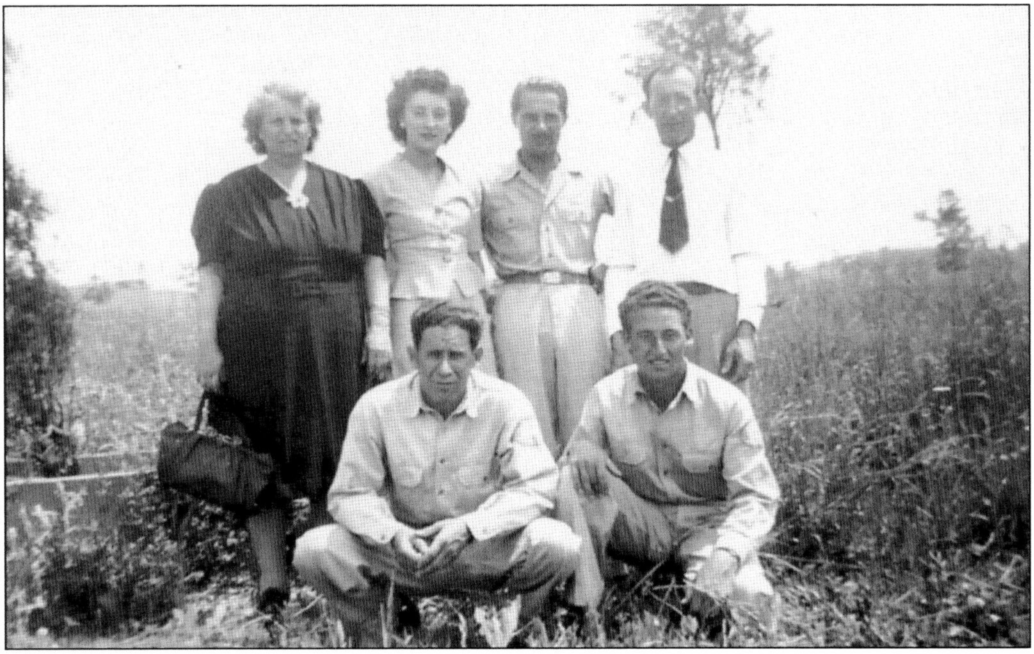

Betty Gilbert, seen here around age 18, had a son named Victor with POW Elio De Angelis. After Elio's repatriation, she began to raise Victor by herself. After Elio's death in 2009, his son Roberto learned in a letter from Betty that he had a brother in America. Victor and Roberto are friends and have remained in contact even after Betty's death on February 13, 2015. In April 2017, Roberto and his wife traveled to Chambersburg to meet Victor. (Courtesy of Roberto De Angelis.)

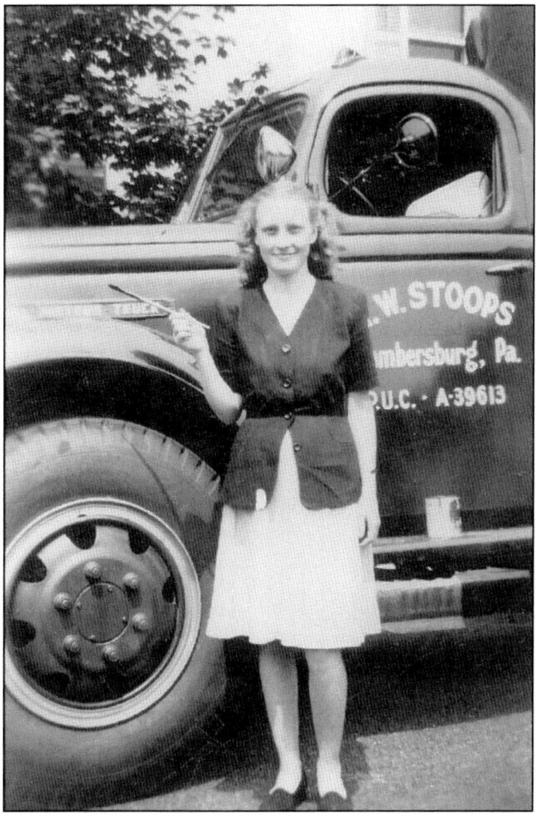

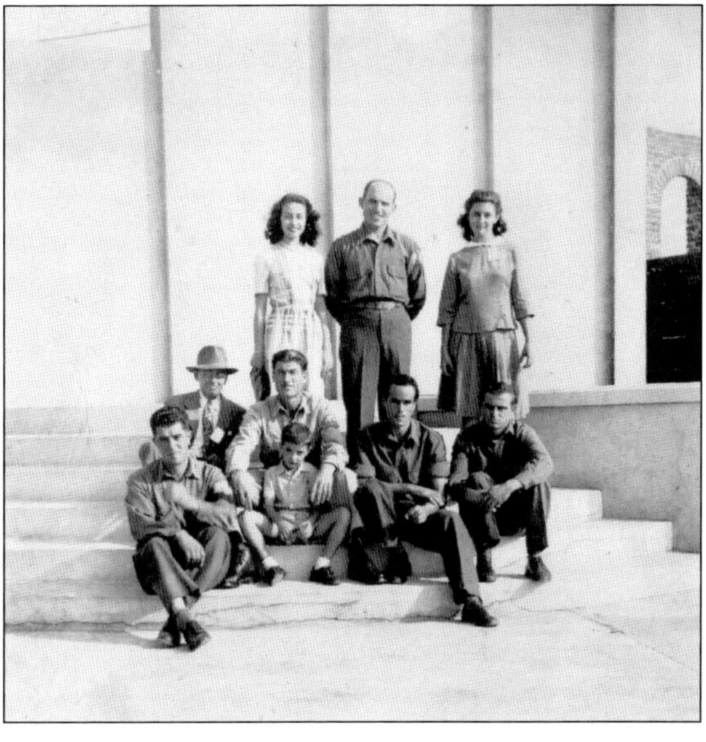

Five cooperators pose together on the steps of the amphitheater with an Italian American family during a visit to Letterkenny. Luigi Brescianini is standing at top between two young women, and Aldo Lorenzi is seated behind an American boy. It is possible that the Italian Americans were relatives of one of the POWs, perhaps even of Lorenzi, given how the boy is cradled by him. (Courtesy of Antonio Brescianini.)

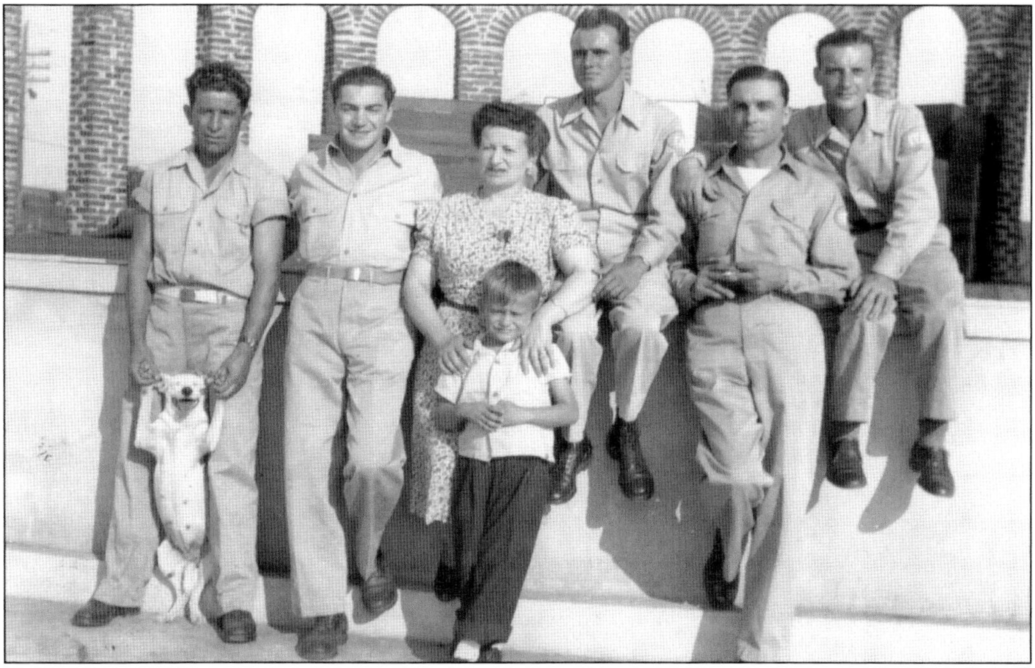

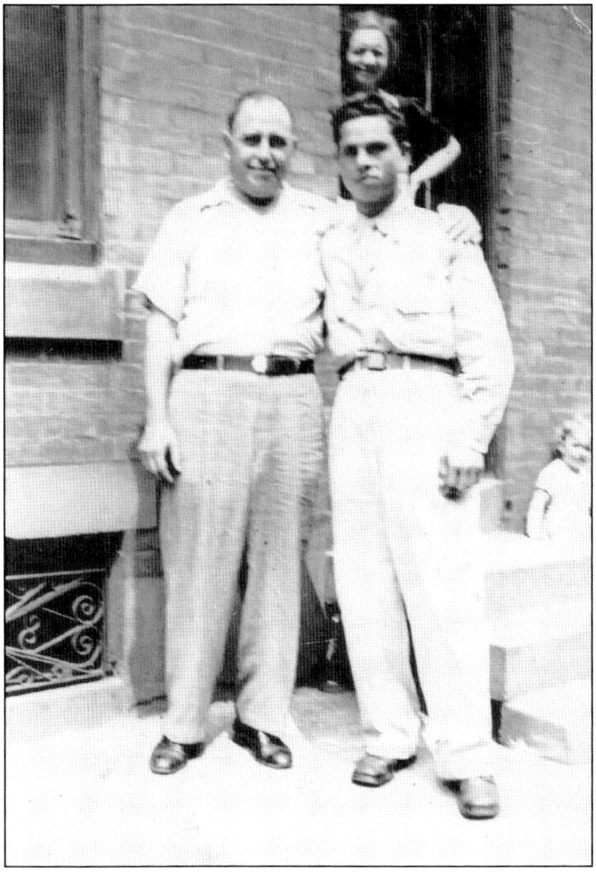

Italian prisoners gather around a woman and boy who have come to visit them at Letterkenny. Standing in front of the amphitheater, the second from the left is Renato Volpi, and the last on the right is Mario Garbagnati. Note how a prisoner holds a dog by its front paws. This canine friend is one of many that the POWs kept for company and within depot regulations. (Courtesy of Luisella Volpi.)

POW Antonio Falanga, on the right, stands next to Frank Caggegi and in front of Maria Gullotto while on a visit to Philadelphia. The Caggegi family, originally from Sicily, hosted Falanga for two days on July 15 and 16, 1944. They toured Philadelphia's Little Italy and danced at a local Sons of Italy club. At the end of his stay, they gifted Falanga a wallet together with $15. (Courtesy of Rosario Falanga.)

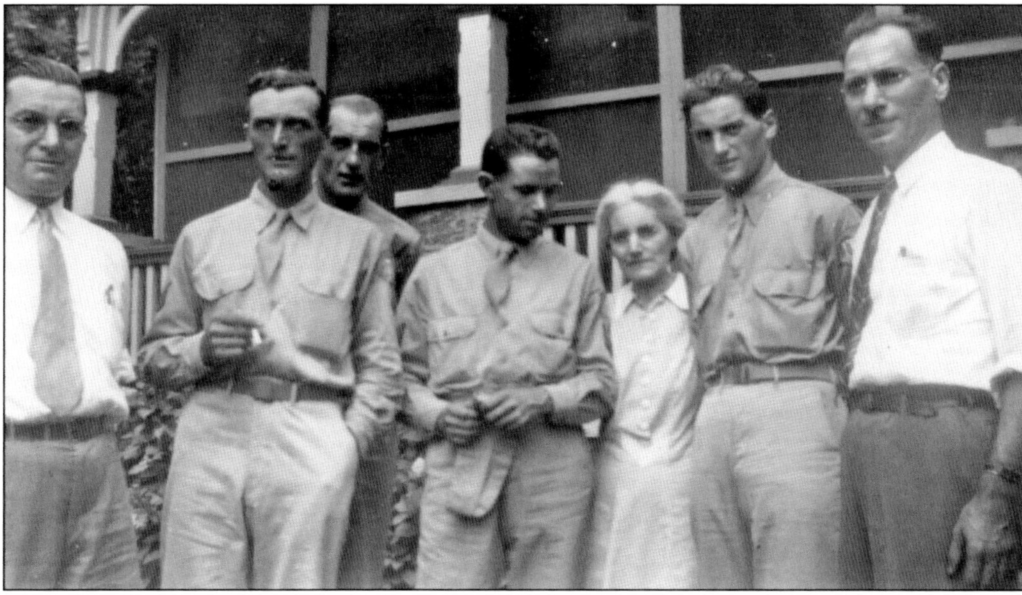

These Letterkenny ISU soldiers pose with a few Italian Americans who are most likely relatives of one of the POWs. Their clothing seems to indicate that these civilians belonged to the middle class. The soldier second from the right is Pvt. Antonio Coin. (Courtesy of Fausta Coin.)

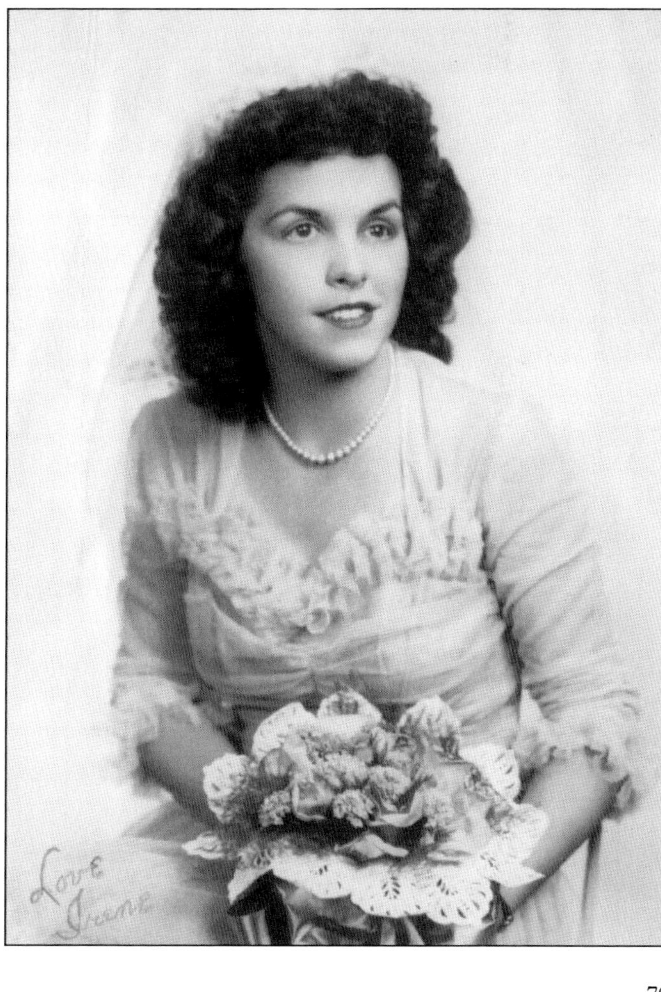

This photograph shows Antonio Coin's American girlfriend, Irene. Coin passed away on January 1, 2017, at the age of 94. Throughout his life, he kept many photographs of Irene, as she posed alone or together with her various family members, a point that indicates how strong their sentimental bonds had been. Unfortunately, the particular details of their relationship are not known. (Courtesy of Fausta Coin.)

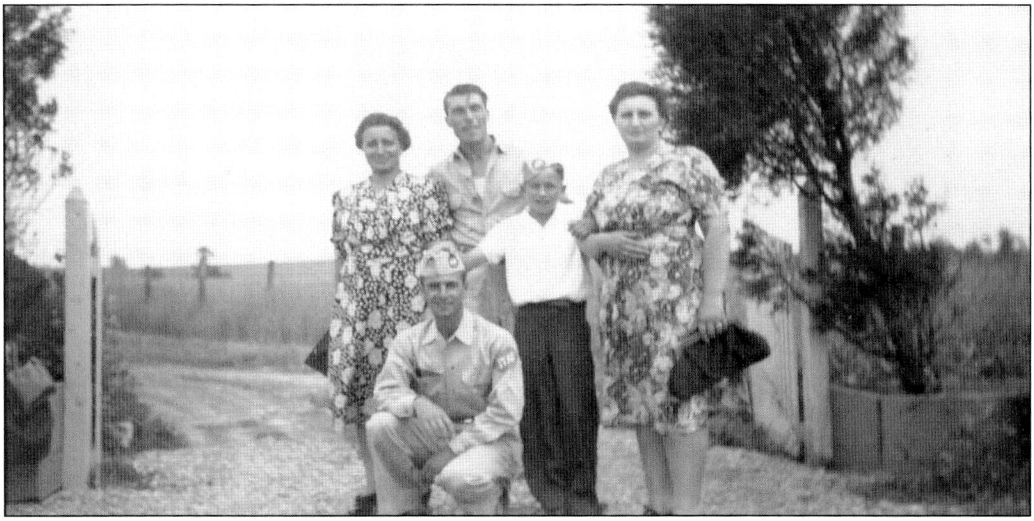

Luigi Sorisio, crouching, and Angelo Erbetta, standing, pose together with two women and an Italian American boy upon a visit to Letterkenny. Note how the child playfully dons Erbetta's garrison cap. Sorisio and Erbetta were both from the Piedmont region, and they often appear together in photographs along with other POWs who hailed from the same region. (Courtesy of Rosi Sorisio and Silvana Erbetta.)

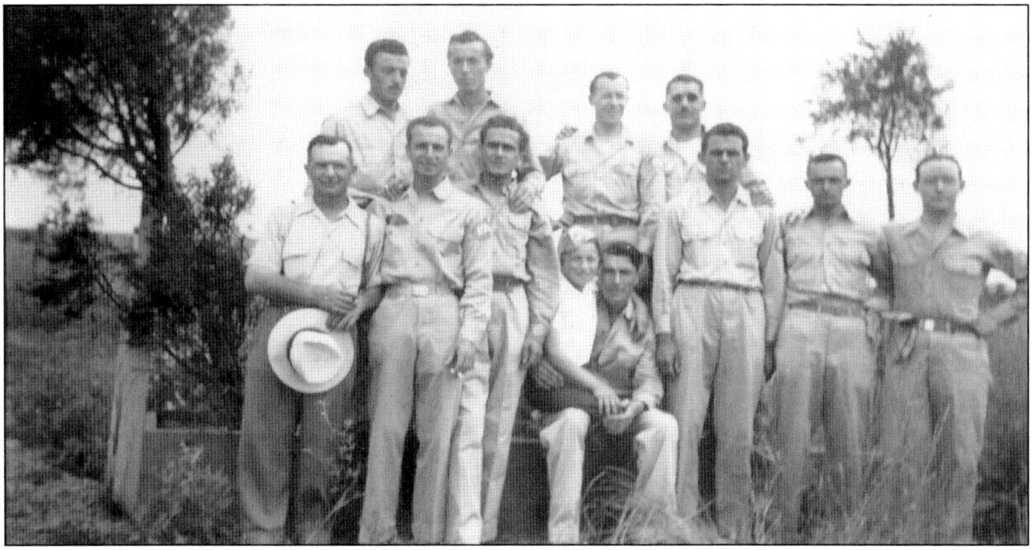

A group of POWs poses with Italian American visitors. Luigi Sorisio is in the first row, second from the left, and Angelo Erbetta sits with a child on his lap. Michele Marchisio is fifth from left, and the first on the left at top is Paolo Muratore. All of the POWs were from Piedmont, as were, most likely, the Italian Americans. (Courtesy of Rosi Sorisio, Govanni Marchisio, and Silvana Erbetta.)

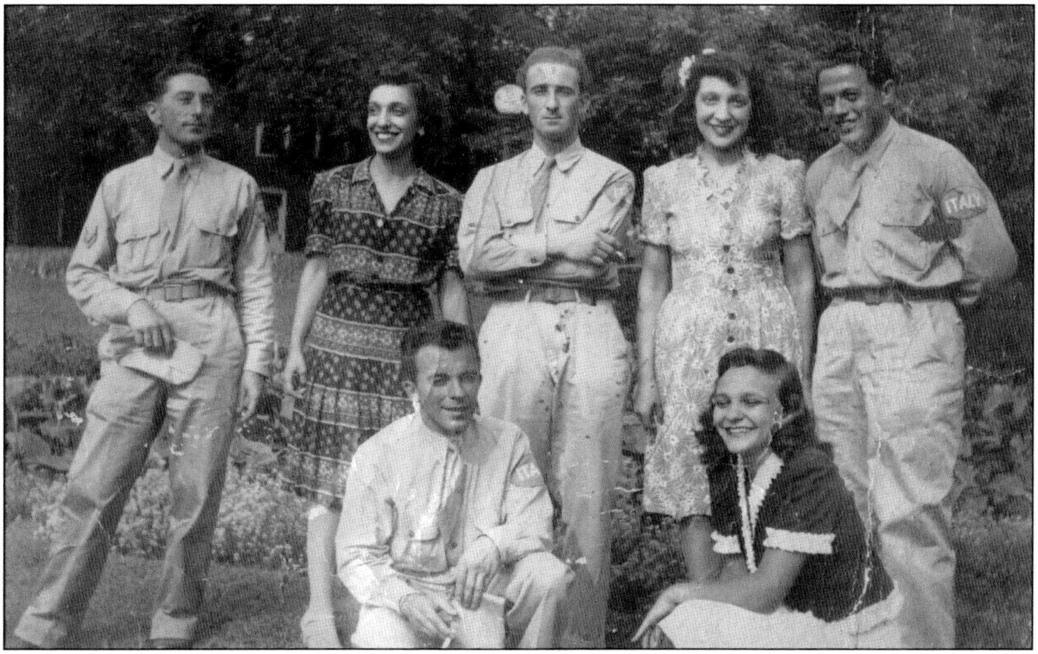

ISU soldiers pose together with Italian American women who have come to the depot for a visit. The first on the right is Angelo Sala. Note that by military regulations, soldiers were always required to wear a cap or hat outdoors, but the Letterkenny Command was lax in enforcing rules and obviously gave the Italian soldiers great freedoms, a further sign of trusted cooperation. (Courtesy of Carlo Sala.)

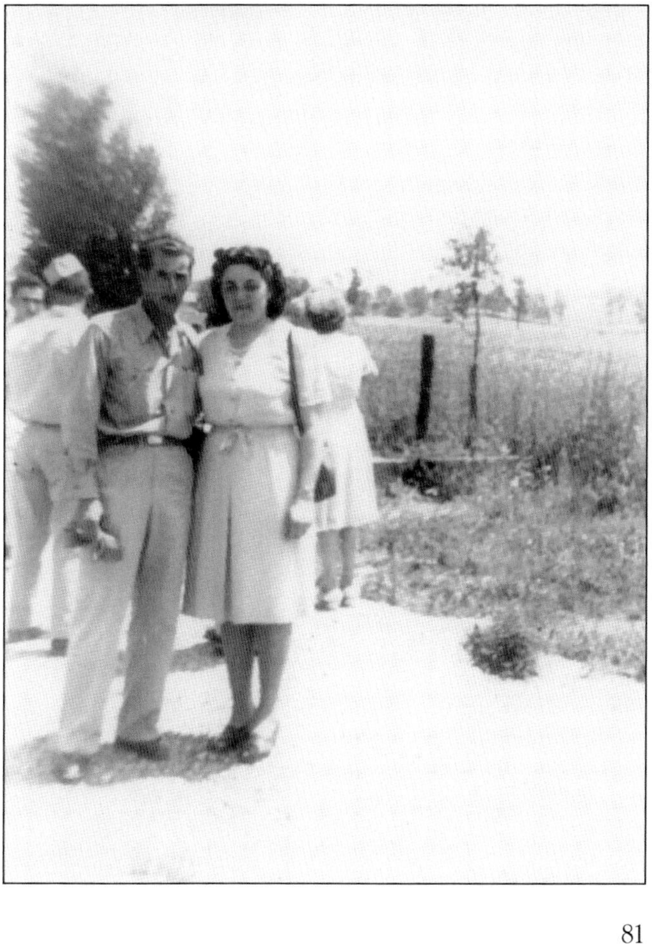

Antonio Arganetto and Bruna D'Angelo pose at Letterkenny in the summer of 1945 before Antonio departed with the 83rd ISU for the Sioux Ordnance Depot in Sidney, Nebraska, on July 21st. Bruna, a daughter of immigrants who were originally from Bologna, had grown up in the Philadelphia area and spoke fluent Italian. The two married in Italy after the war and returned to live in the United States. (Courtesy of Vittoria Buffoni.)

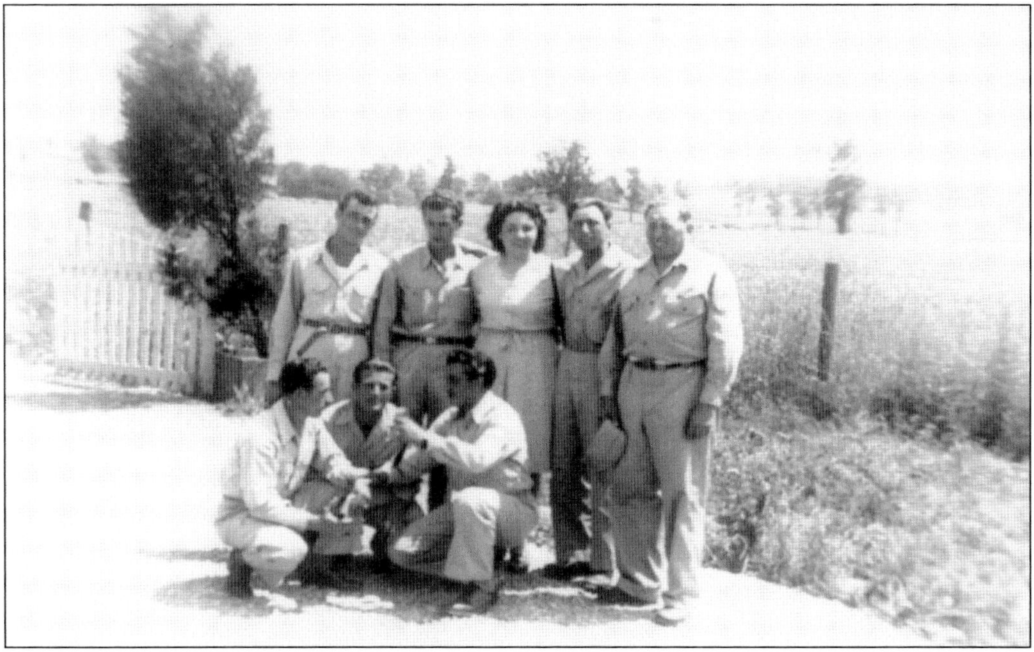

Carlo Buffoni, standing at left, poses with Antonio Arganetto, second from left, alongside Bruna D'Angelo, and Zefferino Trevisan, fifth from left. They were all photographed in the summer of 1945, most likely during Bruna's last visit to the depot before Buffoni and Arganetto's unit, the 83rd ISU, departed for Sioux Ordnance Depot in Sidney, Nebraska. (Courtesy of Vittoria Buffoni.)

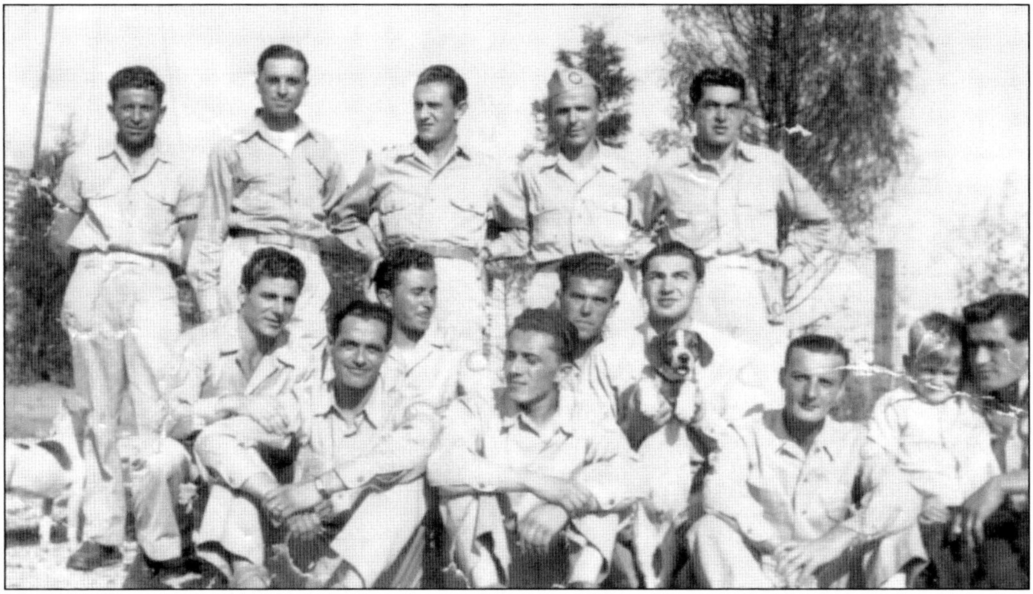

A large group of POWs poses with an Italian American boy, most likely during the summer of 1945. Mario Garbagnati is second from the right, seated, next to the child, and Renato Volpi is behind Garbagnati cradling a beagle. On the left, another dog stands near the soldiers, testifying that numerous dogs provided good company for the ISU members. (Courtesy of Ferdinando Garbagnati.)

Five

Music and Entertainment

Music provided great comfort as a means to cope with detainment. Several Letterkenny prisoners played an instrument prior to the war, and the Red Cross, YMCA, and Catholic Church generously donated pieces to the soldiers, who then organized themselves into a marching band and orchestra. The band played at official ceremonies and formations, often to honor visiting dignitaries. The orchestra, called the "Chicken Band," directed by Mario Luigini, played for the POWs and guests at dances and weekend parties. Beyond these two groups, the POWs formed a choir that performed at Mass. ISU musicians included Giovanni Barbè, Renato Volpi, Federico Cavicchi, Mario Garbagnati, Mario Mattarozzi, Mario Viscardi, Carlo Ferrario, and Giovanni Noè. Singers in the choir included Giovanni Barbè, Zefferino Trevisan, Renato Scattolini, and Pasquale Salvemini.

A few soldiers managed to bring their instruments back to Italy upon repatriation, and their symbolic meaning was never lost on them for the rest of their lives. When the ex-ISU members who had played an instrument at Letterkenny would get together, they gladly performed again for each other and others.

One episode tied to Letterkenny music defies belief. Mario Garbagnati composed a hymn for the Chapel Consecration Mass that took place on May 13, 1945. He titled it "Sacrum Convivium." After his return to Italy, he went to see *The Green Years*, a 1946 film directed by Victor Saville. During a Communion scene, the soundtrack plays music that Garbagnati immediately recognized, and he was stunned. That piece is "Sacrum Convivium," the very one that Garbagnati himself had written as a POW. With great wonderment, he sought help from an American friend who then contacted the right people involved with the film's production, asking how Garbagnati's music had ended up in the film. Amazingly, Garbagnati received a response, and even more thrilling, he found out that the person in charge of the film's soundtrack had found Garbagnati's written composition in a small church in rural Pennsylvania (obviously the chapel at Letterkenny), and, since there was no name written upon the score, had attributed it as "Author Unknown."

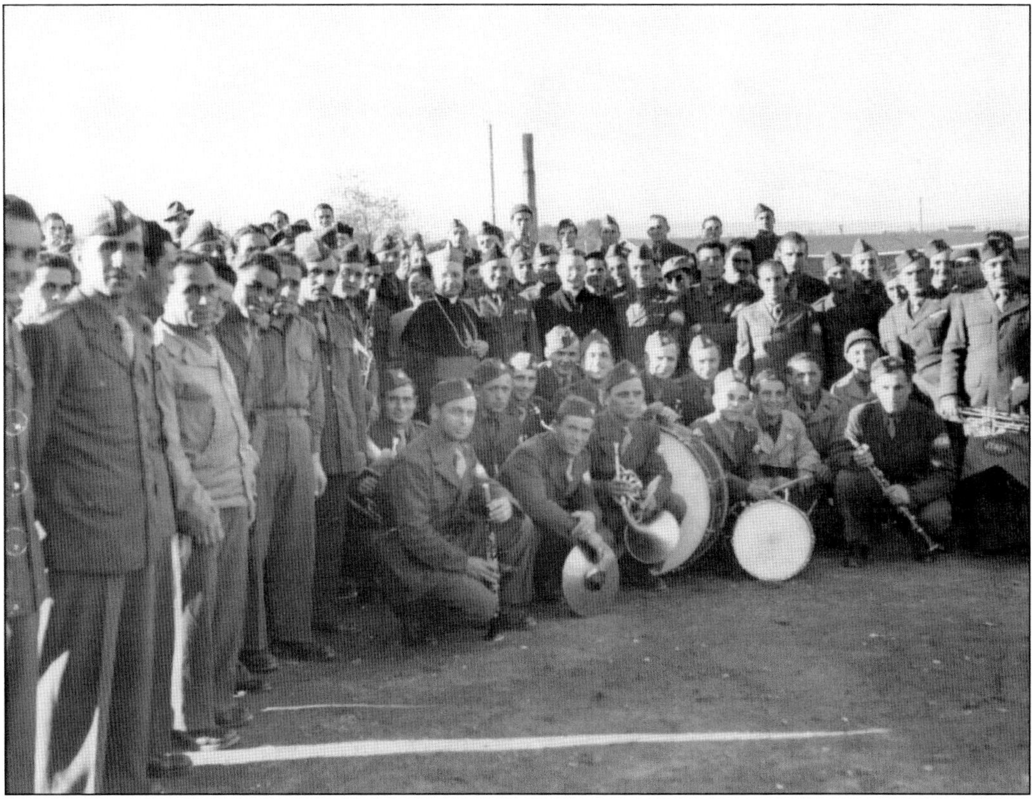

Members of the ISU marching band and other POWs pose together with the Vatican's apostolic delegate, Msgr. Amleto Cicognani, upon his October 22, 1944, visit to Letterkenny. Standing on Cicognani's left is Maj. Angelo Bassi, commander of the 321st Italian QM Battalion. Crouching in the first row with his clarinet is Giovanni Barbè, and last on the right with his trumpet is Mario Luigini. (Courtesy of Giancarla Barbè Biandrate.)

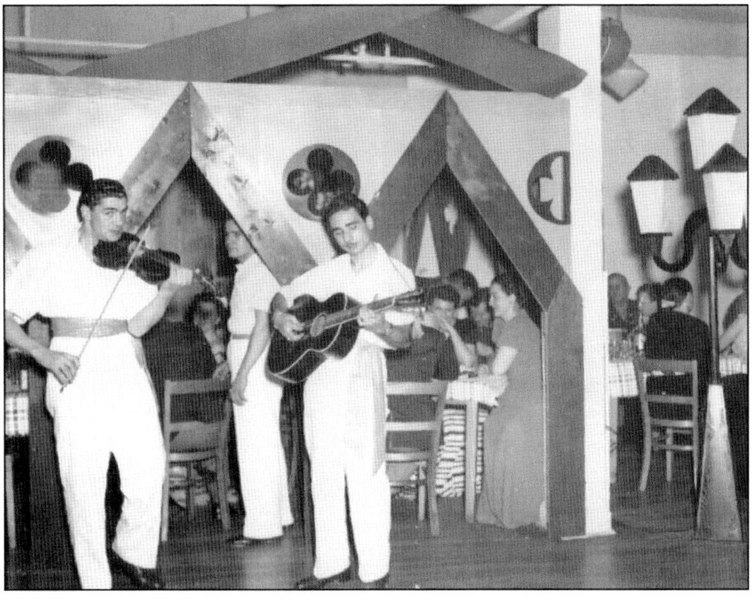

Renato Volpi, with violin, and Carlo Ferrario, with guitar, dressed as Venetian gondoliers, entertain American officers at Letterkenny during a gala called "Una notte a Venezia" (A Night in Venice). Volpi and Ferrario were two musicians who played with the POW orchestra that frequently performed at dances during weekends on the depot. (Courtesy of Luisella Volpi.)

An unidentified Letterkenny POW sings during a party. On the left is Mario Luigini, director of the orchestra that was jokingly called the "Banda Pollastri" (Chicken Band) because of the symbol on the music stands. Mario Viscardi peers out over Luigini's left shoulder, and Renato Volpi sits behind the music stand and in front of Viscardi. Adamo Pedoni is behind the singer, and Carlo Ferrario plays the guitar. (Courtesy of Claudia Rita Pedoni.)

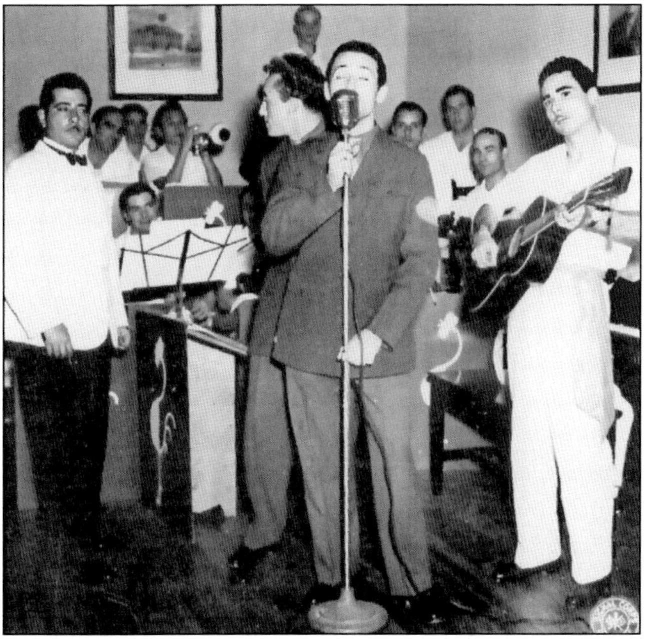

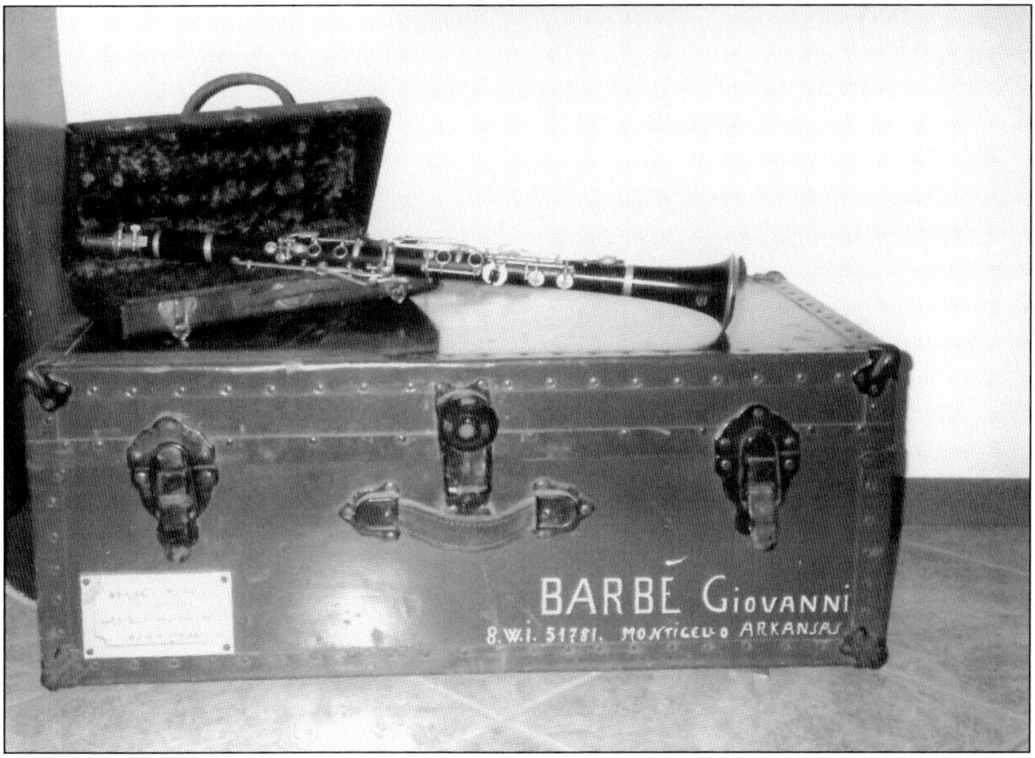

This clarinet carrying case and footlocker belonged to Giovanni Barbè. The footlocker indicates Barbè's POW identification number along with the detention camp, Monticello, Arkansas, where Barbè had been detained prior to Letterkenny. Luckily, Barbè was able to bring these items with him back to Gravellona Lomellina (Pavia) upon repatriation from the United States. (Courtesy of Giancarla Barbè Biandrate.)

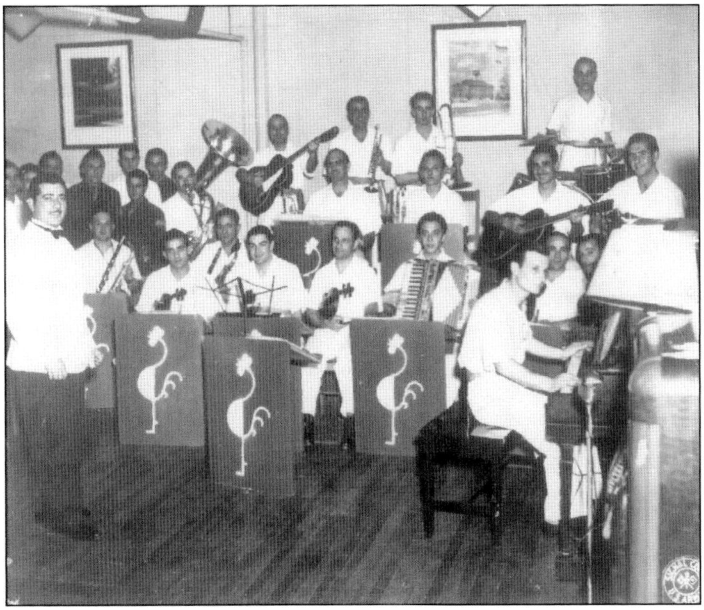

The POW orchestra is pictured in December 1944. From the left are director Mario Luigini, Alessandro Popolizio (with clarinet), Federico Cavicchi (with violin), Giovanni Noè (with clarinet), Renato Volpi (with violin), Giovanni Barbè (with violin), Mario Mattarozzi (with accordion), Mario Garbagnati (at the piano), Mario Viscardi (behind Barbè with trumpet), Carlo Ferrario (on the right with guitar), and Adamo Pedoni (under the picture on the left). (Courtesy of Claudia Rita Pedoni.)

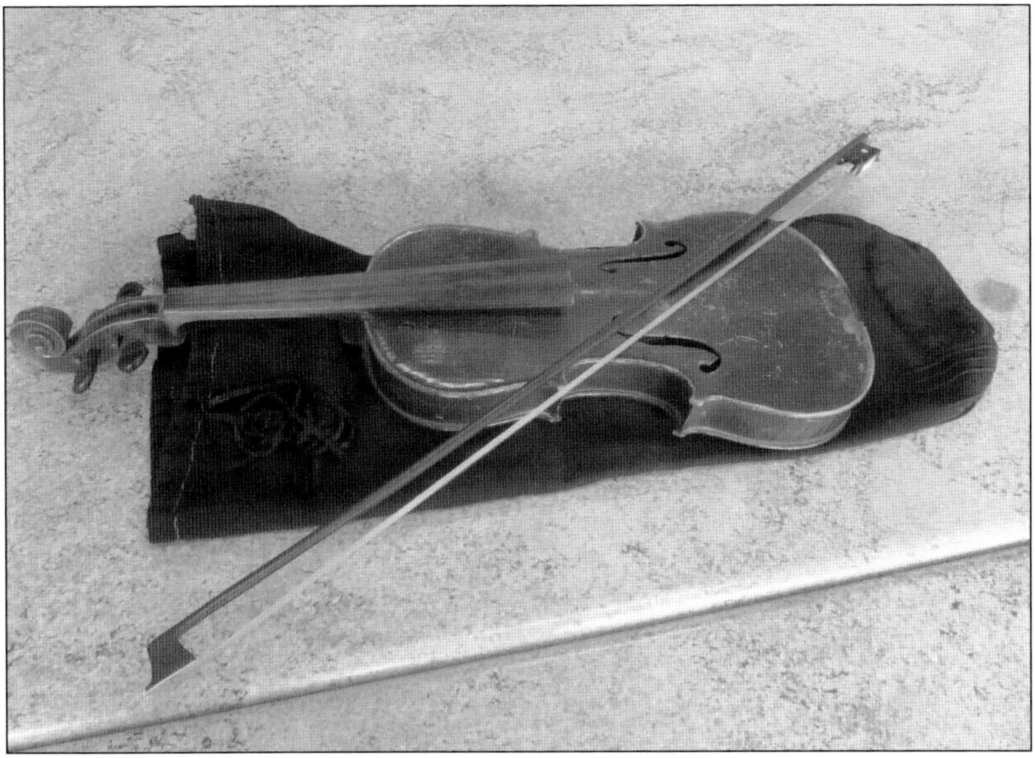

Renato Volpi brought this violin, acquired in the States, back to Italy with him after the war. Originally from Abbiategrasso (Milan), Volpi often appears in photographs of the orchestra while playing his favorite instrument. Upon his return, Volpi and other Letterkenny prisoners would meet periodically to remember their Letterkenny experience, and during those occasions they would play their instruments that they had brought back with them. (Courtesy of Luisella Volpi.)

Six

Faith Activities

Religion was a source of tremendous comfort for many Letterkenny POWs, allowing them to face detention with greater resolve and to believe that no wartime horror would come to their families and friends in Italy. Mass was celebrated for the first several months in the warehouse where Msgr. Amleto Cicognani presided during his visit on October 22, 1944.

At the beginning of 1945, the US command had the POWs begin to build a chapel exclusively dedicated as a place of worship. Most likely it was Sgt. Maj. Giuliano Orzali, a Tuscan master mason who undertook the project shortly after the depot commander, Colonel Hare, had dissuaded him from taking his own life when he had found out that his wife had been killed in Italy. The construction was meant to alleviate his grief. Bricklayers and carpenters, working on a design by Marcello Iovine, and under the direction of this Tuscan foreman, made exclusive use of whatever secondhand material they could find, with no cost to the US government. ISU members who took part during their off-duty time on this special endeavor included the above-mentioned Iovine, Alessio Cerri, Giovanni Barbè, Aldo Lorenzi, Alfredo Tonolo, Pietro Bracchi, Aristodemo Fabbri, Valentino Pauro, Giovanni Borelli, Luigi Grasso, and Alfredo Arienti. The Letterkenny command was very impressed by their work and turned to the Navy for help in locating a ship's bell for the bell tower.

Fr. T.B. Johnson, the local parish priest of Corpus Christi in Chambersburg, often came to celebrate Mass, and, at the evening call of the bell, several POWs would regularly gather to recite the rosary. Monsignor Cigognani traveled from Washington, DC, on May 13, 1945, to consecrate the chapel. During the years following the war, various faith denominations used the chapel, and over time, the State of Pennsylvania placed it on its Register of Historic Places. Today, the Historic Letterkenny Chapel and Franklin County Veterans and 9/11 Memorial Park oversees its upkeep.

On October 24, 2015, a very meaningful Mass took place in the chapel to commemorate the 70th anniversary of Letterkenny POW repatriation to Italy. Several children and grandchildren of former ISU soldiers were in attendance.

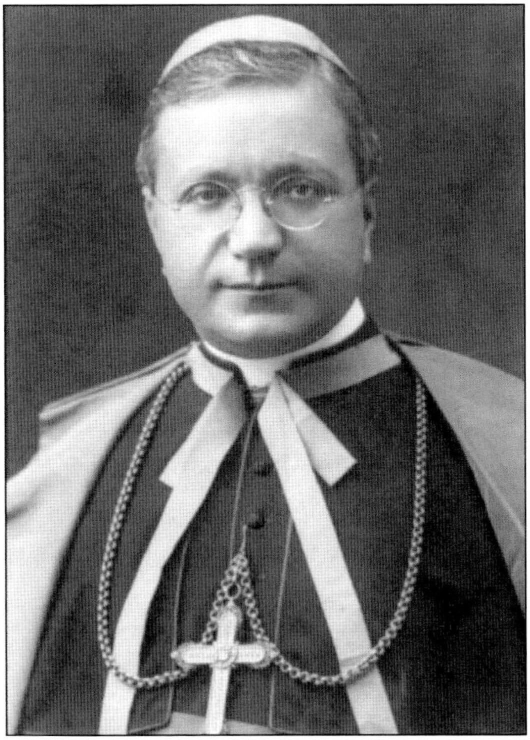

This photograph of apostolic delegate Msgr. Amleto Cicognani was given to Letterkenny ISU members upon his visit to Letterkenny on October 22, 1944. For this occasion, Cicognani distributed 1,100 copies of *Il mio Messale della Domenica* (*My Sunday Missal*), 100 copies of the New Testament, and many small crucifixes and rosaries. (Courtesy of Keti Melotto.)

Msgr. Amleto Cicognani celebrates Mass at Letterkenny on October 22, 1944. Throughout the war, Cicognani worked tirelessly for all Italian POWs, both those who collaborated and those who did not. Besides actual site visits to detention camps, Cicognani fielded innumerable queries from family members and government officials alike as to the welfare of soldiers and served as an excellent Vatican representative in the United States. (Courtesy of Giovanni Serpe.)

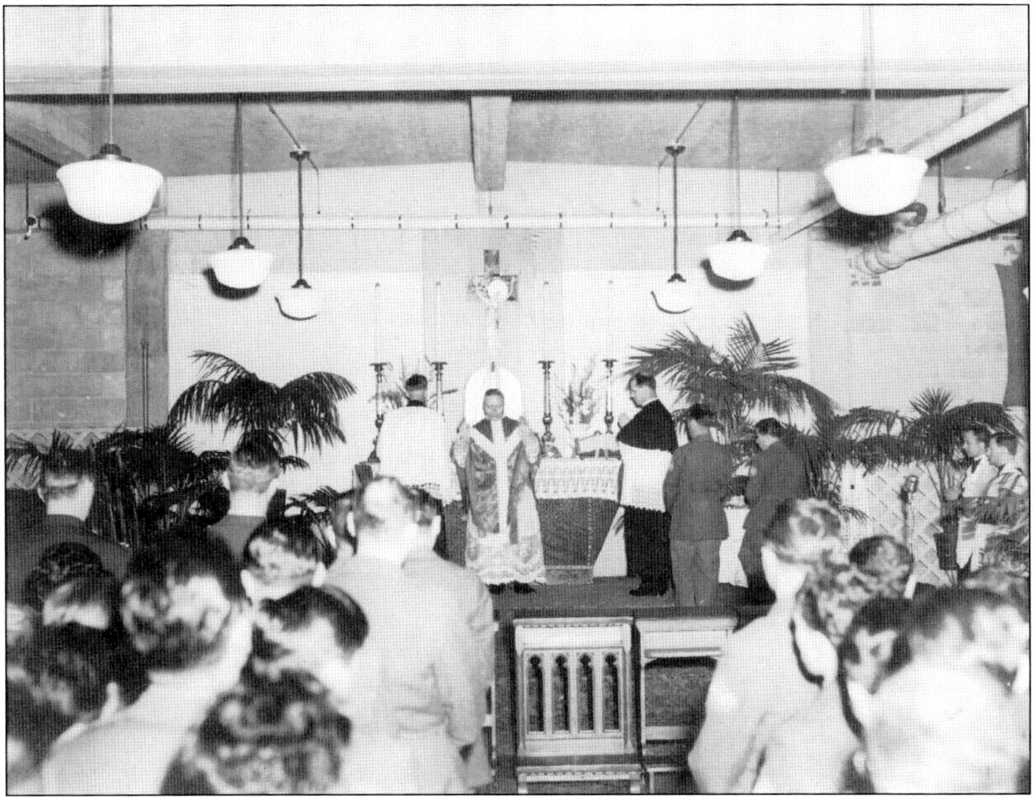

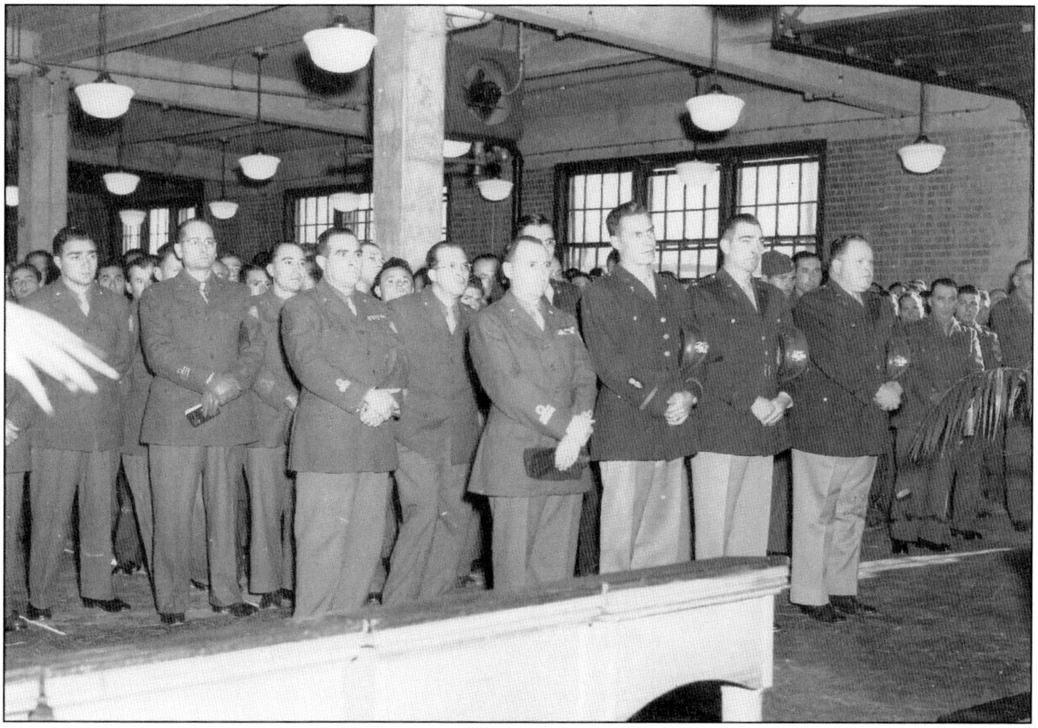

Italian and American officers attend a Mass celebrated by Msgr. Amleto Cicognani on October 22, 1944. Maj. Angelo Bassi stands on the left in the first row. Capt. Girolamo Bellavista is second from the left in the second row, and Capt. Roberto Cardinale is on the left in the third row with glasses, wearing gloves, and holding a missal. Slightly behind him to his right in the fourth row is Lt. Marcello D'Orsogna. (Courtesy of Giuseppe Grasso.)

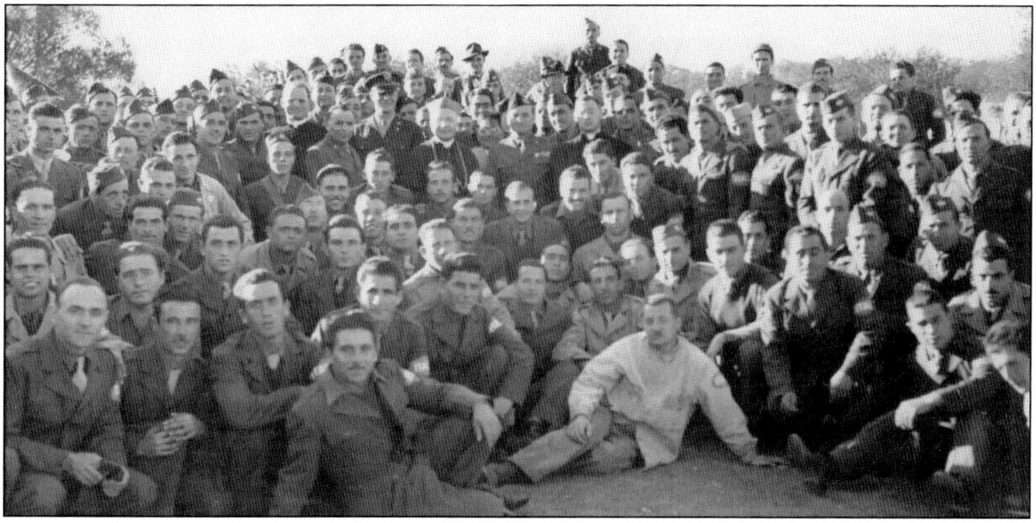

Msgr. Amleto Cicognani is pictured with Letterkenny ISU soldiers on October 22, 1944. Directly to his left is Maj. Angelo Bassi. On his right is Maj. Earl L. Lovelace, American commander of the 321st Italian Battalion. Angelo Marzano, wearing his garrison cap, is behind the POW with the white jacket sitting in the first row. (Courtesy of Giuseppe Marzano, Edoardo Ranzoni, and Fabrizio Campanini.)

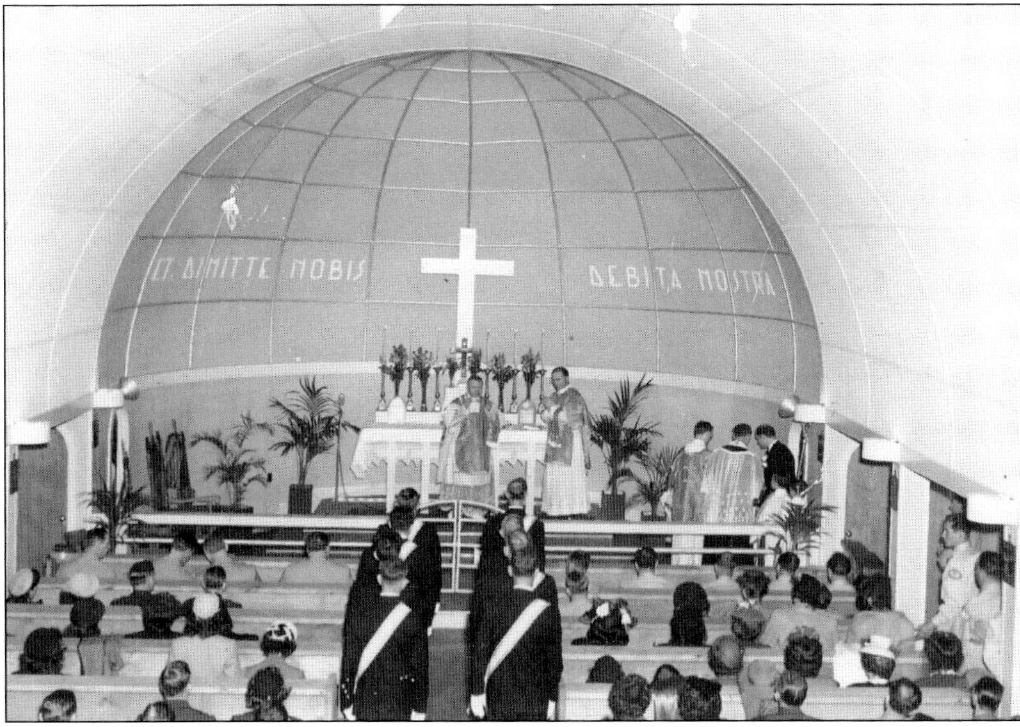

Msgr. Amleto Cicognani celebrates the Mass to consecrate the chapel that Letterkenny POWs had built, on May 13, 1945. In attendance are several POWs, many civilians, and eight Knights of Columbus, the well-known fraternal benefit society. Clearly discernable in the apse are the words "Et dimitte nobis debita nostra" (And forgive us our trespasses). (Courtesy of Keti Melotto.)

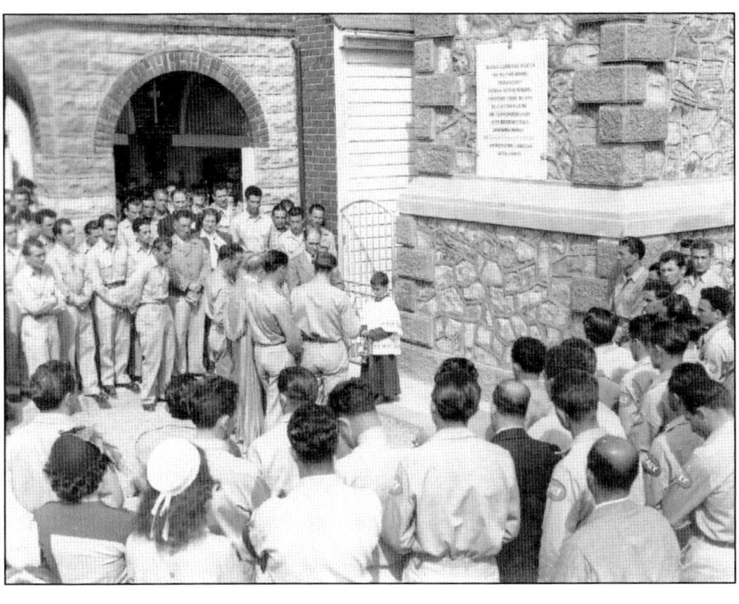

Father T.B. Johnson, parish priest of Corpus Christi Catholic Church, Chambersburg, blesses the church and bell tower constructed by the POWs on May 13, 1945. Capt. Girolamo Bellavista wrote the Latin words etched into the plaque and placed on the bell tower. To the right of the very tall POW standing in front of the arch and by the metal gate is Luigi Guglielmino. (Courtesy of Fabrizio Campanini.)

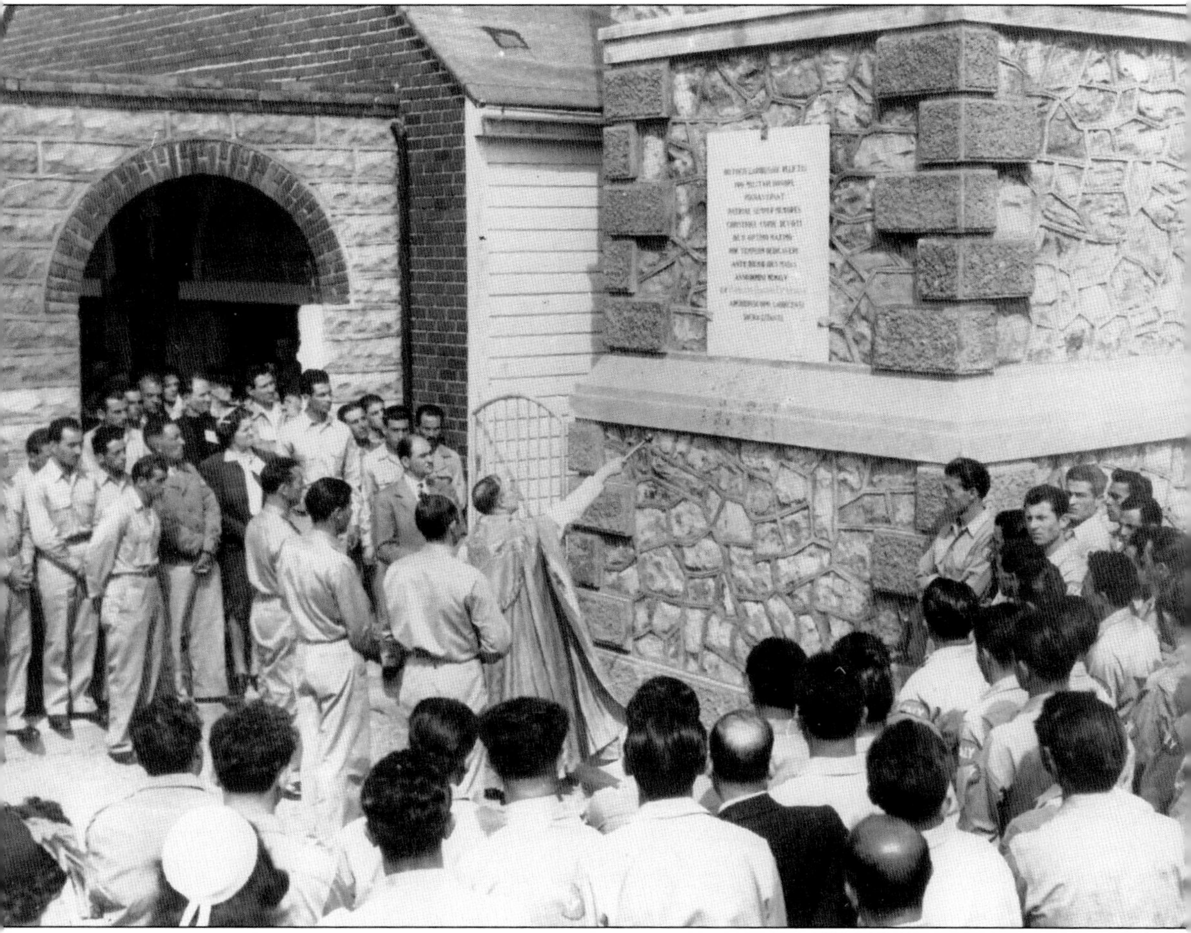

This image shows Father T.B. Johnson precisely at the moment of consecrating the bell tower with holy water on May 13, 1945. Several civilians are also present at this special ceremony. The English translation of the Latin script on the plaque reads in part, "Those who left their homes to fight for military honor . . . dedicated this temple to Almighty God." (Courtesy of Giancarla Barbè Biandrate.)

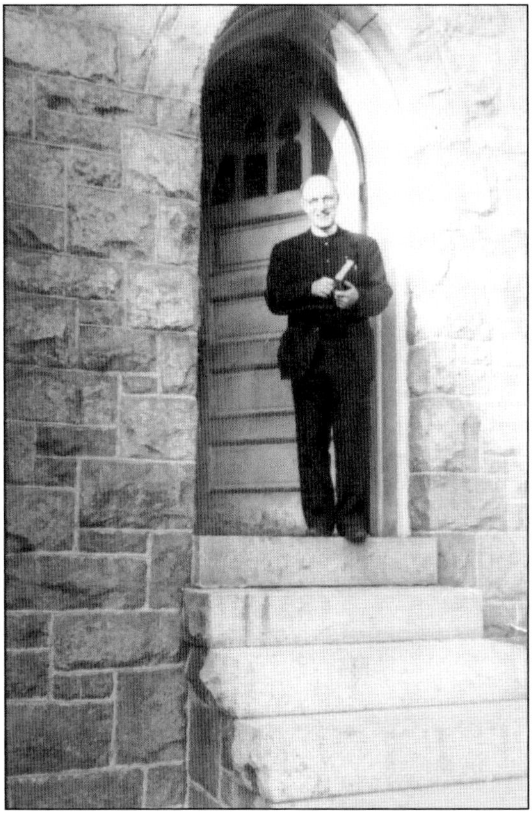

Father T.B. Johnson would often go to the depot to celebrate Mass for the POWs, and many POWs would go into town to attend Mass at Corpus Christi. Accomplished prisoner-artist Corrado Linares worked many hours on behalf of Father Johnson and also decorated a new entrance to the Catholic cemetery for free. (Courtesy of Valeria Conconi.)

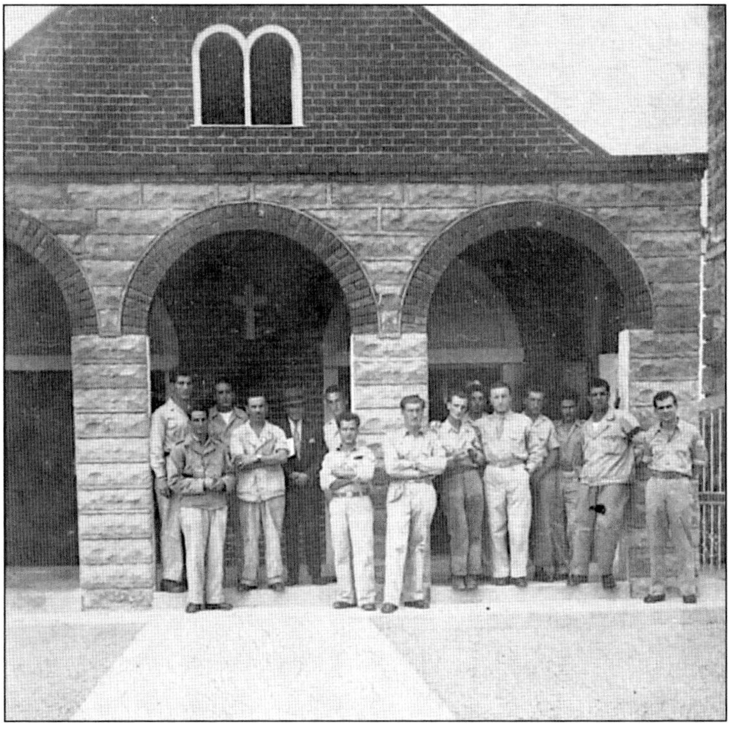

A group of ISU soldiers and an American civilian pose in front of the chapel on May 13, 1945, a few hours after its consecration. Four POWs are identifiable: Almerindo Briganti, sixth from the left, peers in front of the entrance on the civilian's left; Aldo Lorenzi stands eighth from the left in front of a pillar; and Luciano Boneschi, who stands eleventh from the left, has his hand over Mario Garbagnati's shoulder. (Courtesy of Valeria Conconi.)

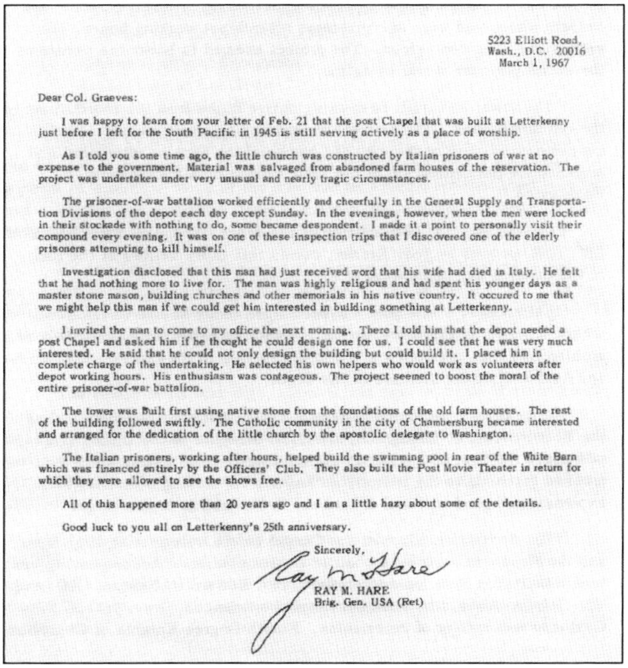

5223 Elliott Road,
Wash., D.C. 20016
March 1, 1967

Dear Col. Graeves:

I was happy to learn from your letter of Feb. 21 that the post Chapel that was built at Letterkenny just before I left for the South Pacific in 1945 is still serving actively as a place of worship.

As I told you some time ago, the little church was constructed by Italian prisoners of war at no expense to the government. Material was salvaged from abandoned farm houses of the reservation. The project was undertaken under very unusual and nearly tragic circumstances.

The prisoner-of-war battalion worked efficiently and cheerfully in the General Supply and Transportation Divisions of the depot each day except Sunday. In the evenings, however, when the men were locked in their stockade with nothing to do, some became despondent. I made it a point to personally visit their compound every evening. It was on one of these inspection trips that I discovered one of the elderly prisoners attempting to kill himself.

Investigation disclosed that this man had just received word that his wife had died in Italy. He felt that he had nothing more to live for. The man was highly religious and had spent his younger days as a master stone mason, building churches and other memorials in his native country. It occured to me that we might help this man if we could get him interested in building something at Letterkenny.

I invited the man to come to my office the next morning. There I told him that the depot needed a post Chapel and asked him if he thought he could design one for us. I could see that he was very much interested. He said that he could not only design the building but could build it. I placed him in complete charge of the undertaking. He selected his own helpers who would work as volunteers after depot working hours. His enthusiasm was contageous. The project seemed to boost the moral of the entire prisoner-of-war battalion.

The tower was built first using native stone from the foundations of the old farm houses. The rest of the building followed swiftly. The Catholic community in the city of Chambersburg became interested and arranged for the dedication of the little church by the apostolic delegate to Washington.

The Italian prisoners, working after hours, helped build the swimming pool in rear of the White Barn which was financed entirely by the Officers' Club. They also built the Post Movie Theater in return for which they were allowed to see the shows free.

All of this happened more than 20 years ago and I am a little hazy about some of the details.

Good luck to you all on Letterkenny's 25th anniversary.

Sincerely,

Ray M. Hare

RAY M. HARE
Brig. Gen. USA (Ret)

Gen. Ray M. Hare, the commanding officer at Letterkenny during the war, writes to a subsequent commander, Colonel Graeves, on March 1, 1967, explaining the story of how he came upon a POW master stonemason who was about to commit suicide. To save his life and lift his spirits, Hare asked him to build the depot a suitable chapel. The original letter is found in the chapel. (Courtesy of Dave Goodman.)

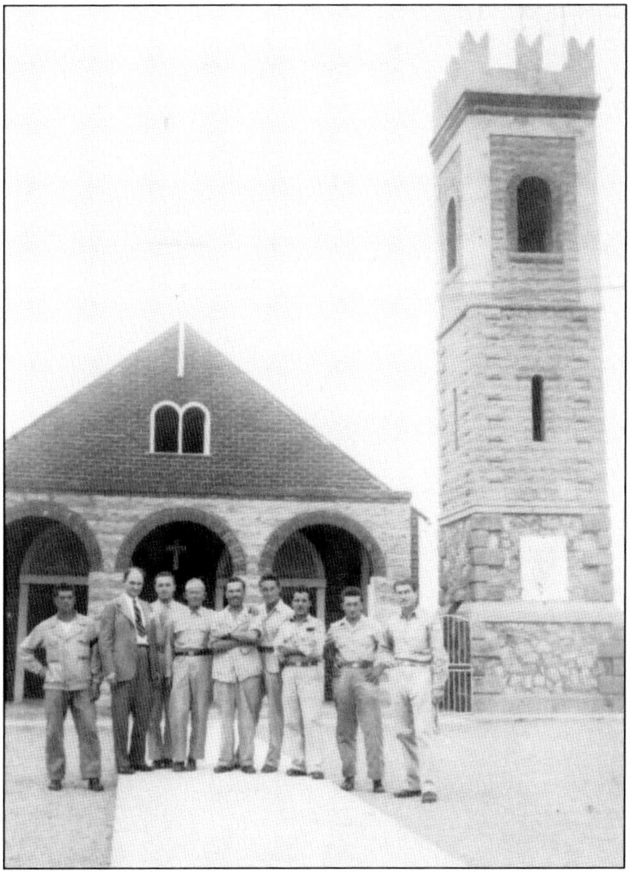

On May 13, 1945, Aldo Lorenzi, on the right, and other POWs stand in front of the chapel and bell tower constructed by POWs. Lorenzi was a devout Christian who had served Mass as an altar boy while growing up in his hometown of Mozzecane (Verona). He was one of the Italian soldiers who helped to build these monuments. (Courtesy of Valeria Conconi [granddaughter of Luciano Boneschi].)

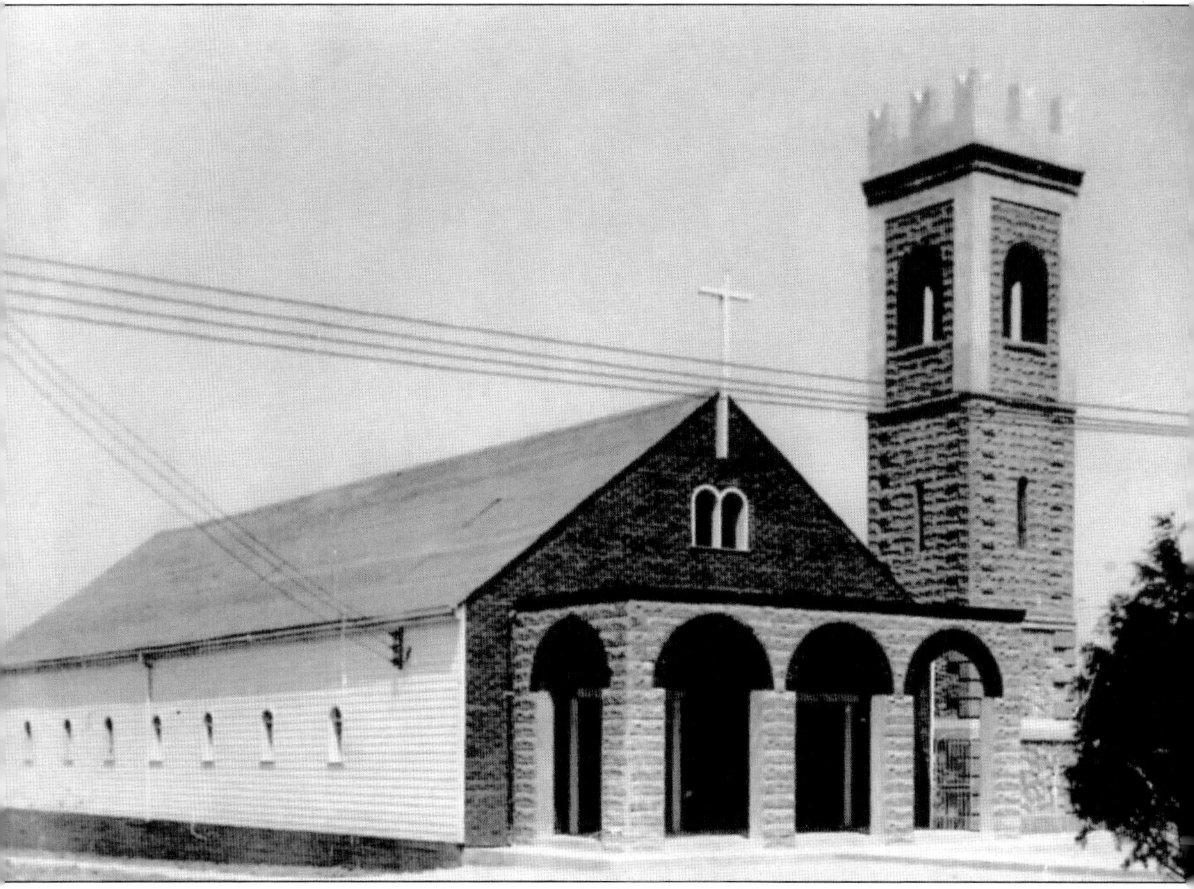

This is a vintage photograph of the chapel and bell tower built by the Italian POWs at Letterkenny. Beginning in January 1945, several carpenters, masons, bricklayers, painters, electricians, and plumbers—under the supervision of 2nd Lt. Marcello Iovine and most likely Sgt. Maj. Giuliano Orzali, an expert stonemason—gave voluntarily of their time during their off-hours to construct this holy site, essentially using secondhand material at no cost to the US government. (Courtesy of Ettore Rovida.)

Seven

Soccer as the Main Sporting Event

The participation in sports was very valuable to Letterkenny POWs, most of whom were young and wanted to have a way to keep in shape, both physically and mentally. Sports also allowed the US command a way to channel the pent-up frustrations and stress POWs experienced, and officers readily permitted institutions such as the YMCA, Red Cross, and Catholic Church to outfit the soldiers with uniforms and necessary equipment.

As with other POW camps in the United States, the sport that had the greatest participation at Letterkenny was soccer, and the command organized several tournaments to decide the best teams among those established at the company level. When Msgr. Amleto Cicognani first visited the depot on October 22, 1944, a tournament took place where the 84th and 86th ISU teams reached the final. The 86th claimed the trophy, and Cicognani donated its players $25, while giving $15 to the runner-up 84th side. The first tournament between the five ISUs already present at the depot had taken place on September 3, 1944, and another all-ISU competition occurred on April 15, 1945.

A special match occurred on June 24, 1945, between an all-star team of ISU soldiers and the Juventus New York club that had made the long trip to Letterkenny. On the ISU side, Antonio Tascione played a brilliant game and scored the decisive goal on a penalty kick to end the match 1-0 in favor of the soldiers. Eugenio Fortunati, Donato Pietra, and Angelo Barcella also played strongly for the Letterkenny side.

From time to time, the matches between company teams were so intense that fights erupted among spectators watching on the sidelines and the MPs had to be called in to restore order. A few prisoners even needed to go to the emergency room to get sutures for cuts or casts for broken bones. The US command preferred that the violence happen there, near the pitch, rather than in downtown Chambersburg.

Beyond soccer, POWs liked to bowl, shoot hoops, and play bocce, tennis, and volleyball.

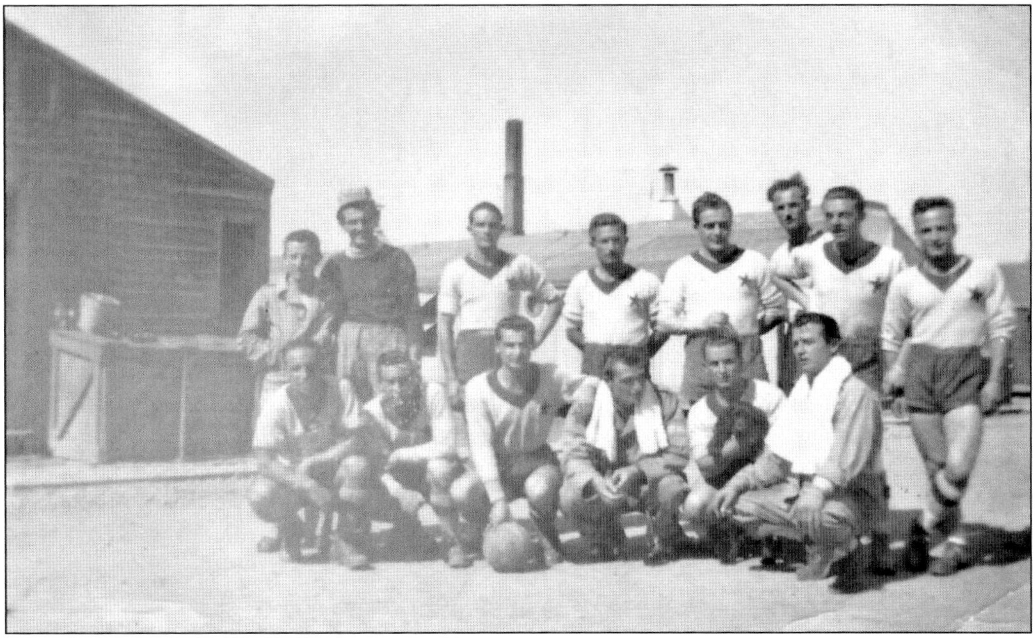

The 85th Italian Service Unit's soccer team poses in front of a few POW billets. Virginio Ranzoni, second from the left, standing, is the coach. Francesco Grossi is fourth from the left, standing. Note the fifth player crouching from the left who is holding a black dog, which is most likely the mascot of the team. (Courtesy of Giovanni Grossi.)

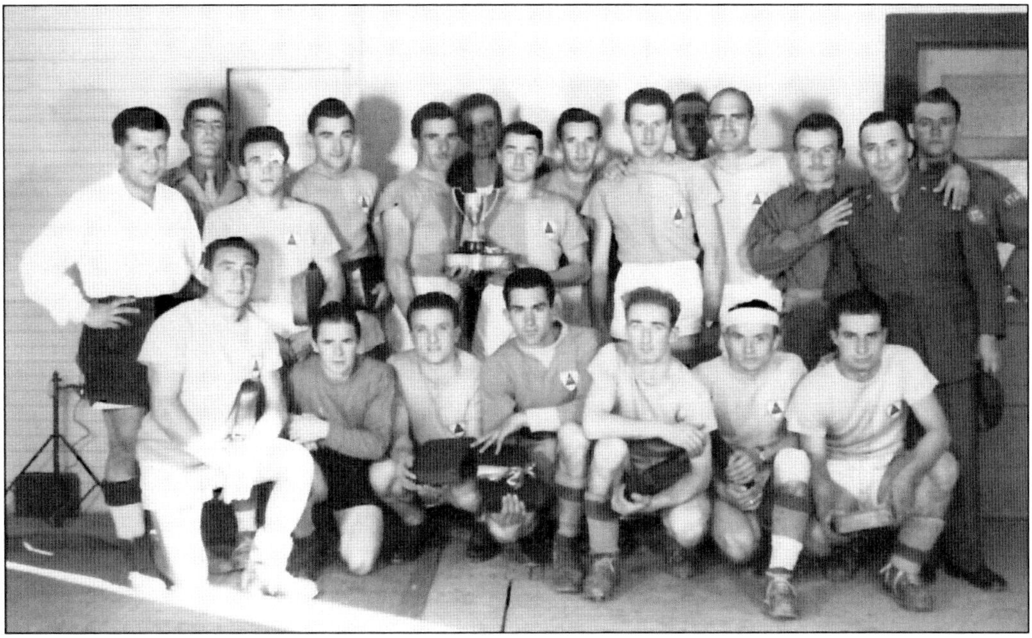

The 86th Italian Service Unit's soccer team poses for a group picture after winning a tournament. Judging from the POWs in uniform, the decisive match occurred most likely during Msgr. Amleto Cicognani's first visit in October 1944. Standing fifth from the left, with a moustache, is Emilio Pizzetti, the eleventh is Mario Viscardi. The player in the center holding the trophy is Antonio Brissoni. (Courtesy of Carlo Viscardi.)

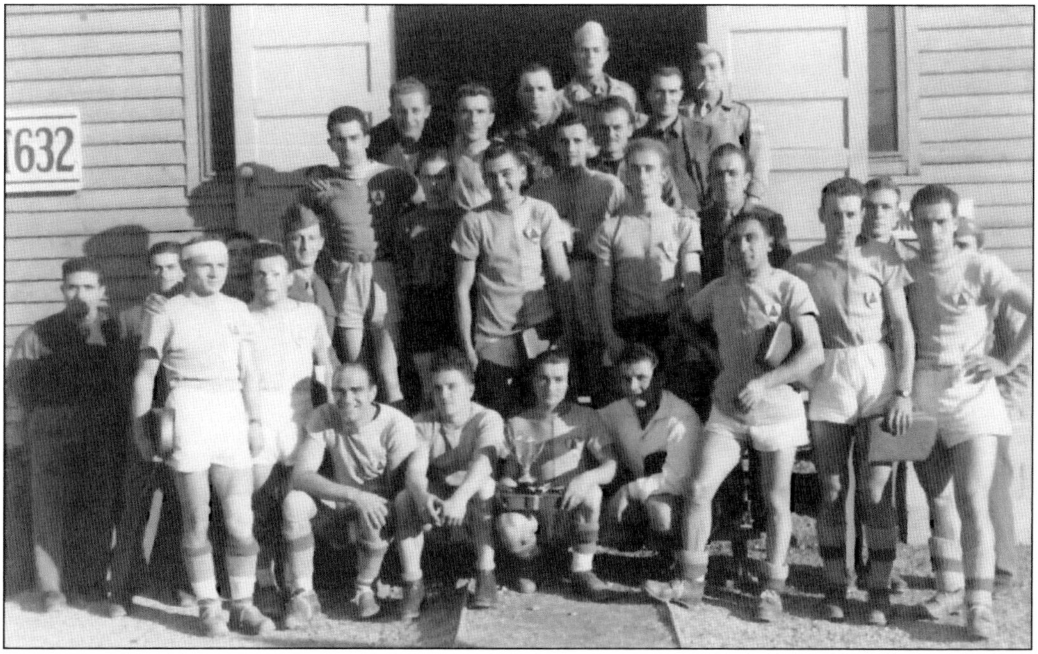

Here is another image of the 86th Italian Service Unit's soccer team upon winning the trophy in October 1944. The first crouching on the left is Mario Viscardi, the third with the trophy is Antonio Brissoni, and the second from the left in the last row is Emilio Pizzetti. The POW in uniform, slightly hidden behind the last player on the right, is Emilio Mosconi. Several players are holding the missal that Msgr. Cicognani gifted to various POWs. (Courtesy of Carlo Viscardi.)

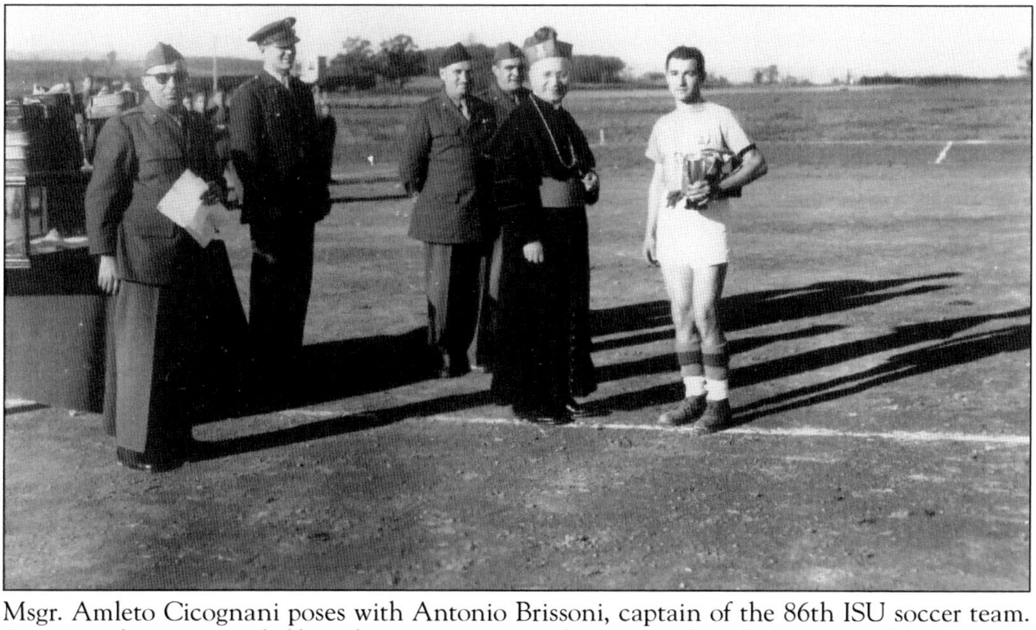

Msgr. Amleto Cicognani poses with Antonio Brissoni, captain of the 86th ISU soccer team. Cicognani has just awarded him the tournament trophy contested on the occasion of the apostolic delegate's October 22, 1944, visit. Standing directly behind the monsignor is Maj. Angelo Bassi, who is next to Maj. Earl L. Lovelace of the United States. Stacks of missals, soon to be distributed, are on the table. (Courtesy of Giancarla Barbè Biandrate.)

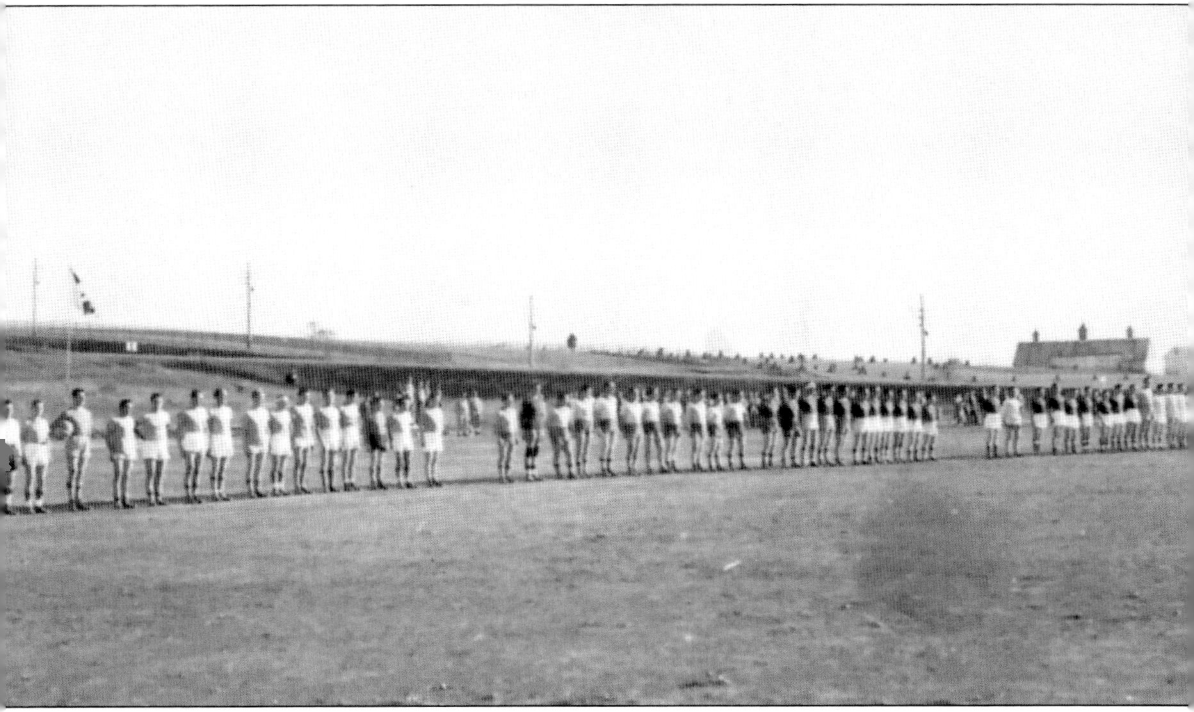

All of Letterkenny's ISU soccer teams stand in review for Msgr. Amleto Cigognani's October 22, 1944, visit. Among the players with the first team on the left are Mario Viscardi, seventh in line from the left, and Donato Pietra, ninth, who is wearing a white headband. Note that one of the two flags flying behind the players is the Italian tricolor with its original House of Savoyard emblem. (Courtesy of Giovanni Serpe and Giovanni Grossi.)

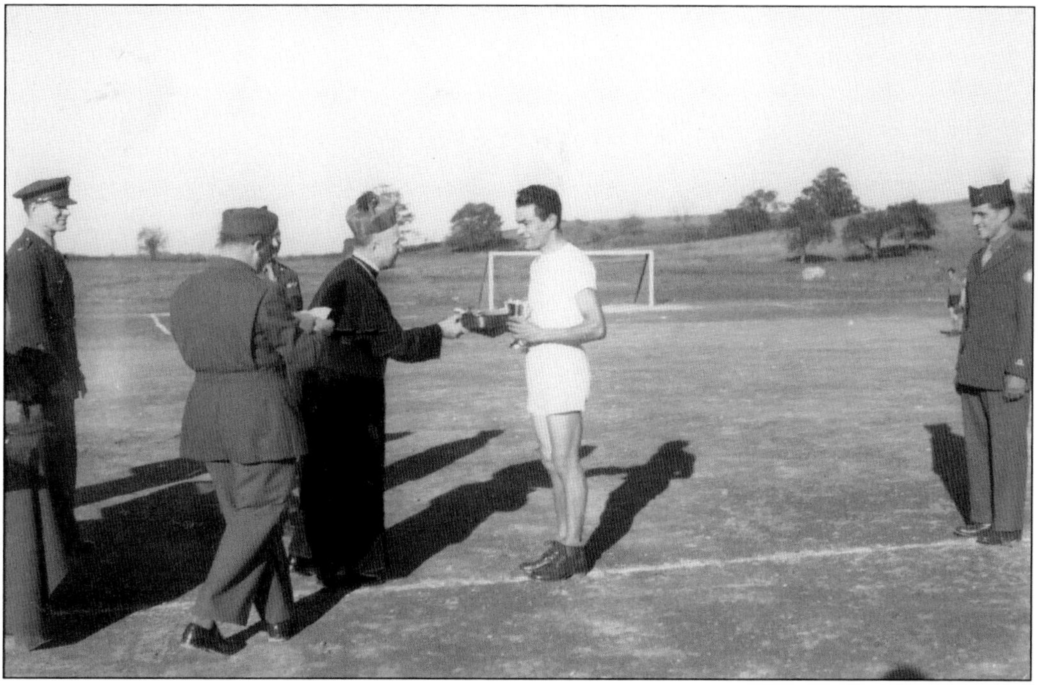

Msgr. Amleto Cicognani awards a trophy to the captain of the 85th ISU side—the runner-up team of the tournament played on the occasion of Cigognani's October 22, 1944, visit. On the left is American major Earl L. Lovelace, and partially hidden to his left is Maj. Angelo Bassi. Standing in front of everyone, on the far right of the picture, is 2nd Lt. Alfredo Tonolo. (Courtesy of Frances Tonolo MacAvoy.)

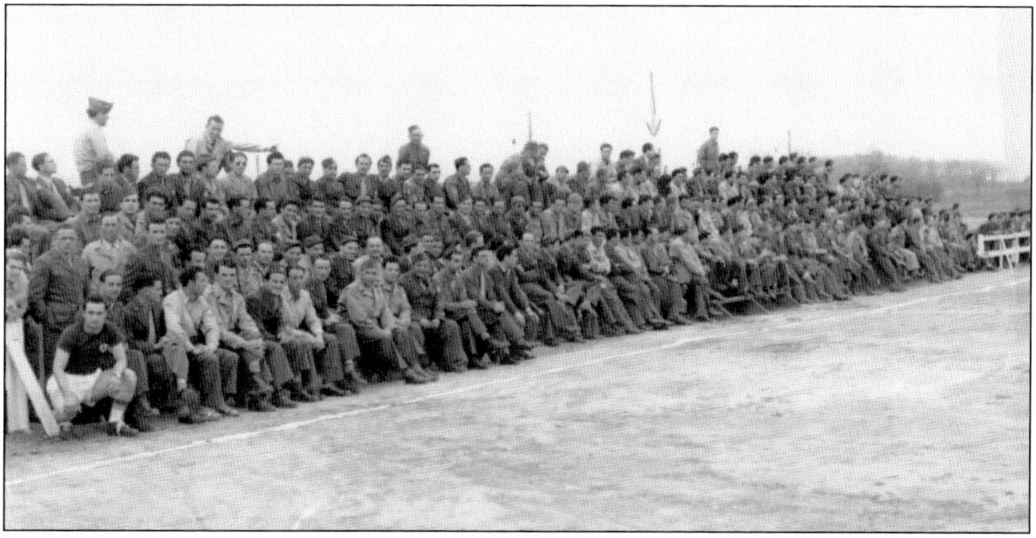

A crowd watches a soccer match between the 84th and 86th ISUs, played on April 15, 1945. The arrow indicates Luigi Sorisio. Francesco Maccione is eighth from the left in the fourth row wearing sunglasses. Almerindo Briganti is in the center of the second row, leaning forward beneath the two soldiers lighting a cigarette. Renzo Foietta sits to the left, second row, behind two soldiers wearing lighter-colored jackets. (Courtesy of Rosi Sorisio, Paola Maccione, Alessandra Briganti and Flavio Foietta.)

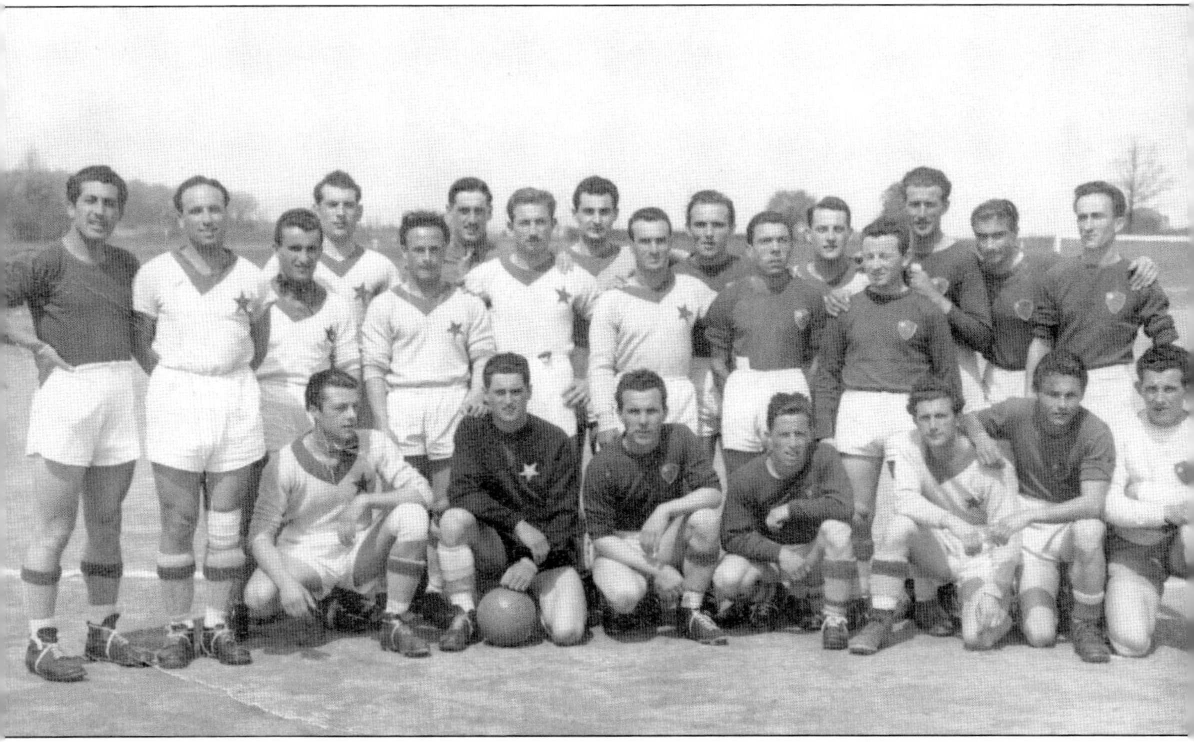

The 85th ISU's soccer team, dressed in white, poses in April 1945 together with the 84th's team, in black. From the left, Alfredo Tonolo is second in the back row, wearing a tie, Francesco Grossi is standing fifth in the second row, Giuseppe Simonini is second to last. Crouching from the left are Antonio Coin, second, and Donato Pietra, fourth. (Courtesy of Anna Grazia Simonini, Donato and Massimo Pietra.)

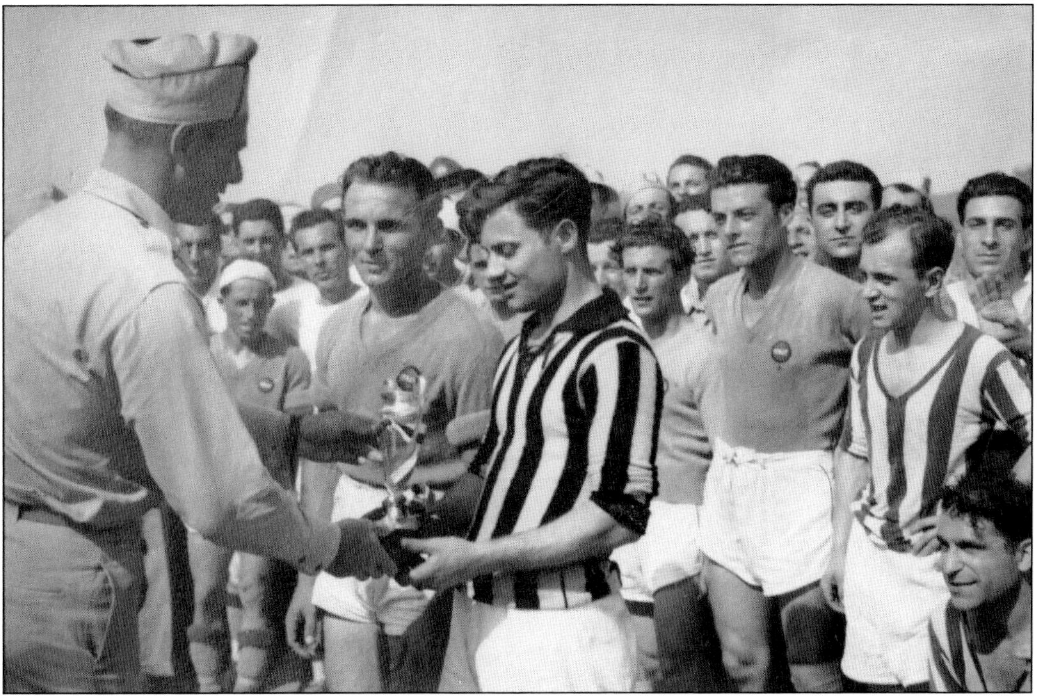

Lt. Col. Edwin L. Colbert, American commander of the 321st Italian QM Battalion, awards the game trophy to the visiting Juventus New York club that had come to the Letterkenny depot to play the 321st team on June 24, 1945. On the left, in the white headband and observing the gesture is Donato Pietra. (Courtesy of Edoardo Ranzoni and Massimo Pietra.)

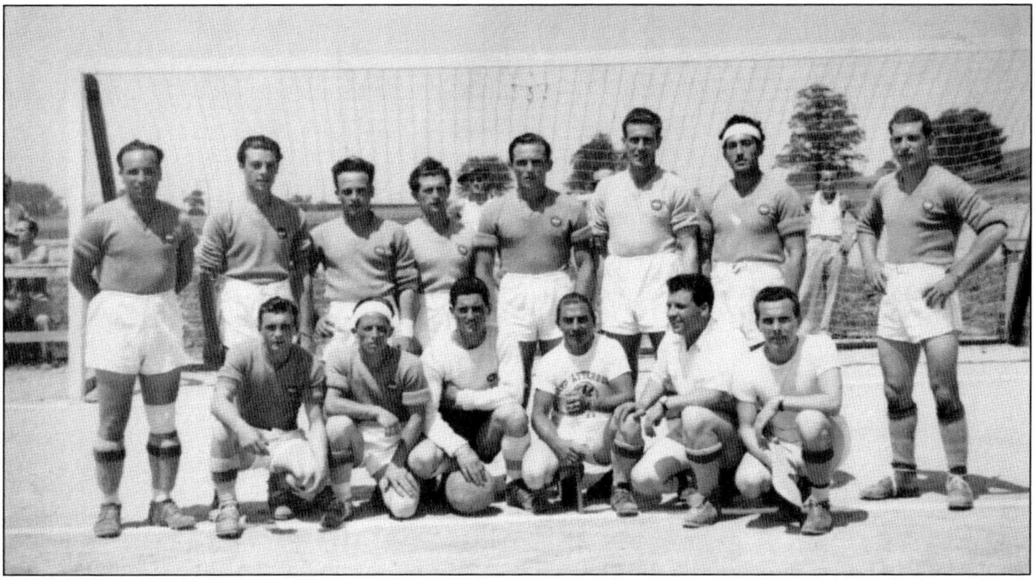

The all-star soccer side comprised of Letterkenny's six ISUs poses as a team. These players defeated the Juventus New York side 1-0 on June 24, 1945. In the first row, crouching, Donato Pietra wears the headband, and to the right of him kneels Antonio Coin. The player to Coin's right with the Camp Atterbury script is probably Angelo Barcella. (Courtesy of Massimo Pietra and Fausta Coin.)

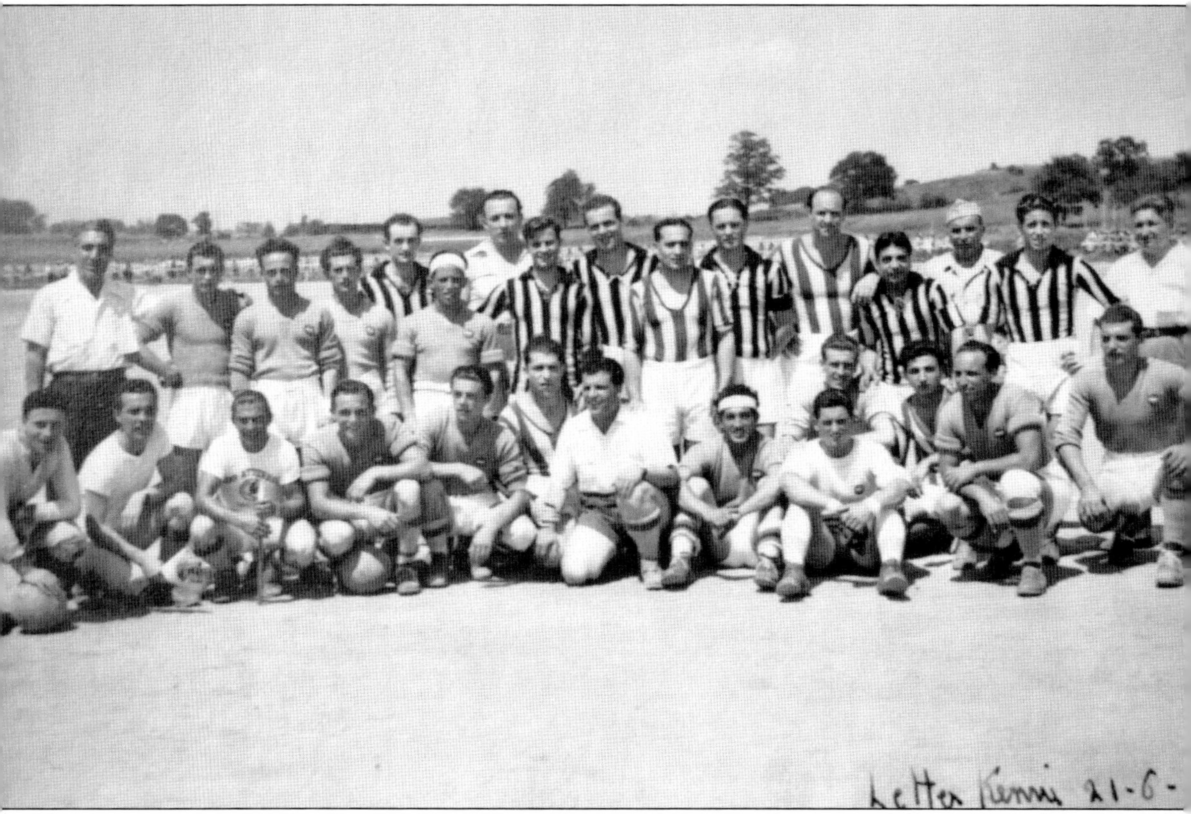

The Letterkenny ISU and Juventus New York soccer teams pose for their match on June 24, 1945. The photograph erroneously carries the date June 21. The third from the left, crouching, may be Angelo Barcella; Antonio Coin sits eighth from the left wearing white socks; Donato Pietra (still living at age 95) stands sixth from the left; and the last on the right crouching is most likely Guglielmo Apostoli. (Courtesy of Massimo Pietra and Fausta Coin.)

Eight

Camp Life

Food, both its quantity and quality, is one of the most important aspects of imprisonment, and without a doubt, Italian POWs at Letterkenny benefited from abundant and tasty fare. The prisoners themselves ran their own mess halls, and they were able to offer typical Italian dishes that were enjoyed by all. Indeed, their food was so good that US soldiers often found ingenious ways to dine with the very soldiers they oversaw.

Prisoners could also purchase goods at the post exchange—everything from sweets and low-alcohol beer to sewing kits and hygiene supplies. They were given $24 a month, $16 of which came in the form of coupons and the other $8 in cash. So they had money to buy authorized items. The POWs could also purchase mail-order goods, and officers in particular took advantage of this liberty. Finally, many POWs used their ticket card to acquire a weekly ration of cigarettes or tobacco.

To become a cooperating soldier, an Italian prisoner had to fill out an official application form, and this chapter includes an example of what one looked like. Once they took their oaths, the POWs received summer- and winter-issue uniforms with a relative garrison cap. The only distinction between these uniforms and the ones normal US soldiers wore came with a large, green oval patch with "Italy" written in white letters upon it that had to be worn on the left sleeve. A similar, smaller, "Italy" patch, round in shape, was sewn on the garrison cap. Apart from the uniform, the cooperating soldiers were also issued a canteen, mess kit, three utensils, and a laundry bag.

Medical care given to the POWs was outstanding: the POWs received vaccinations for smallpox, typhus, and various bacterial infections, and each detention camp had a hospital or clinic where the POWs could seek assistance if needed.

The most tragic event that occurred among Letterkenny ISU soldiers took place on June 3, 1944, when Pasquino Savini committed suicide by hurling himself underneath a road grader as he was working on building a depot road.

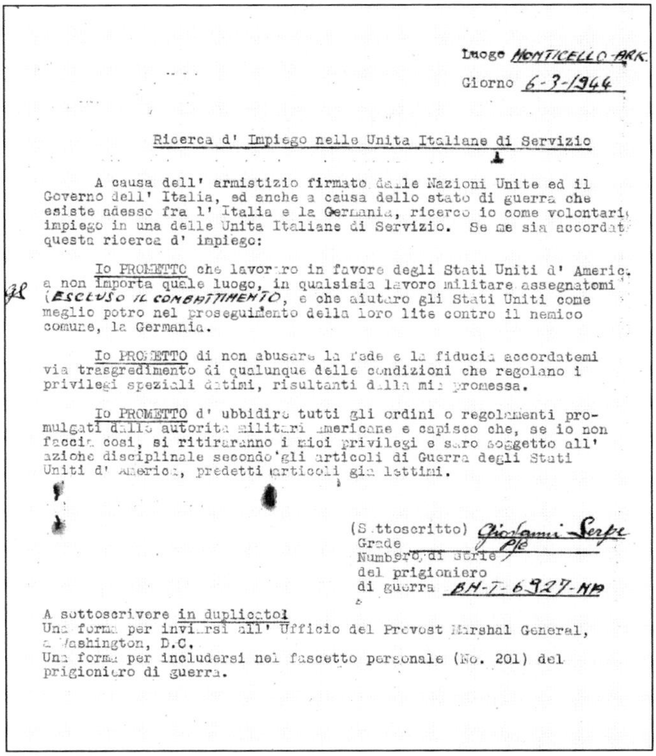

Luogo *MONTICELLO-ARK.*

Giorno *6-3-1944*

Ricerca d' Impiego nelle Unita Italiane di Servizio

A causa dell' armistizio firmato dalle Nazioni Unite ed il Governo dell' Italia, ed anche a causa dello stato di guerra che esiste adesso fra l' Italia e la Germania, ricerco io come volontari impiego in una delle Unita Italiane di Servizio. Se me sia accordat questa ricerca d' impiego:

Io PROMETTO che lavorero in favore degli Stati Uniti d' Americ a non importa quale luogo, in qualsisia lavoro militare assegnatomi (*ESCLUSO IL COMBATTIMENTO*, e che aiutero gli Stati Uniti come meglio potro nel proseguimento della loro lite contro il nemico comune, la Germania.

Io PROMETTO di non abusare la fede e la fiducia accordatemi via trasgredimento di qualunque delle condizioni che regolano i privilegi speziali datimi, risultanti dalla mia promessa.

Io PROMETTO d' ubbidire tutti gli ordini o regolamenti promulgati dalle autorita militari americane e capisco che, se io non faccia cosi, si ritireranno i miei privilegi e saro soggetto all' azione disciplinale secondo'gli articoli di Guerra degli Stati Uniti d' America, predetti articoli gia lettimi.

(Sottoscritto) *Giovanni Serpe*
Grade *P/e*
Numbero di Serie del prigioniero di guerra *BH-T-6927-MA*

A sottoscrivere in duplicato!
Una forma per inviarsi all' Ufficio del Provost Marshal General, a Washington, D.C.
Una forma per includersi nel fascetto personale (No. 201) del prigioniero di guerra.

Giovanni Serpe completed this application form in order to be a cooperator and officially assigned to an Italian Service Unit. The Italian translation of the original English contains many grammatical errors. Serpe signed his request on March 6, 1944, when he was at Camp Monticello, Arkansas. Duty as a collaborator in the ISUs officially began on May 1, 1944, and many cooperators arrived at Letterkenny around that date. (Courtesy of Giovanni Serpe.)

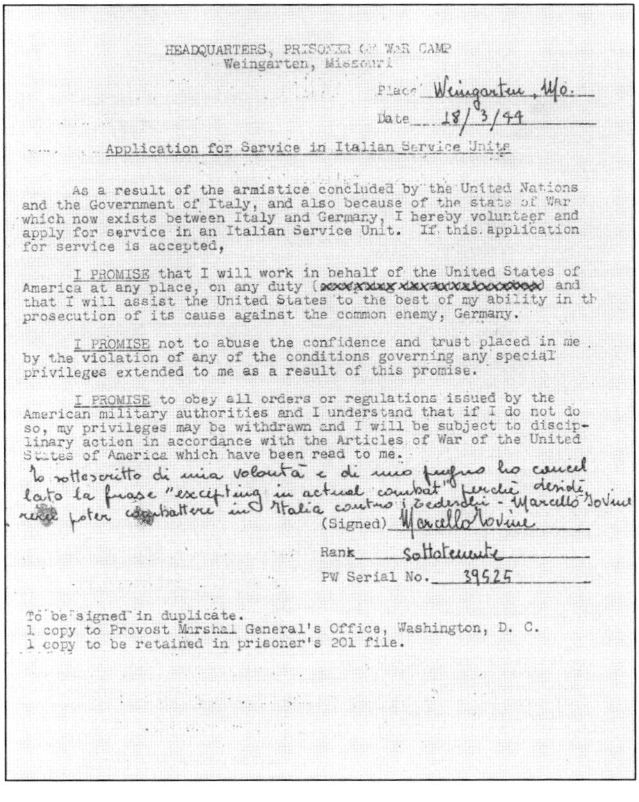

HEADQUARTERS, PRISONER OF WAR CAMP
Weingarten, Missouri

Place *Weingarten, Mo.*

Date *18/3/44*

Application for Service in Italian Service Units

As a result of the armistice concluded by the United Nations and the Government of Italy, and also because of the state of War which now exists between Italy and Germany, I hereby volunteer and apply for service in an Italian Service Unit. If this application for service is accepted,

I PROMISE that I will work in behalf of the United States of America at any place, on any duty (xxxxxxxxxxxxxxxxxxxxxxxx) and that I will assist the United States to the best of my ability in th prosecution of its cause against the common enemy, Germany.

I PROMISE not to abuse the confidence and trust placed in me by the violation of any of the conditions governing any special privileges extended to me as a result of this promise.

I PROMISE to obey all orders or regulations issued by the American military authorities and I understand that if I do not do so, my privileges may be withdrawn and I will be subject to disciplinary action in accordance with the Articles of War of the United States of America which have been read to me.

Io sottoscritto di mia volontà e di mio pugno ho cancellato la frase "excepting in actual combat" perchè desidererei poter combattere in Italia contro i tedeschi - Marcello Iovine

(Signed) *Marcello Iovine*

Rank *Sottotenente*

PW Serial No. *39525*

To be signed in duplicate.
1 copy to Provost Marshal General's Office, Washington, D. C.
1 copy to be retained in prisoner's 201 file.

This is 2nd Lt. Marcello Iovine's application form, written in English, to serve as a cooperating soldier. Unlike Serpe, Iovine was an officer, and his form did not explicitly delineate his duty as "excepting in actual combat." Most likely, US authorities understood that a majority of Italian enlisted soldiers had no intention to return to the front lines while officers were perceived as more open to serve in this capacity. (Courtesy of the MDDGCSGA, Rome, Iovine file.)

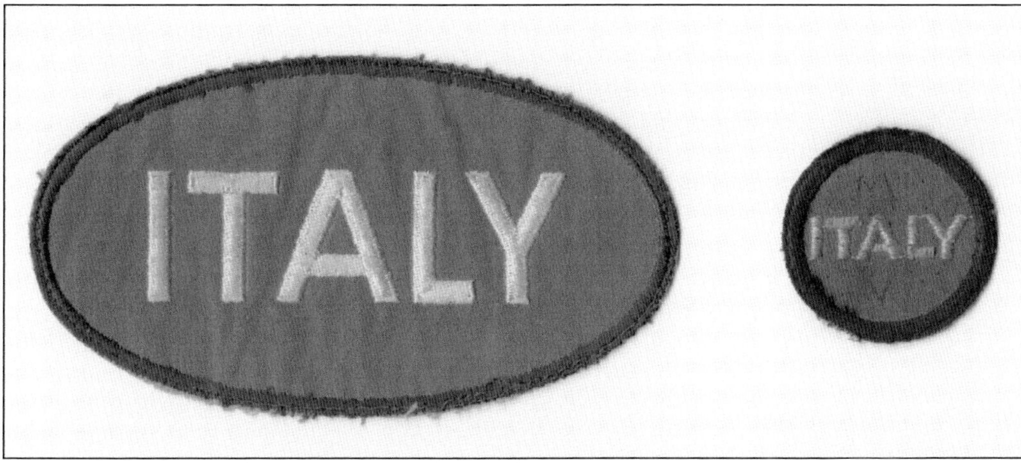

Italian cooperators wore this "Italy" oval patch on the left sleeve of their uniforms while the round patch was sewn on their hats. It was not difficult for the POWs to remove this insignia in order to resemble a normal US serviceman when they had liberty to leave the depot since all other aspects of their uniform were identical. (Courtesy of Carlo Viscardi and others.)

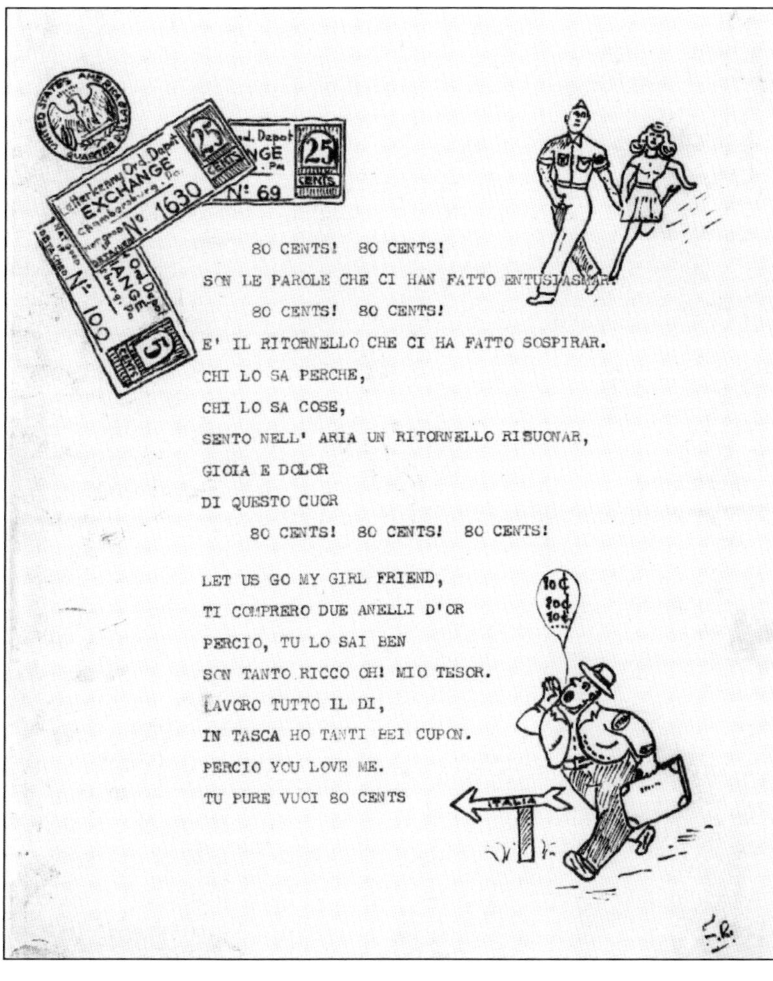

80 CENTS! 80 CENTS!
SON LE PAROLE CHE CI HAN FATTO ENTUSIASMAR.
80 CENTS! 80 CENTS!
E' IL RITORNELLO CHE CI HA FATTO SOSPIRAR.
CHI LO SA PERCHE,
CHI LO SA COSE,
SENTO NELL' ARIA UN RITORNELLO RISUONAR,
GIOIA E DOLOR
DI QUESTO CUOR
80 CENTS! 80 CENTS! 80 CENTS!

LET US GO MY GIRL FRIEND,
TI COMPRERO DUE ANELLI D'OR
PERCIO, TU LO SAI BEN
SON TANTO RICCO OH! MIO TESOR.
LAVORO TUTTO IL DI,
IN TASCA HO TANTI BEI CUPON.
PERCIO YOU LOVE ME.
TU PURE VUOI 80 CENTS

This poem pokes fun at the pay the cooperators earned. As the verses jokingly relate, with 80¢, a POW was rich and could buy his girlfriend two rings of gold. He even worked all day long and accumulated coupons like those reproduced in the upper left corner of the page. The POWs earned coupons as part of their pay and could redeem them at their exchange store. (Courtesy of Canclini family and others.)

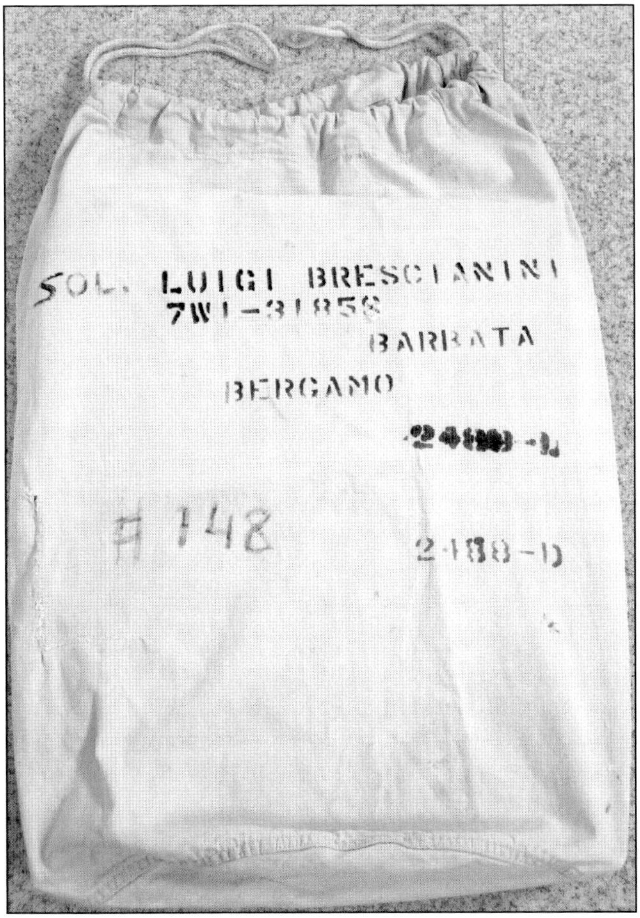

Luigi Brescianini brought back this US Army–issue laundry sack with him upon repatriation. Several POWs did the same as a souvenir, but a few continued to use them for other purposes. 2nd Lt. Giuseppe Avancini's son, Giampaolo Avancini, for instance, relates how his family still uses his father's sack to gather a well-known variety of apples found near Trento, the city where he lives. (Courtesy of Antonio Brescianini.)

This monthly meal ticket was issued to Antonio Falanga. A hole was punched for every meal taken at the mess hall. Many POWs were struck by the abundance of food they were given, a marked increase over the rations that they had received in the Italian army and even vastly more to what they normally ate at home before the war. Cigarettes were also allotted similarly. (Courtesy of Rosario Falanga.)

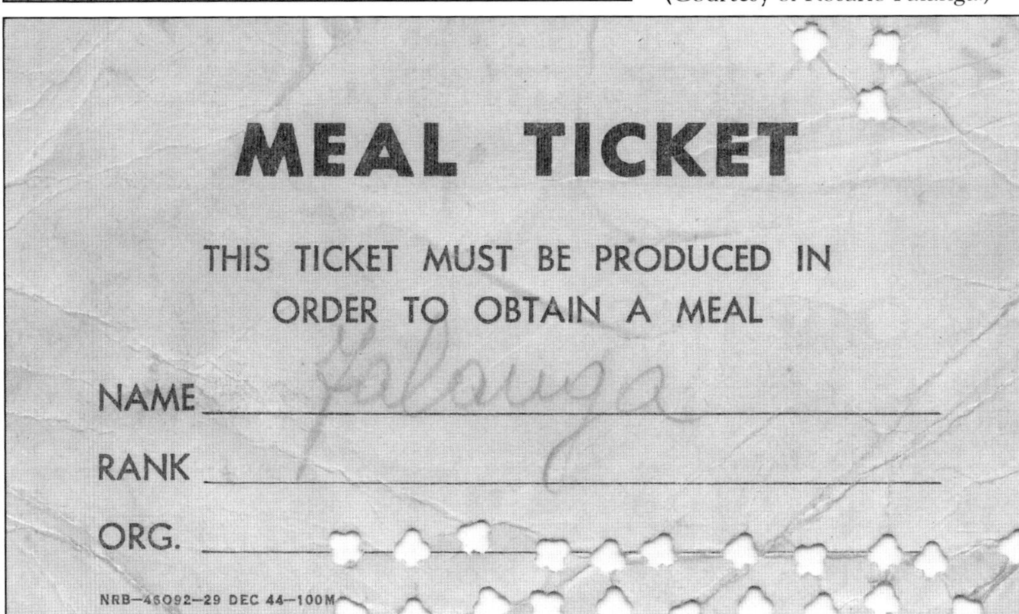

MEAL TICKET

THIS TICKET MUST BE PRODUCED IN ORDER TO OBTAIN A MEAL

NAME Falanga

RANK

ORG.

NRB—46092—29 DEC 44—100M

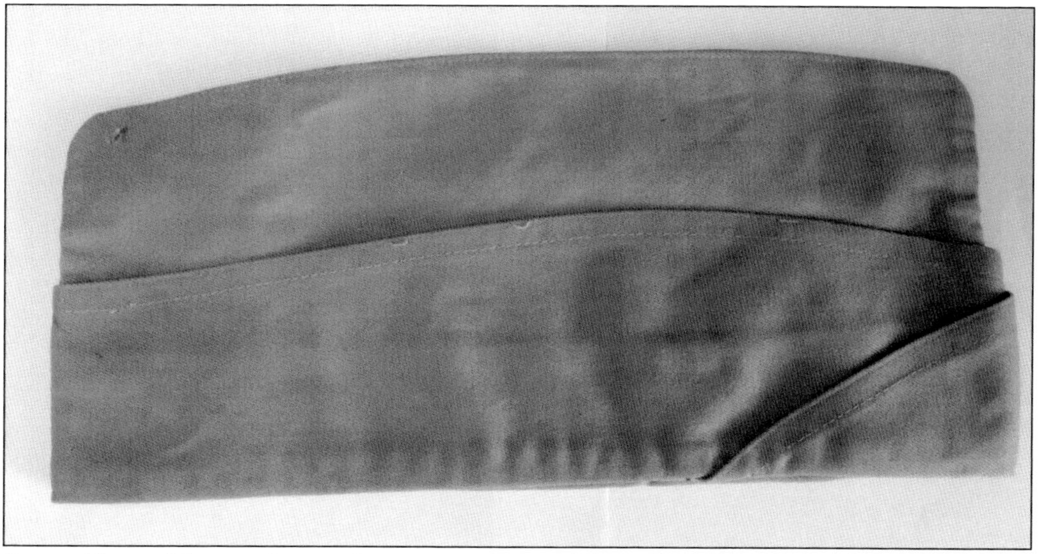

Pictured here is Virginio Ranzoni's garrison cap, one of those that POWs serving in Italian Service Units were authorized to wear. Many photographs show how a round "Italy" patch with white letters on a green background was sewn on the left front side. Garrison caps were standard issue for the various military branches during the war. (Courtesy of Edoardo Ranzoni.)

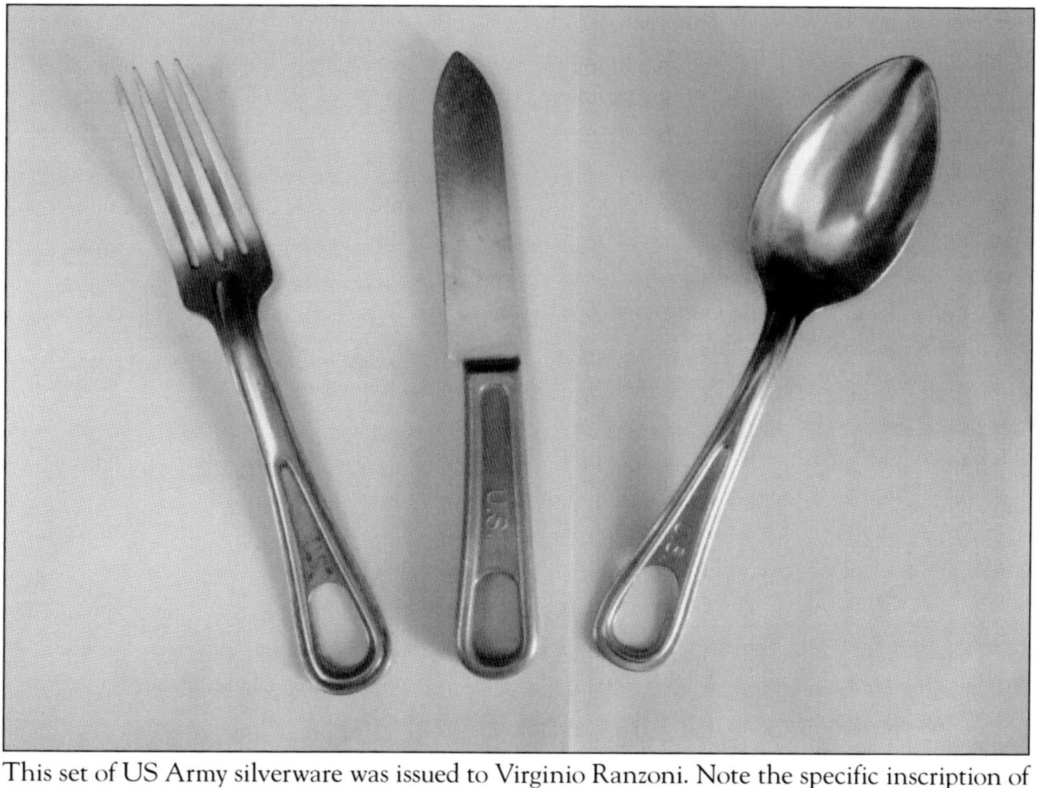

This set of US Army silverware was issued to Virginio Ranzoni. Note the specific inscription of "U.S." on the handles. Numerous prisoners were able to bring American dining utensils, plates, and canteens back to Italy as souvenirs—even if part of incomplete sets. Ranzoni proudly displayed his US fork, knife, and spoon for family and guests. (Courtesy of Edoardo Ranzoni.)

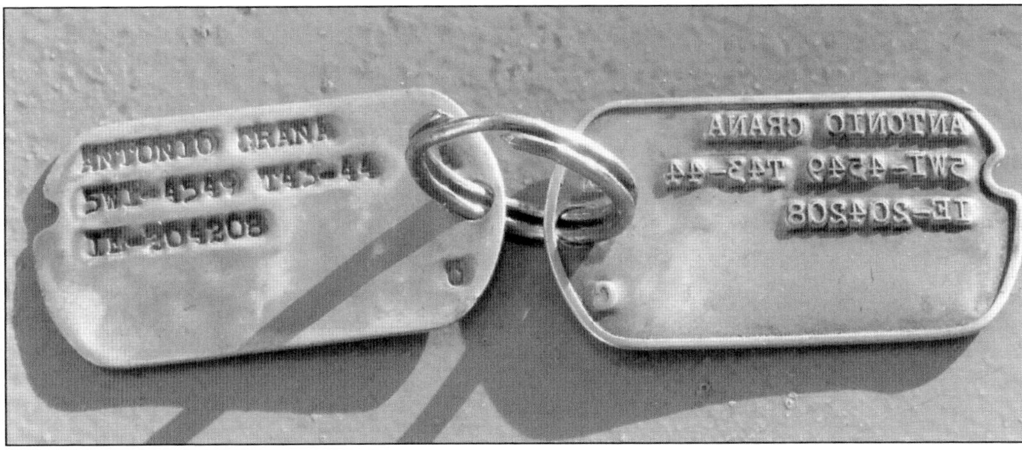

These prisoner-issued dog tags belonged to Antonio Crana. Great numbers of POWs brought their tags back with them to Italy upon repatriation. With Crana's number, 5WI-4549, the "5" indicates that he had been assigned to the 5th Service Command (SC), the "W" indicates the War Department, and the "I," Italy. (Courtesy of Giuseppe Crana.)

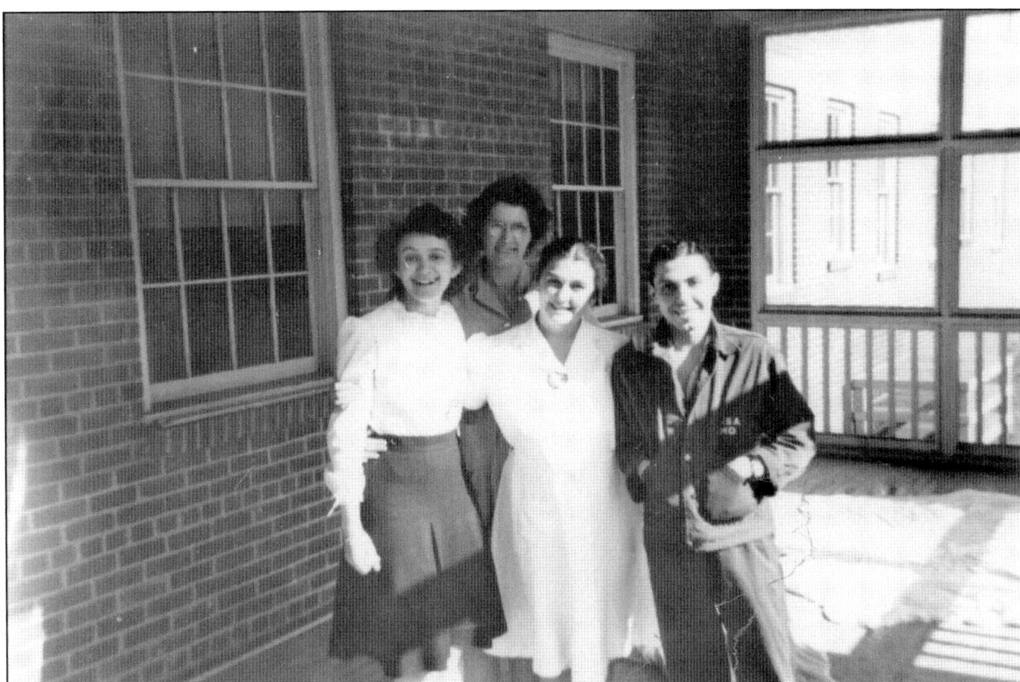

Ettore Calizza stands with medical staff members of the Valley Forge Hospital in Phoenixville, Pennsylvania. Calizza was admitted to the hospital three times—at the end of October 1943, once in 1944, and again in 1945 in order to be treated for both myositis (muscle inflammation) and kidney failure. He was only able to return to full duty at Letterkenny by the middle of March 1945. (Courtesy of Maurizio Calizza.)

Letterkenny Ordnance Depot
EXCHANGE
Chambersburg, Penna.
NOT GOOD IF DETACHED
No. 15857
25 CENTS

The monthly salary for cooperating Italian POWs spanned from $24 a month for enlisted soldiers to $64 a month for generals. One-third was actually paid in cash and the rest given in coupons that each detention camp issued for the exclusive use to purchase goods at the military exchange outlets at that base. Here is Antonio Falanga's coupon for 25¢ that was issued at Letterkenny. (Courtesy of Rosario Falanga.)

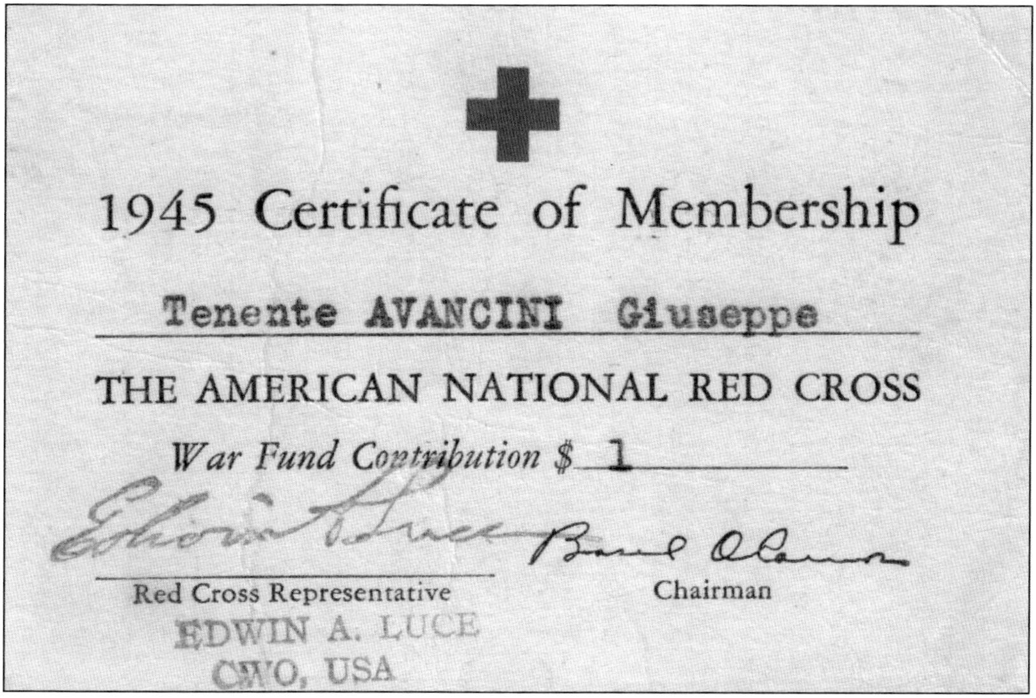

1945 Certificate of Membership
Tenente AVANCINI Giuseppe
THE AMERICAN NATIONAL RED CROSS
War Fund Contribution $ 1
Red Cross Representative
EDWIN A. LUCE
CWO, USA
Chairman

Lt. Giuseppe Avancini acquired this 1945 certificate of membership in the American National Red Cross for having generously donated his blood. Other Letterkenny POWs did likewise on multiple occasions, and the particular gesture of giving blood contributed greatly to enhance the positive relationship between the POWs and townsfolk in Chambersburg. (Courtesy of Giampaolo Avancini.)

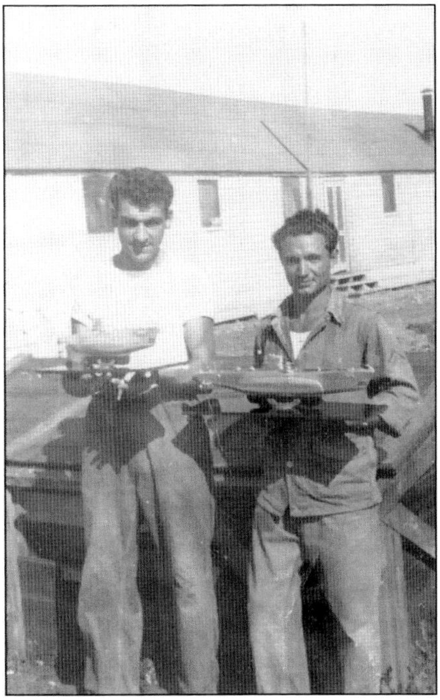

Mario Fioretti, on the right, and an unidentified POW proudly display their model submarines. Model building was an important and popular hobby for many POWs, especially in the evening hours after work during the winter months when bad weather often kept them indoors. Other POWs who constructed models of ships include Almo Meniconi and Gino Baldacci. (Courtesy of Giovanni Serpe.)

This is the Caterpillar road grader under which Pasquino Savini, a 47-year-old private from Santo Stefano, Ravenna, tragically threw himself and committed suicide on June 3, 1944. At the time, he was digging postholes with other POWs for road construction. Unfortunately, Savini's name was misspelled on official documents, and this error caused several problems for his widow, who tried to obtain his retirement pay from the Italian government. (Courtesy of the MDDGCSGA, Rome, Savini file.)

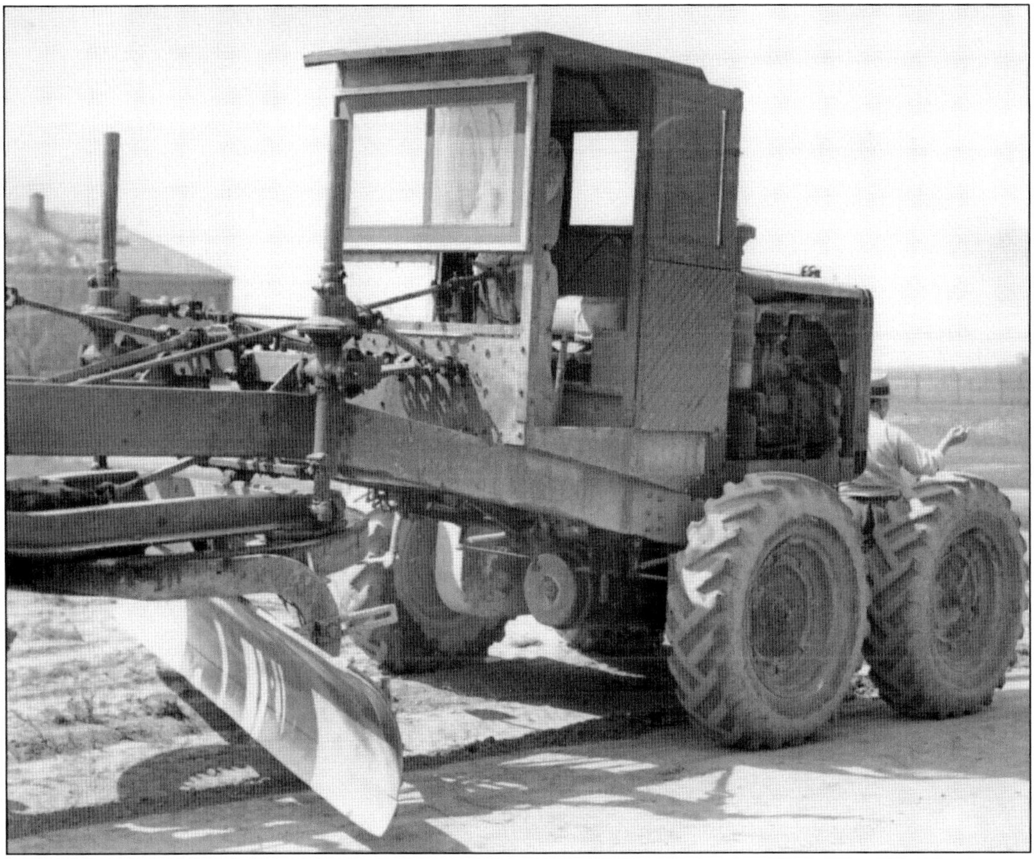

The Vatican apostolic delegate, Msgr. Amleto Cicognani, wrote this December 7, 1944, letter to US provost marshal general Brig. Gen. B.M. Bryan to support Capt. Girolamo Bellavista's request for early repatriation. Cicognani supported Bellavista a second time with another letter to Bryan on April 3, 1945. Indeed, in part perhaps because of Cicognani's help, Bellavista was repatriated a few months ahead of most other Letterkenny POWs. (Courtesy of the MDDGCSGA, Rome, Bellavista file.)

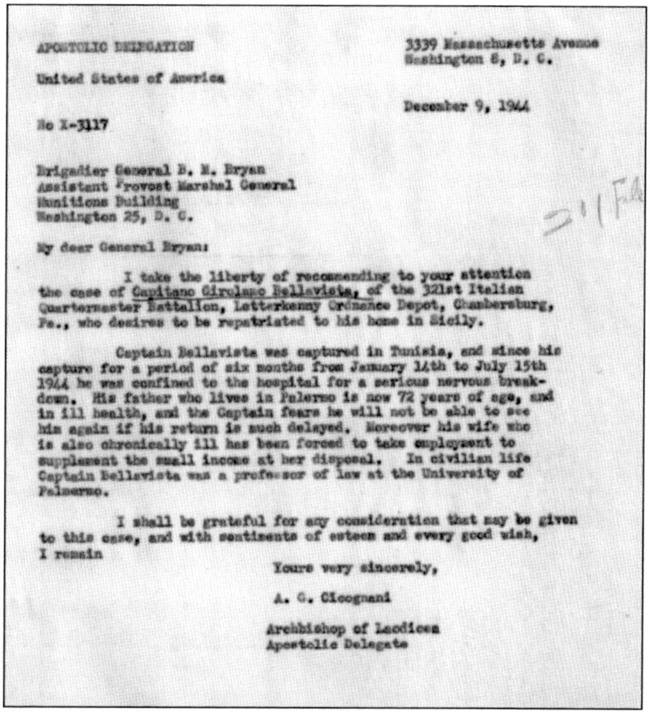

APOSTOLIC DELEGATION
United States of America

3339 Massachusetts Avenue
Washington 8, D. C.

December 9, 1944

No X-3117

Brigadier General B. M. Bryan
Assistant Provost Marshal General
Munitions Building
Washington 25, D. C.

211 FA

My dear General Bryan:

I take the liberty of recommending to your attention the case of Capitano Girolamo Bellavista, of the 321st Italian Quartermaster Battalion, Letterkenny Ordnance Depot, Chambersburg, Pa., who desires to be repatriated to his home in Sicily.

Captain Bellavista was captured in Tunisia, and since his capture for a period of six months from January 14th to July 15th 1944 he was confined to the hospital for a serious nervous breakdown. His father who lives in Palermo is now 72 years of age, and in ill health, and the Captain fears he will not be able to see him again if his return is much delayed. Moreover his wife who is also chronically ill has been forced to take employment to supplement the small income at her disposal. In civilian life Captain Bellavista was a professor of law at the University of Palmerno.

I shall be grateful for any consideration that may be given to this case, and with sentiments of esteem and every good wish, I remain

Youre very sincerely,

A. G. Cicognani

Archbishop of Laodicea
Apostolic Delegate

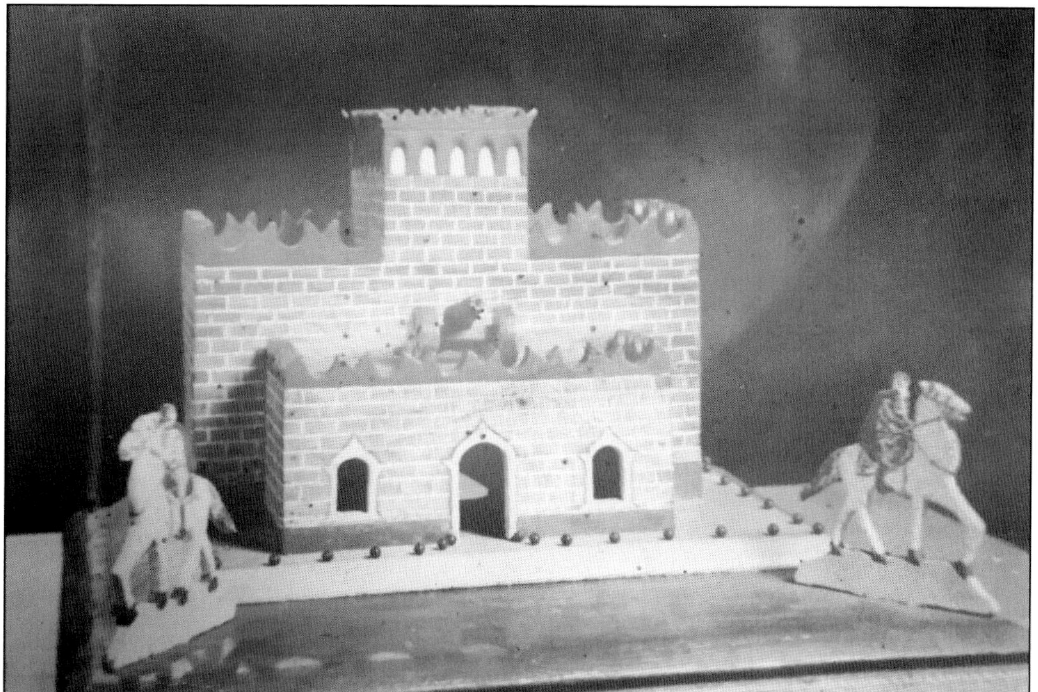

Letterkenny ISU member Carlo Buffoni constructed this model of a castle. Artistic endeavors of this type allowed POWs an important outlet both to express their own talents and to pass away time that seemed to move very slowly, given the tedium of being prisoners and the longing to return to family and loved ones in Italy. (Courtesy of Vittoria Buffoni.)

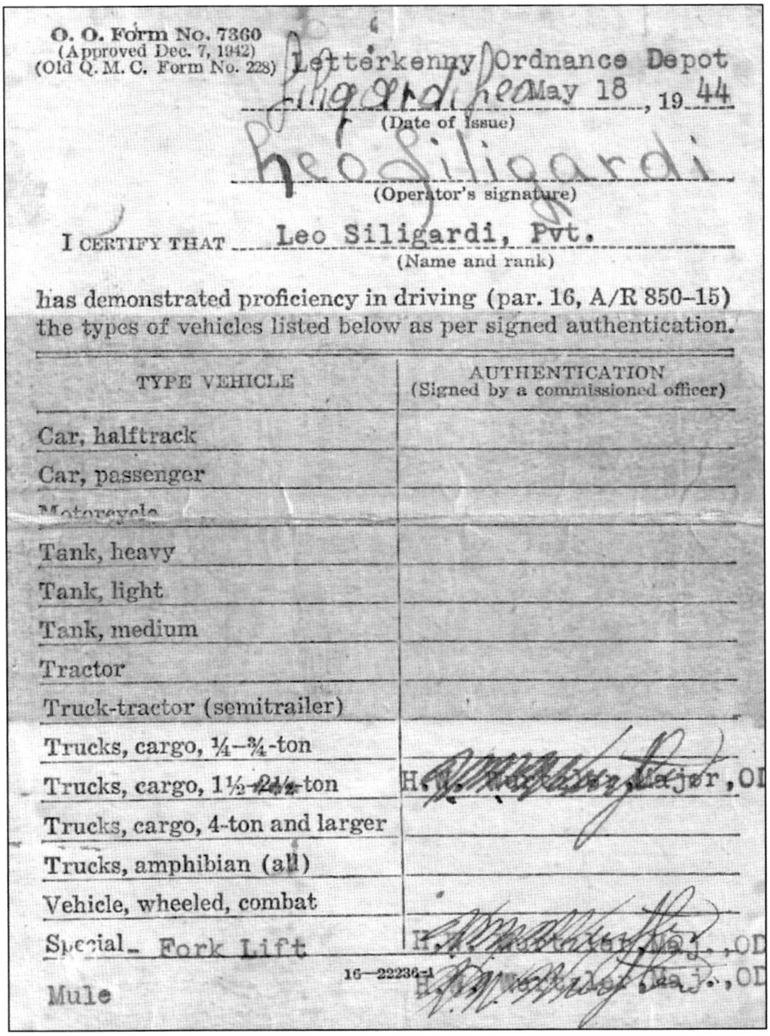

O. O. Form No. 7360
(Approved Dec. 7, 1942)
(Old Q. M. C. Form No. 228)

Letterkenny Ordnance Depot
May 18, 1944
(Date of Issue)

Leo Siligardi
(Operator's signature)

I CERTIFY THAT Leo Siligardi, Pvt.
(Name and rank)

has demonstrated proficiency in driving (par. 16, A/R 850–15) the types of vehicles listed below as per signed authentication.

TYPE VEHICLE	AUTHENTICATION (Signed by a commissioned officer)
Car, halftrack	
Car, passenger	
Motorcycle	
Tank, heavy	
Tank, light	
Tank, medium	
Tractor	
Truck-tractor (semitrailer)	
Trucks, cargo, ¼–¾-ton	
Trucks, cargo, 1½–~~2½~~-ton	H. [illegible] Major, OD
Trucks, cargo, 4-ton and larger	
Trucks, amphibian (all)	
Vehicle, wheeled, combat	
Special – Fork Lift	H. [illegible] Maj., OD
Mule	H. [illegible] Maj., OD

16—22236-1

The US Army Quartermaster Corps issued this military vehicle drivers license on May 18, 1944, to Leo Siligardi while he was at Letterkenny. With this license, Siligardi could drive cargo trucks up to 1.5 tons, forklifts, and the motorized M274 Mule. The fact that the cooperators were authorized to drive any number of military vehicles further attests to their special status. (Courtesy of Sandra Siligardi.)

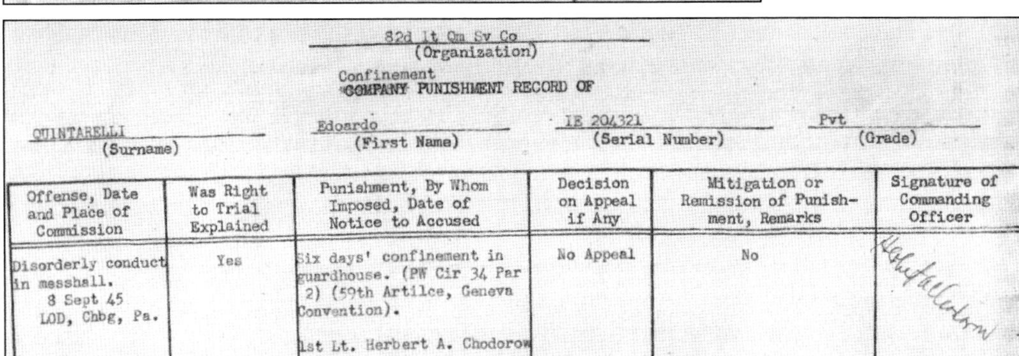

82d Lt Qm Sv Co
(Organization)

Confinement
~~COMPANY~~ PUNISHMENT RECORD OF

QUINTARELLI (Surname) — Edoardo (First Name) — IE 204321 (Serial Number) — Pvt (Grade)

Offense, Date and Place of Commission	Was Right to Trial Explained	Punishment, By Whom Imposed, Date of Notice to Accused	Decision on Appeal if Any	Mitigation or Remission of Punishment, Remarks	Signature of Commanding Officer
Disorderly conduct in messhall. 8 Sept 45 LOD, Chbg, Pa.	Yes	Six days' confinement in guardhouse. (PW Cir 34 Par 2) (59th Artilce, Geneva Convention). 1st Lt. Herbert A. Chodorow	No Appeal	No	H. A. Chodorow

This documentation shows that Lt. Herbert A. Chodorow, US company commander of the 82nd ISU, punished Edoardo Quintarelli with six days of confinement in the guardhouse for disorderly conduct in the mess hall on September 8, 1945, just a few days before repatriation. There is no documentation that describes the actual infraction, but most likely it was much more serious than a simple food fight. (Courtesy of the MDDGCSGA, Rome, Quintarelli file.)

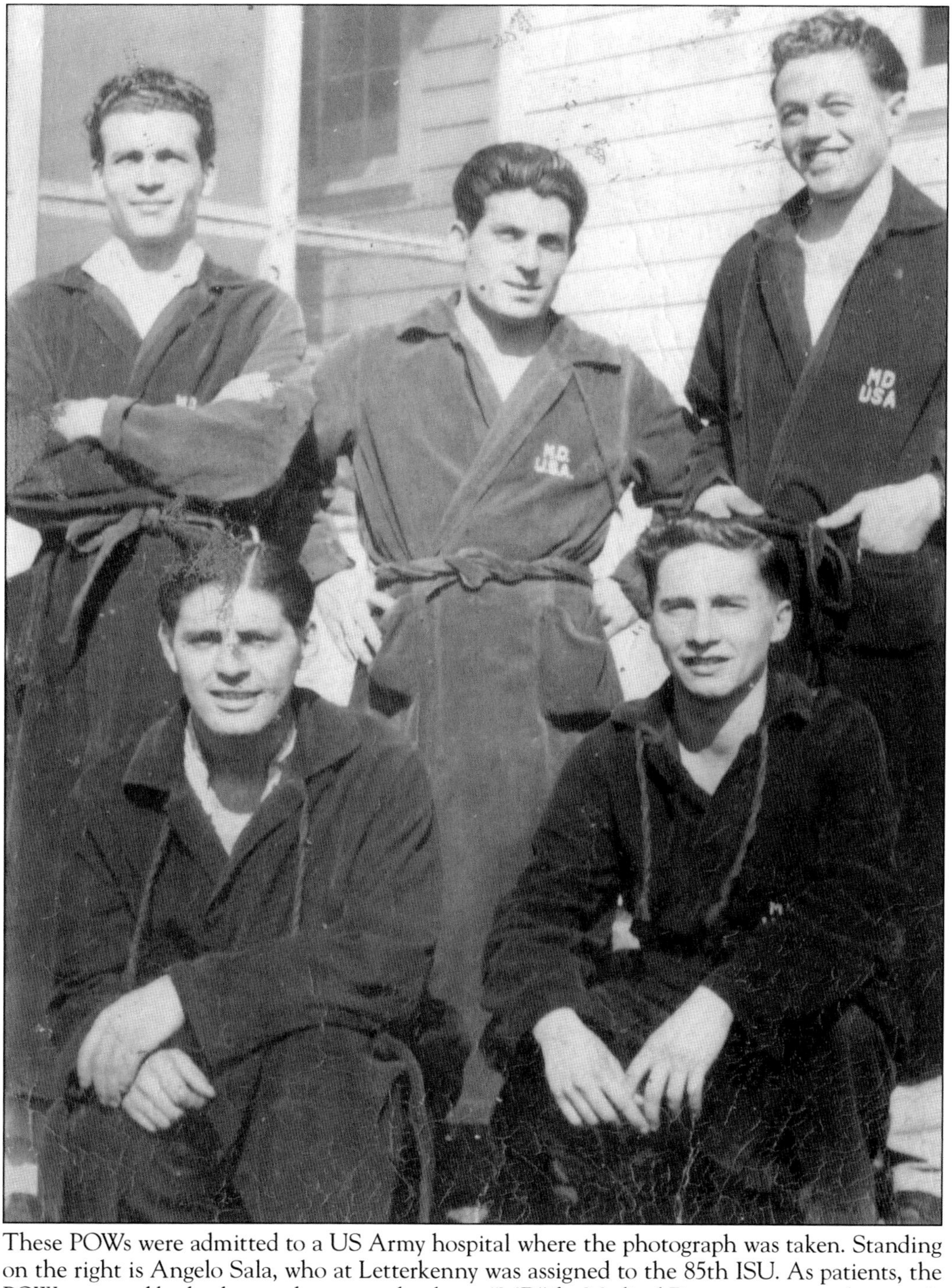

These POWs were admitted to a US Army hospital where the photograph was taken. Standing on the right is Angelo Sala, who at Letterkenny was assigned to the 85th ISU. As patients, the POWs wore red bathrobes, and one can clearly see "MD" for Medical Department over the initials "USA." (Courtesy of Carlo Sala.)

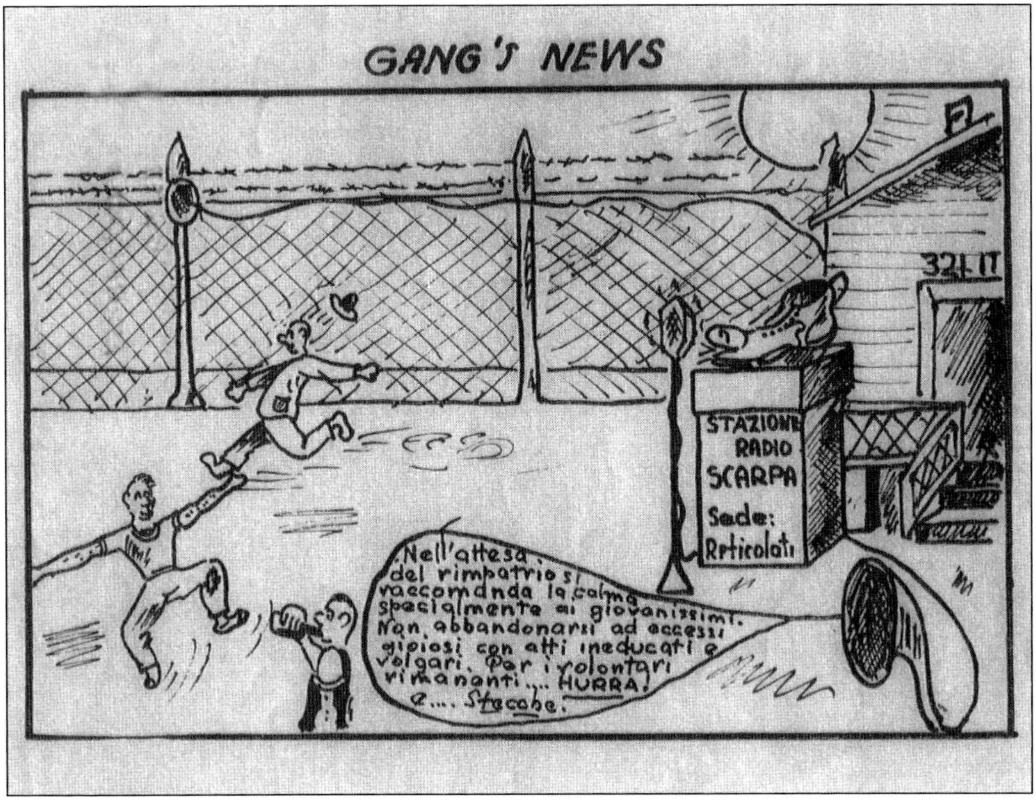

This POW-designed vignette shows how prisoners were absolutely ecstatic to be informed about their imminent repatriation. The script reads, "While waiting repatriation we recommend that especially young soldiers keep calm. Do not give yourselves over to excessive joy through vulgar and uneducated behavior. For the volunteers still here . . . Hurrah and we're turning it over to you!" (Courtesy of Dave Goodman.)

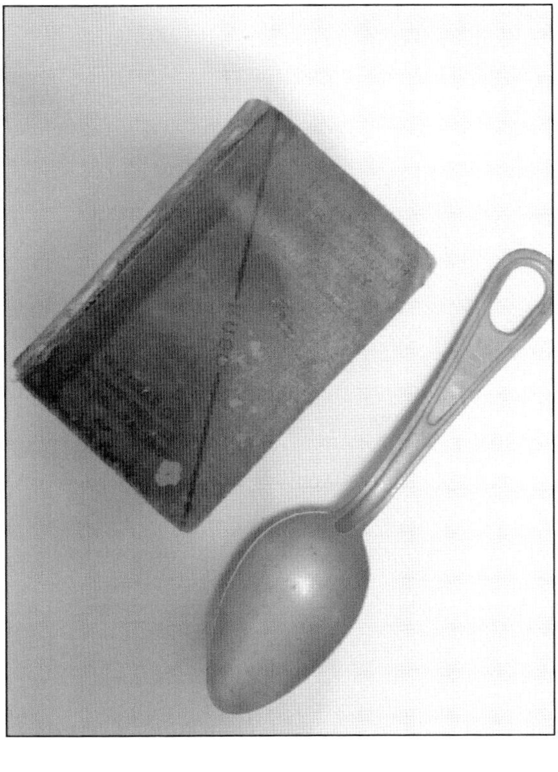

This is Antonio Torneo's spoon and pocket Italian-English/English-Italian dictionary that he used while detained at Letterkenny. For many POWs, it was obviously important to be able to communicate in English, and, upon repatriation to Italy, many of them were able to bring their knowledge of English to increase their opportunities to gain employment. (Courtesy of Salvatore Torneo.)

This service stationery belonged to Pvt. Savio Cavagna, who had been captured in Mazara del Vallo (Trapani), Sicily, on July 22, 1943. Perhaps no other activity was more meaningful and crucial to morale than the exchange of letters—a precarious link to loved ones in war-torn Italy. After the end of the war in Europe, the use of stationery and regular envelopes was authorized. (Courtesy of Marco Cavagna.)

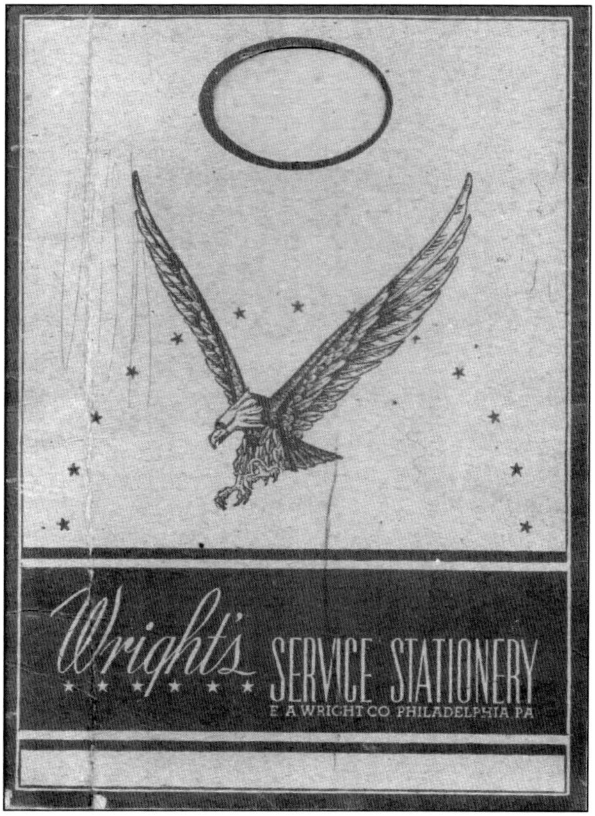

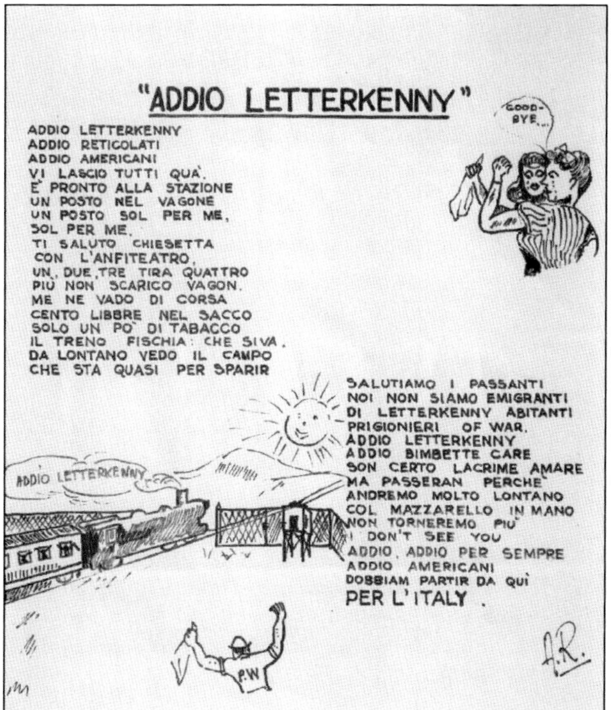

This POW poem was liberally circulated upon repatriation in the early fall of 1945. "So Long, Letterkenny" may have been written with a tune for a song in mind. Its spirit conveys a joy for leaving a life behind and makes special mention of the chapel and amphitheater. But in design and words, it also references the tears the sweethearts will shed as the POWs head back to Italy. (Courtesy of Maurizio Calizza.)

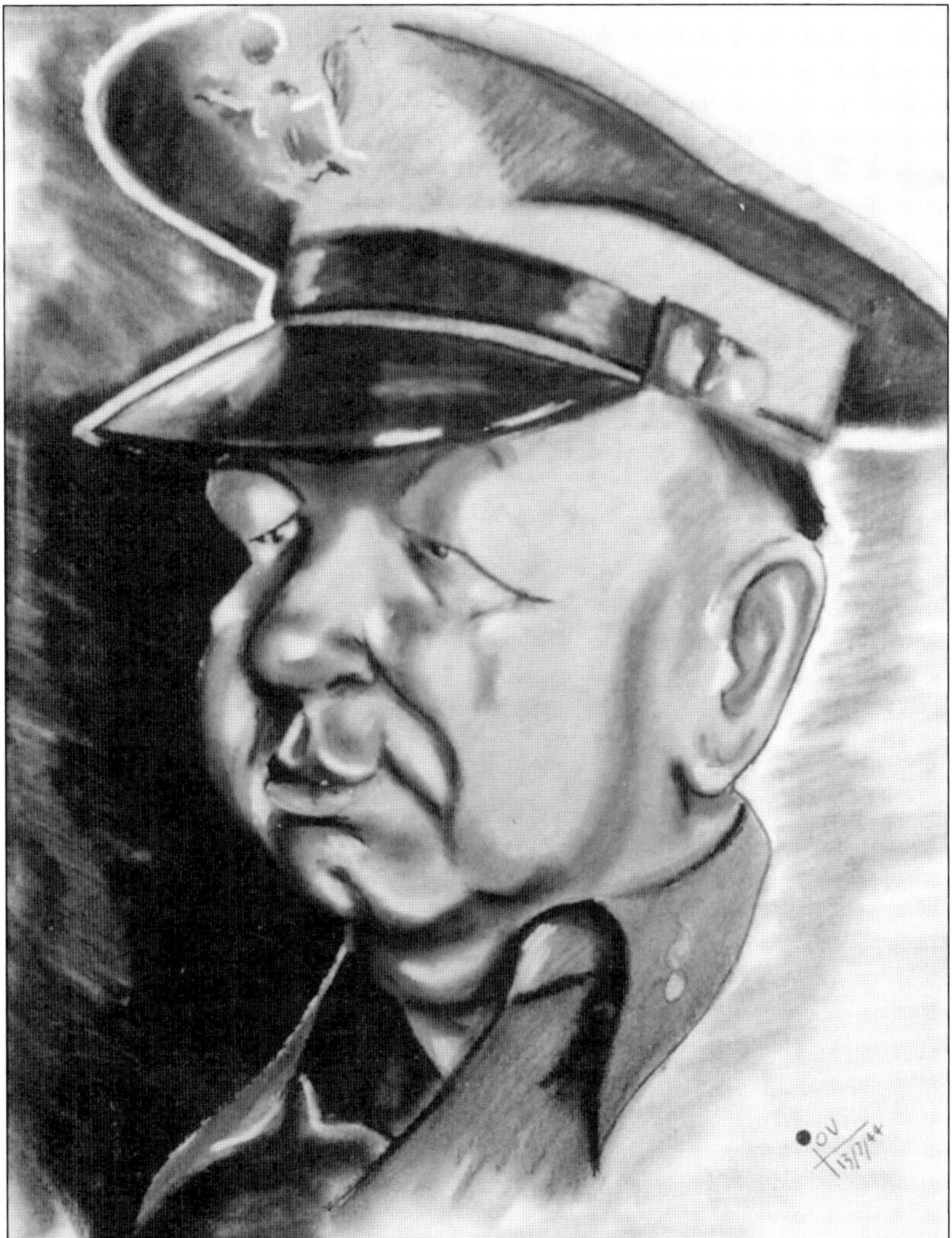

2nd Lt. Marcello Iovine drew this caricature of Col. Raymond Hare, the commanding officer at Letterkenny. Overall, in July 1944, Iovine sketched 20 caricatures in crayon of both military and civilian officials that worked on the depot. In turn, the images were sold for $1,000 each to support the 5th War Loan Drive at Letterkenny. (Courtesy of Marcia and Andrea Jovine, copyright 2017.)

Nine

AFTER THE WAR

Between the end of September and middle of October 1945, all of the Letterkenny Italian POWs were repatriated. When they arrived in Italy, they found their country in truly dire straits: countless bridges, roads, and large parts of cities lay in ruins. Economically, many of the ISU soldiers had to start over from scratch, "roll up their sleeves," and create a new life.

Msgr. Amleto Cicognani, the former apostolic delegate general to the United States who had been so important to the POWs, was nominated a cardinal in 1958 and in 1961 became the Vatican's secretary of state. He died in 1973 and was buried in the Basilica of San Clemente in Rome. In 1991, a few former Letterkenny POWs and their families dedicated a special plaque to him in commemoration of his service to the 321st Italian Quartermaster Battalion.

Some Letterkenny ISU members immigrated to other countries after they spent a few years in Italy, heading off to Argentina, Australia, Brazil, Canada, France, and mainly to the United States since several had married, or were to marry, their American girlfriends in time. Among those ex-prisoners that have been identified who came back to the United States are Antonio Arganetto, Antonio Brissoni, Gaetano Capurso, Alessio Cerri, Filippo Dilisciandro, Marcello D'Orsogna, Marcello Iovine, Mario Mazzacchi, Marcello Pomi, Armando Ravera, Donato Rinaldi, Antonio Tescione, Lelio Tomasina, Alfredo Tonolo, Giuseppe Tuttolomondo, and Guido Vincenzi. Iovine, in particular, had enormous success as a toy maker and medallion designer. Tonolo also had a wonderful academic career as a professor of Spanish. Over the years, many former POWs would often visit each other, both in the United States and Italy.

Over the last two years, the authors of this book have been greatly aided by Antonio Brescianini and Sara De Giorgis, respectively a son and granddaughter of a Letterkenny POW. They have helped to locate many relatives of former ISU soldiers, both in the United States and in Italy, who have then been able to meet, share family stories, and reveal cherished photographs of their grandparents, parents, and uncles.

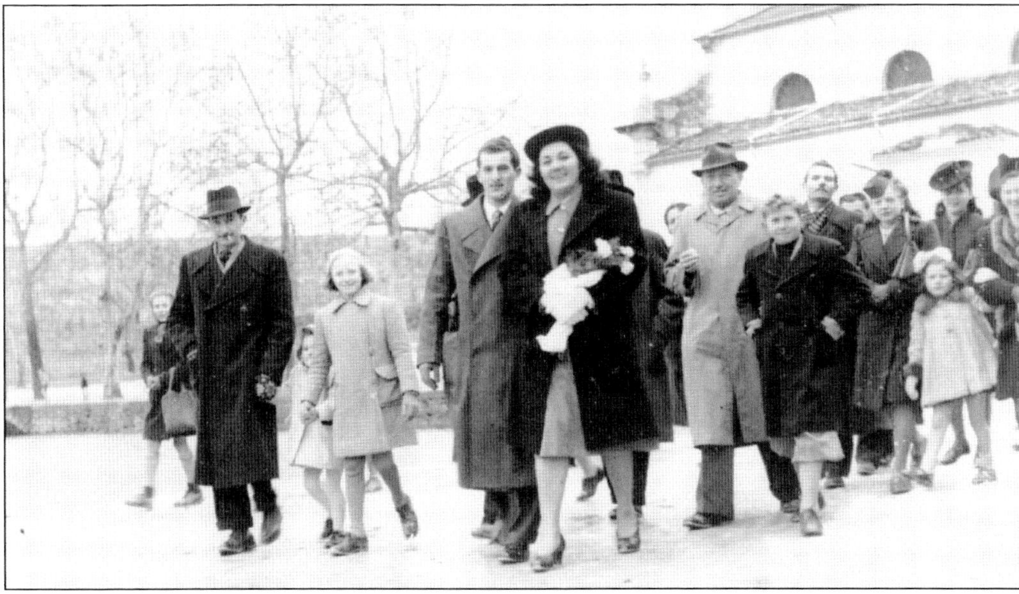

Antonio Arganetto and Bruna D'Angelo process out of church on May 5, 1947, after their nuptial Mass in Pitigliano, a town near Grosseto in the region of Tuscany. Zefferino Trevisan, a close friend of Arganetto since his Letterkenny days, follows closely behind the couple. Antonio and Bruna returned to the United States to the Philadelphia area, where Antonio had a career as a barber. (Courtesy of Mark and Michael Arganetto.)

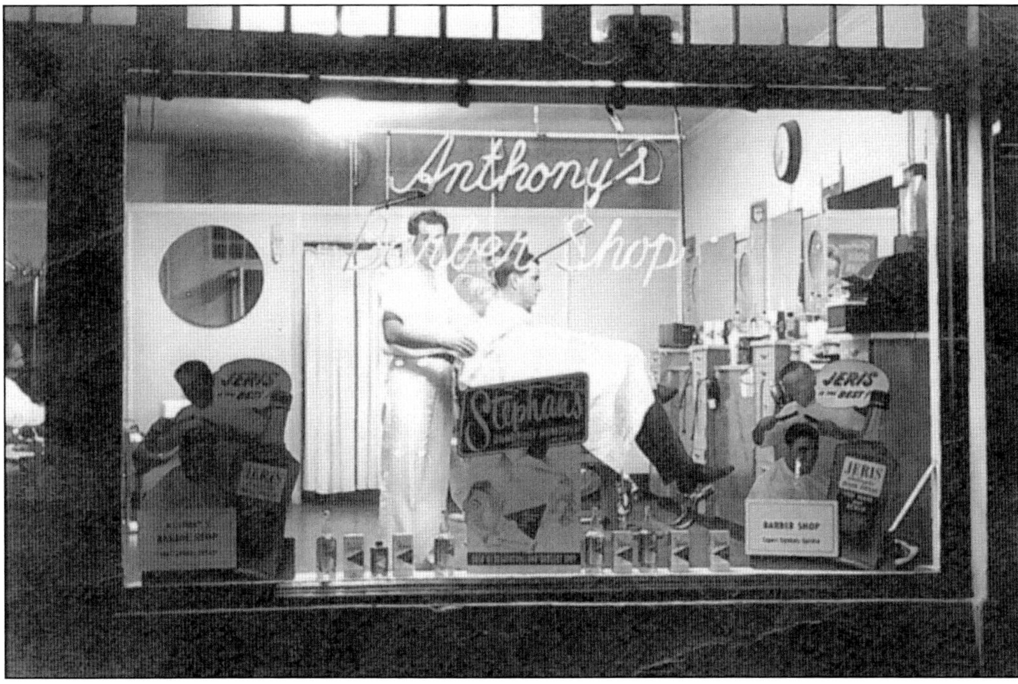

Antonio Arganetto is seen here in his barbershop in Penn Wynne, Pennsylvania, during the early 1950s. Arganetto practiced his profession in Italy even prior to this military service; and at Letterkenny, American authorities gave him clippers, scissors, and razors, since his original barber kit had been confiscated upon his capture in North Africa. (Courtesy of Fabio Trevisan.)

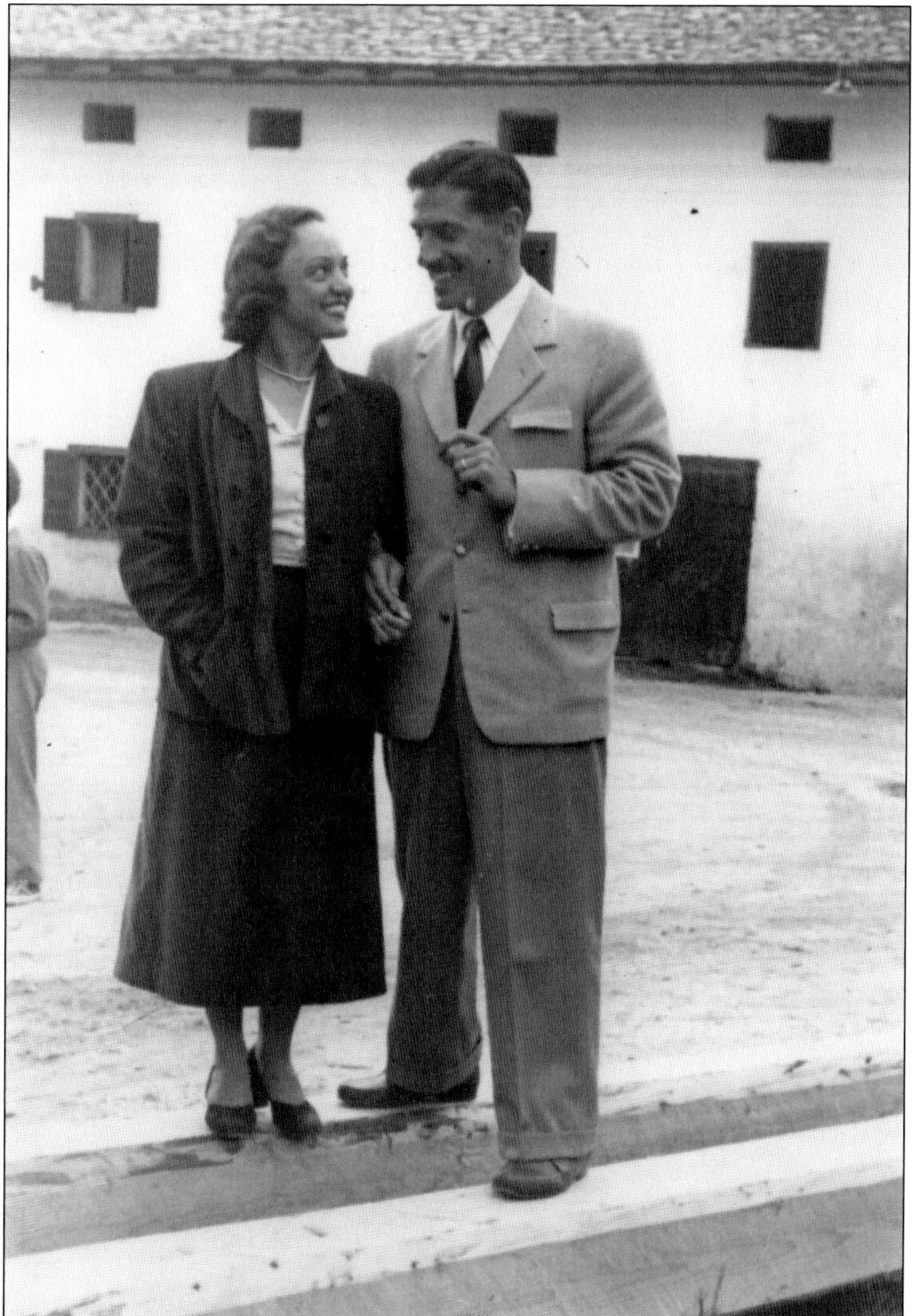

Alfredo Tonolo and Tina Norce, his new bride, are seen in this 1949 photograph taken in Italy. After Alfredo's repatriation, they corresponded via letters for over four years. Tina accepted Alfredo's proposal for marriage and traveled to Genoa to meet him. After a year spent in Italy, they returned to the United States, where Alfredo eventually became a professor of Spanish at Bloomsburg University. (Courtesy of Frances Tonolo MacAvoy.)

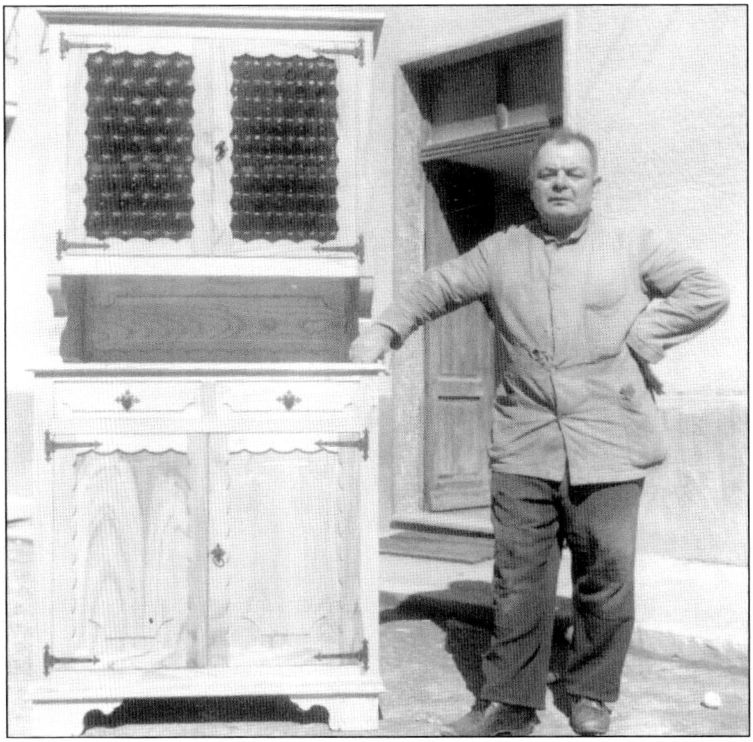

Pietro Bracchi proudly poses with one of his handmade furniture cabinets made during the 1960s. Born in Saluzzo (Cuneo) on February 7, 1910, he was captured in Sicily. At Letterkenny, Bracchi was an accomplished cabinetmaker and worked in the woodshop as a carpenter. He was so good, in fact, that many US officers requested his finishing skills in their homes and quarters. (Courtesy of Carmela Bracchi and Sara De Giorgis.)

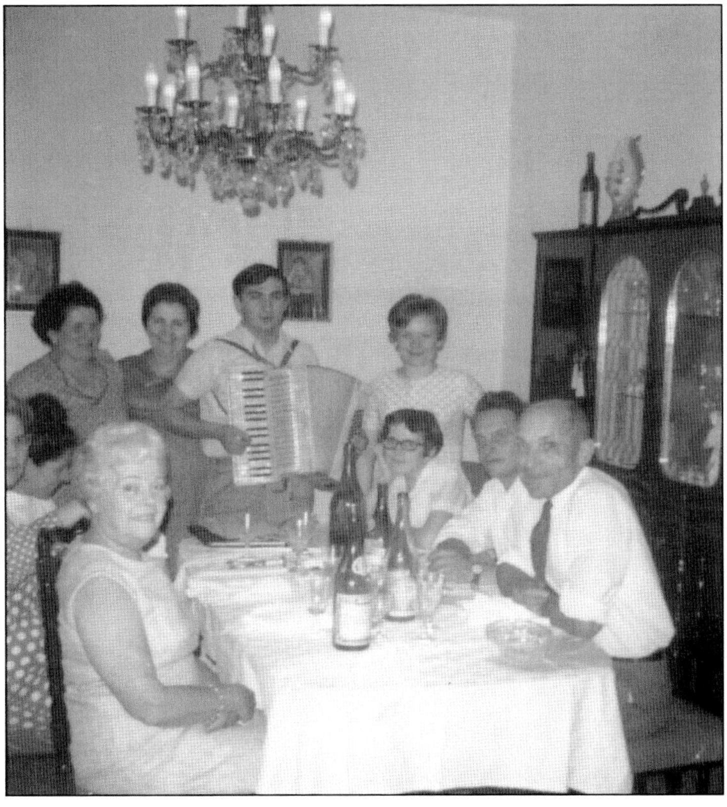

Irene Melotti, left, an Italian American who often visited Italian POWs at Letterkenny during the war, is here pictured with the Luigi Brescianini family in Italy, around 1963. Antonio Brescianini is playing the accordion. Melotti stayed in contact with several ex-prisoners whom she often visited during her travels back to Italy in the decades following the war. (Courtesy of Antonio Brescianini.)

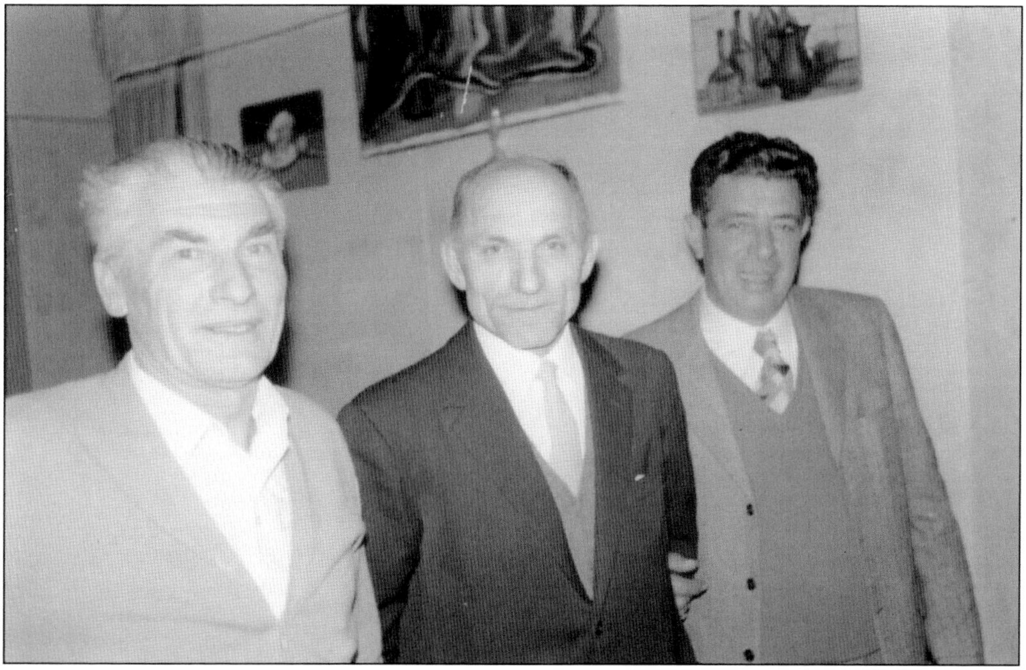

Three former Italian Letterkenny POWs pose during a 1971 informal reunion. From the left are Aldo Lorenzi, from Mozzecane (Verona); Luigi Brescianini, from Barbata (Bergamo); and Fortunato Brunino, from Abano Terme (Padua). Many ex-POWs worked hard to maintain thriving friendships with their buddies they had lived and worked with at Letterkenny, often meeting for special occasions, such as the holidays. (Courtesy of Antonio Brescianini.)

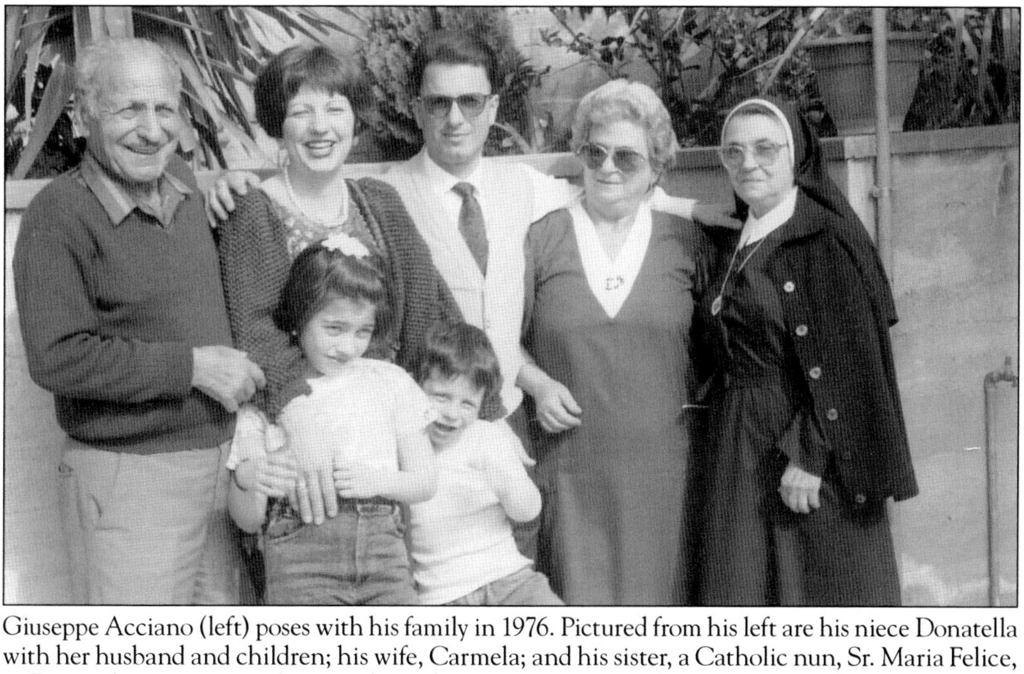

Giuseppe Acciano (left) poses with his family in 1976. Pictured from his left are his niece Donatella with her husband and children; his wife, Carmela; and his sister, a Catholic nun, Sr. Maria Felice, in Rocca di Capri Leone (Messina), Sicily. It was Giuseppe's first trip back to Italy after having immigrated to Australia on March 21, 1952. (Courtesy of Anthony Acciano.)

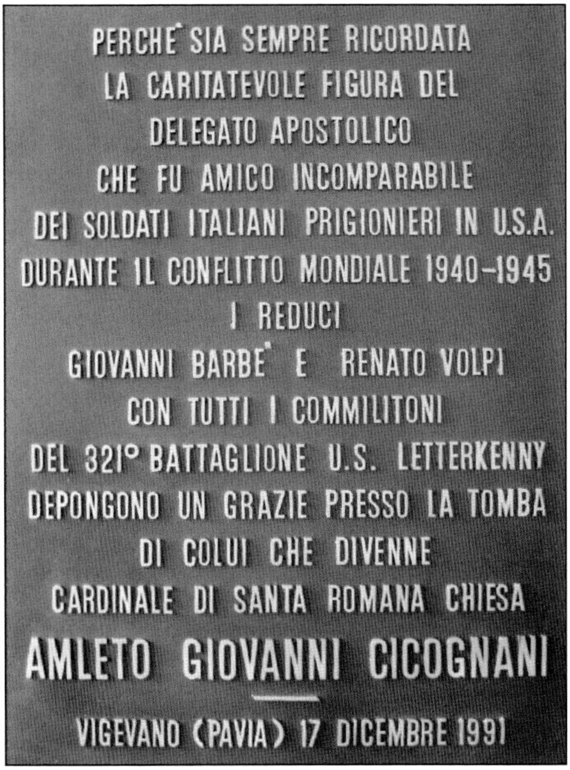

On December 17, 1991, ex–Letterkenny POW Renato Volpi, his family, and Giovanni Barbè's family helped to dedicate Card. Amleto Cicognani's memorial plaque in the ancient Basilica of San Clemente (Rome) in the name of all former 321st Letterkenny ISU soldiers. As the Vatican's apostolic delegate during the war, Cicognani had provided exceptional spiritual help to them. (Courtesy of Luisella Volpi.)

Brig. Gen. Roberto Cardinale accompanies Pope Paolo VI on a visit to a Roman neighborhood in a Carabinieri jeep, probably in 1965. Cardinale was one of a handful of former Letterkenny POWs who reached the rank of general in the Italian armed forces. The others were Giovanni Fresta, Gregorio Lucia, and Francesco Agate. (Courtesy of Giuseppe Grasso.)

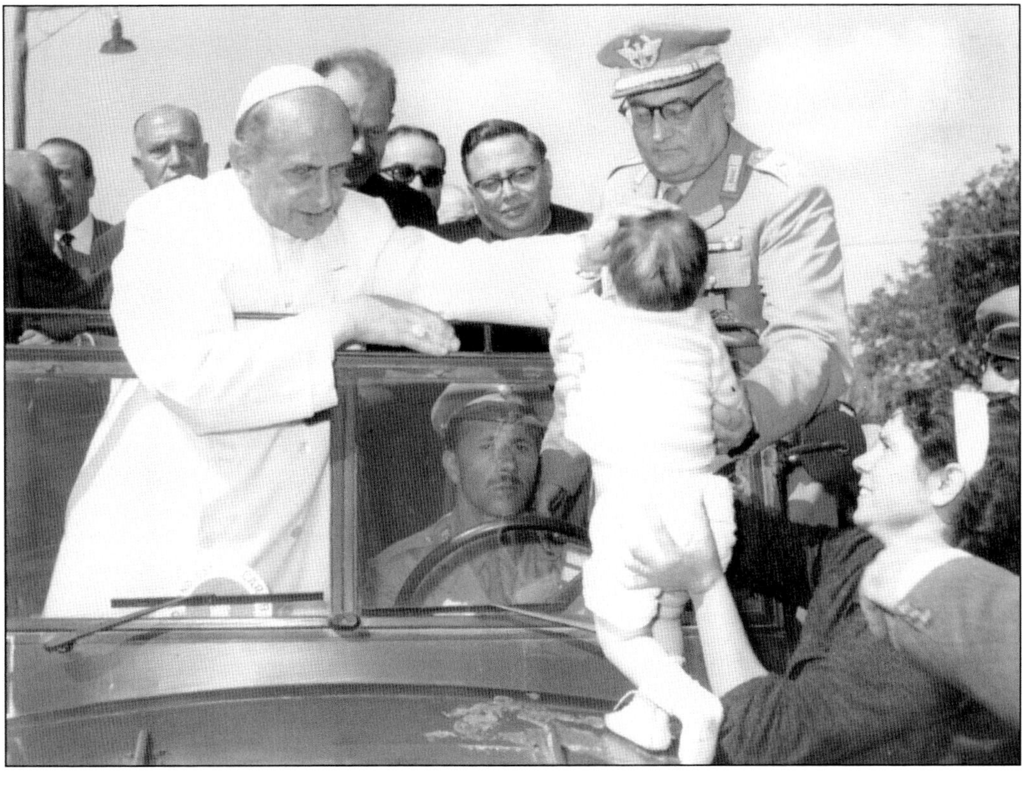

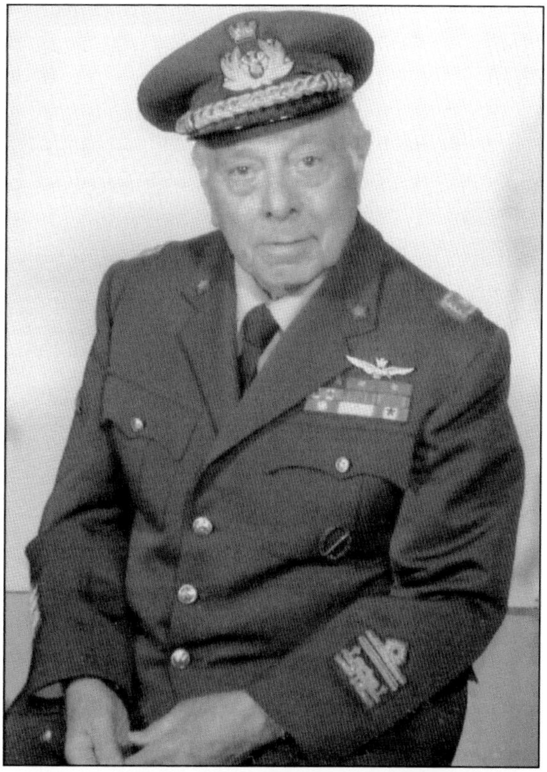

Giovanni Fresta, born in 1918 in Giarre (Catania), poses while wearing his Italian air force major general uniform during the 1990s, when he had been in retirement for several years. At Letterkenny, Fresta commanded the 159th ISU that arrived at the depot in March 1945. He had been captured in May 1943 when his plane was shot down in the Mediterranean. (Courtesy of Isidoro Fresta.)

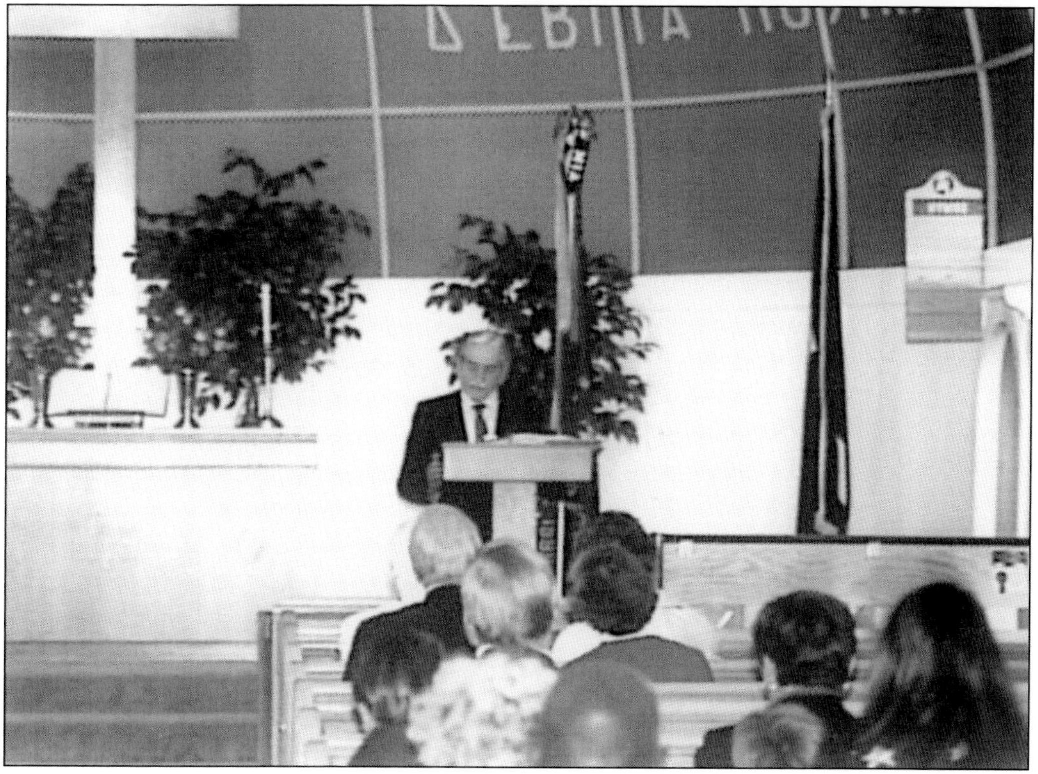

Alfredo Tonolo speaks at the Letterkenny chapel during a memorial service honoring the Italian POWs on November 11, 1998. Tonolo was one of several ex–Letterkenny POWs who came back to live in the United States after marrying their American sweethearts. As a proud bersagliere, he often attended important ceremonies at the chapel until his death on December 4, 2006, at the age of 85. (Courtesy of Edoardo Ranzoni.)

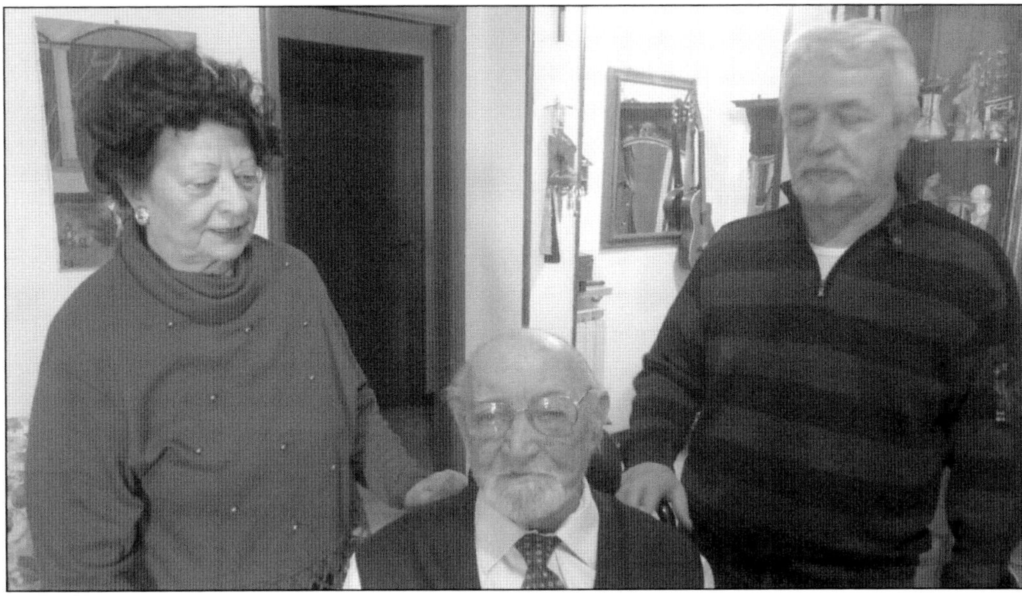

Edoardo Quintarelli, born on March 16, 1922, poses with his second wife and his son during an oral history interview conducted by Flavio G. Conti at Sant'Ambrogio Valpolicella (Verona) on March 13, 2015. As of April 2017, Quintarelli is one of three ex–Letterkenny POWs known to still be alive. His reflections have given great insights into the daily life ISU members experienced at the depot. (Courtesy of Antonio Brescianini.)

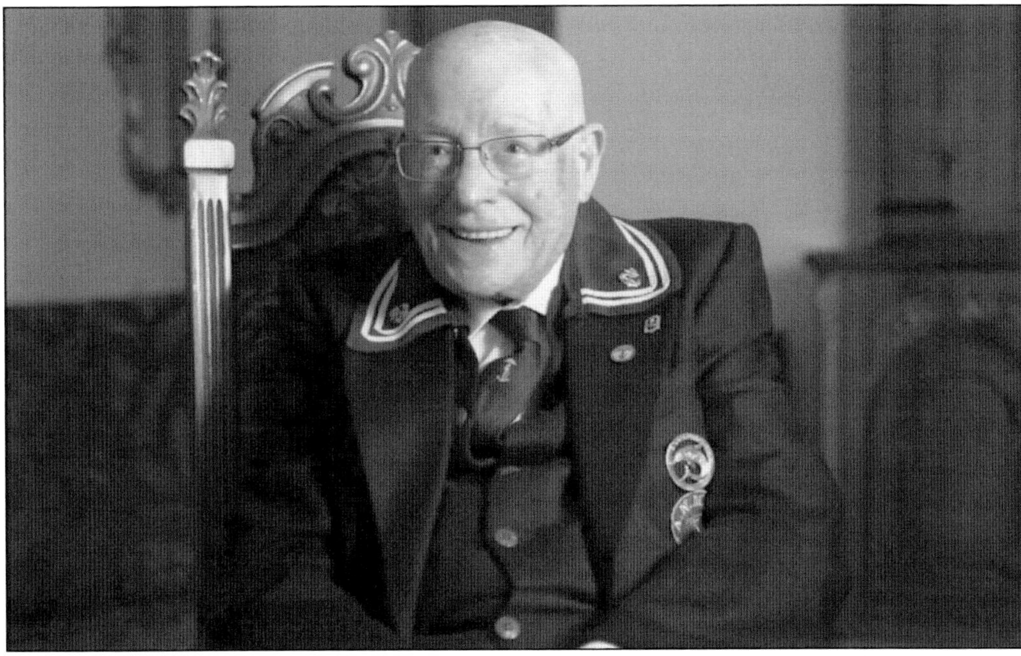

Giovanni Serpe, here wearing his dress submariner uniform with various medals, poses during an oral history interview conducted by Flavio G. Conti at Gaeta on March 6, 2015. After the war, Serpe maintained contact with Americans through the presence of the US Sixth Fleet stationed at Gaeta. Serpe died on May 20, 2016, following a brief sickness, three weeks after his 95th birthday. (Courtesy of Tommaso Cassinis.)

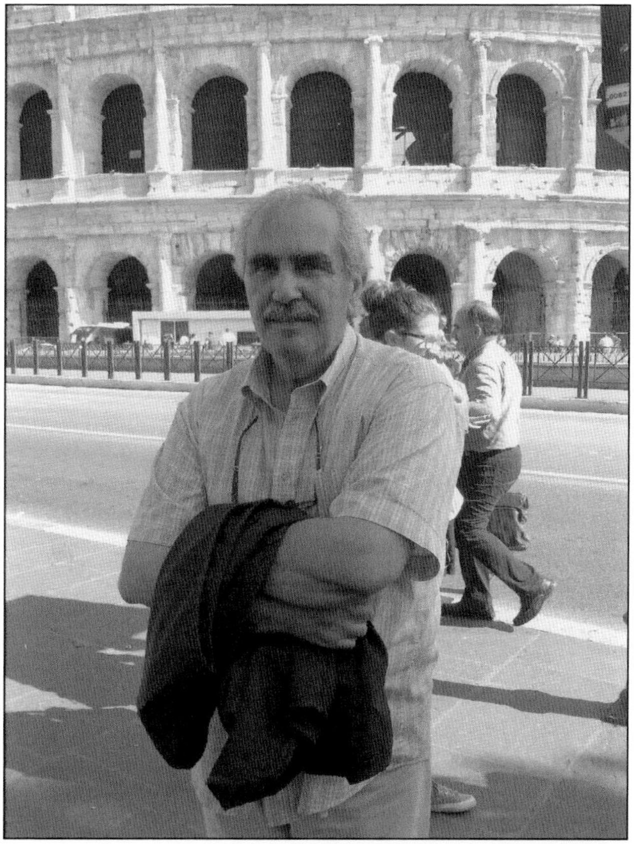

Roberto De Angelis, son of POW Elio, and half brother of Victor Fogelsonger through Elio, stands in front of the Roman Colosseum on June 10, 2015. After the two first made contact in 2009, they continued to correspond, and finally in April 2017, Robert traveled to Chambersburg to meet Victor in person. (Courtesy of Flavio G. Conti.)

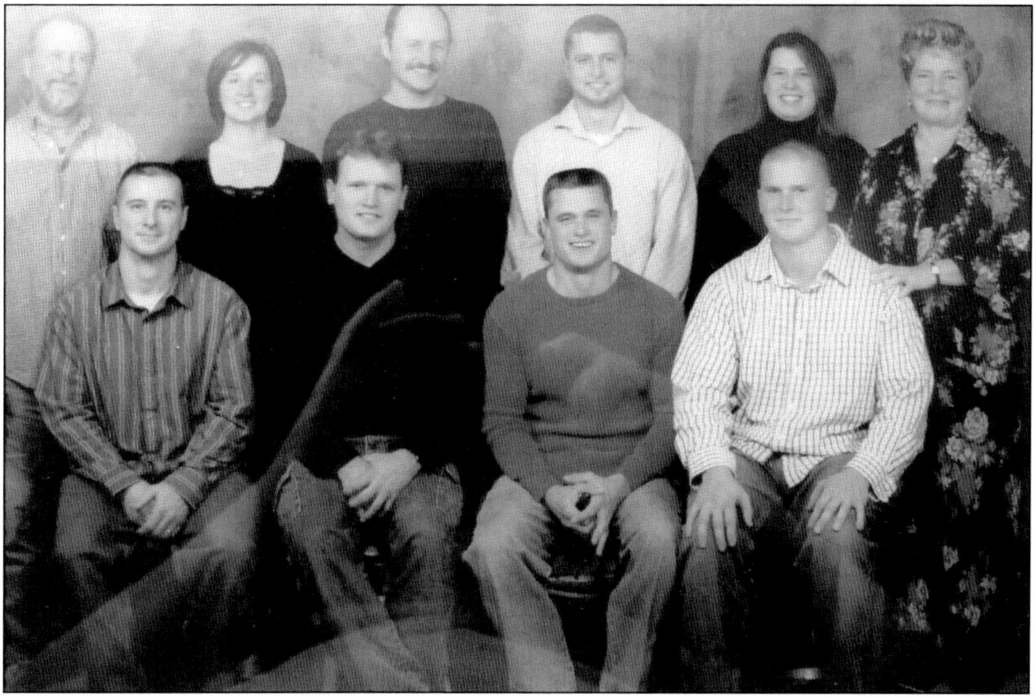

Victor Fogelsonger, in the back row, far left, is the son of POW Elio De Angelis and Betty Gilbert, and half brother of Roberto De Angelis through Elio. Here, he is pictured with his former wife, Mary, and his family, on June 17, 2015. Betty had told Victor about her relationship with Elio, but Roberto only found out that he had a brother by Betty in 2009, after Elio had died. (Courtesy of Victor Fogelsonger.)

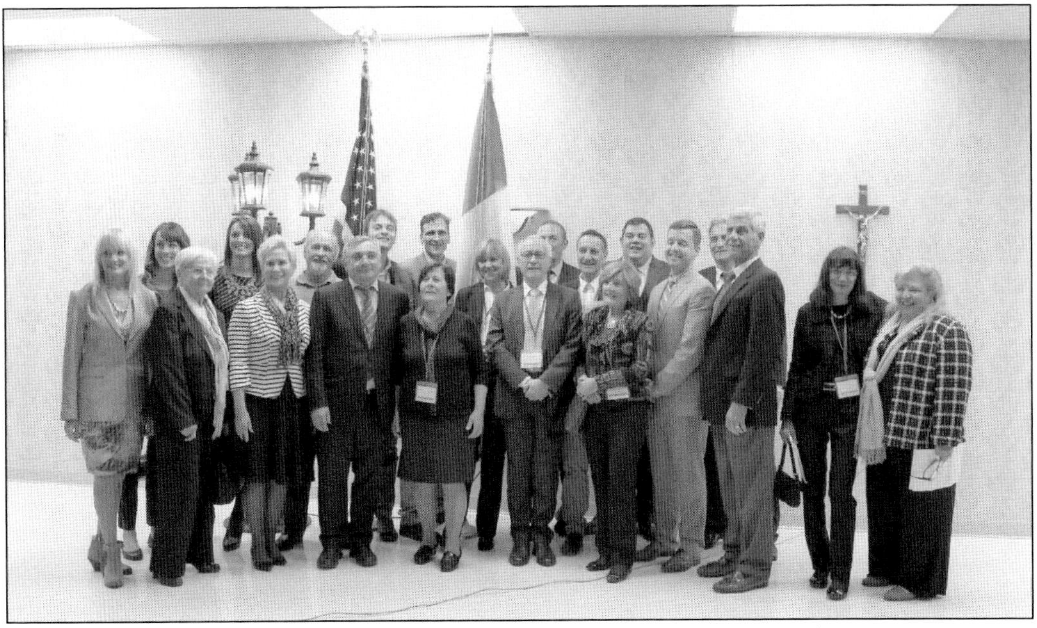

Children and grandchildren of Letterkenny Italian prisoners of war pose during a repatriation anniversary celebration in Chambersburg, Pennsylvania, on October 24, 2015. The authors of this book are also present: Flavio G. Conti is in the first row, fifth from the left, and Alan R. Perry is in the back row, sixth from the left. (Courtesy of Mattia Brusati.)

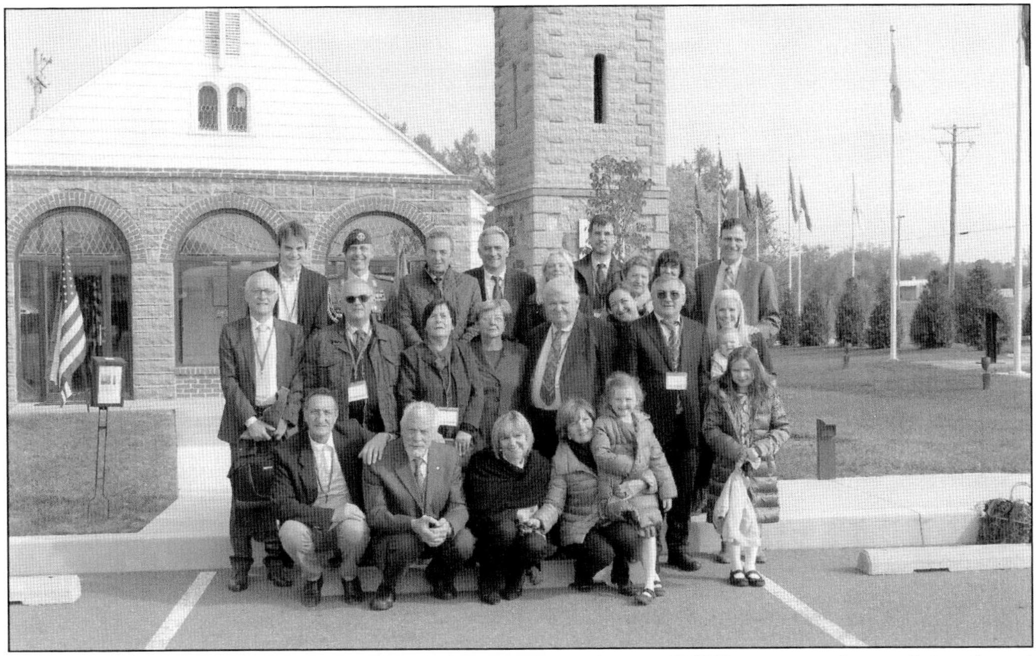

A special delegation of family members of former Letterkenny POWs poses in front of the chapel and bell tower with a few friends on October 24, 2015: Flavio G. Conti (first on the left in the second row), Col. Rodolfo Sganga, Italian military embassy attaché in Washington (back row, second from left), and Alan R. Perry (back row, far right, with wife and family). (Courtesy of Antonio Brescianini.)

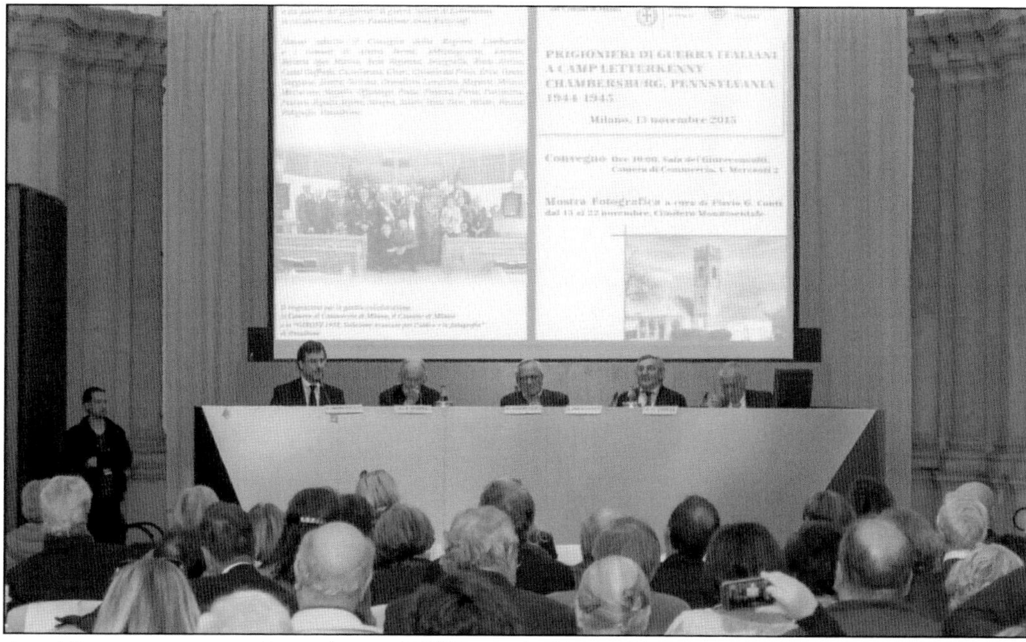

A public symposium on Letterkenny POWs was held in Milan on November 13, 2015. From the left at the presenter's table are Carlo Borghetti, council member for the region of Lombardy; Giuseppe Cassini, ambassador and former Italian consul general in Philadelphia; Walter Galbusera, president of the Anna Kuliscioff Foundation; Antonio Brescianini, mayor of Vimodrome and son of Letterkenny POW Luigi; and Flavio G. Conti, historian, author, and conference organizer. (Courtesy of Mario Luigini [grandson].)

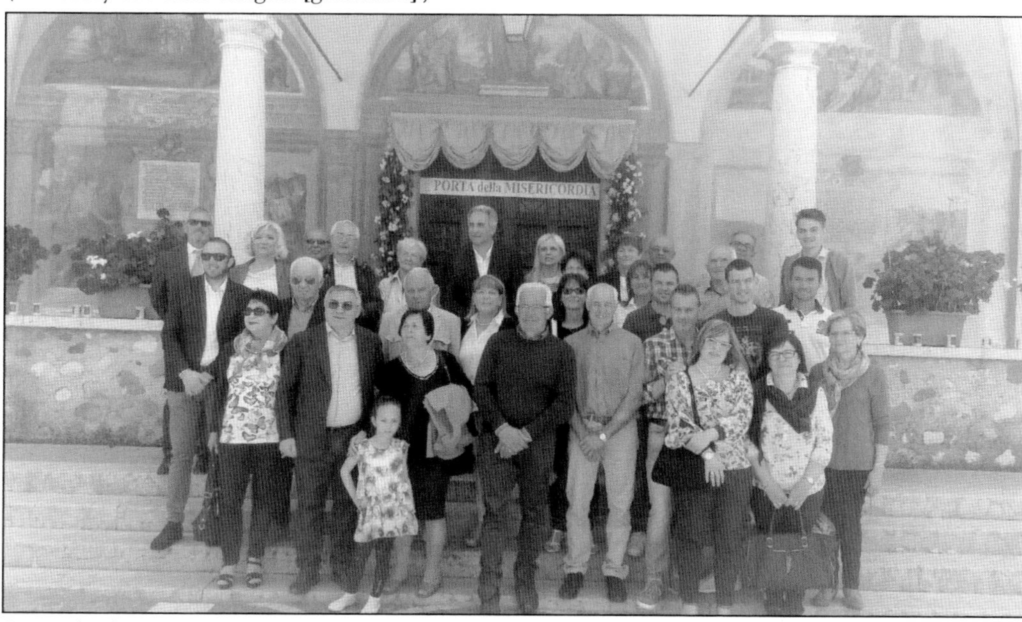

Several relatives of former Letterkenny POWs and a few friends pose during a meeting at the Madonna del Frassino Sanctuary in Peschiera del Garda (Verona), on May 22, 2016. Relatives of the following POWs were present: Luigi Brescianini, Renato Volpi, Zefferino Trevisan, Renato Scattolini, Giovanni Barbè, Aldo Lorenzi, and Aldo Storari. (Courtesy of Antonio Brescianini.)